Dutch and Flemish Drawings

from the Royal Library
Windsor Castle

D0939909

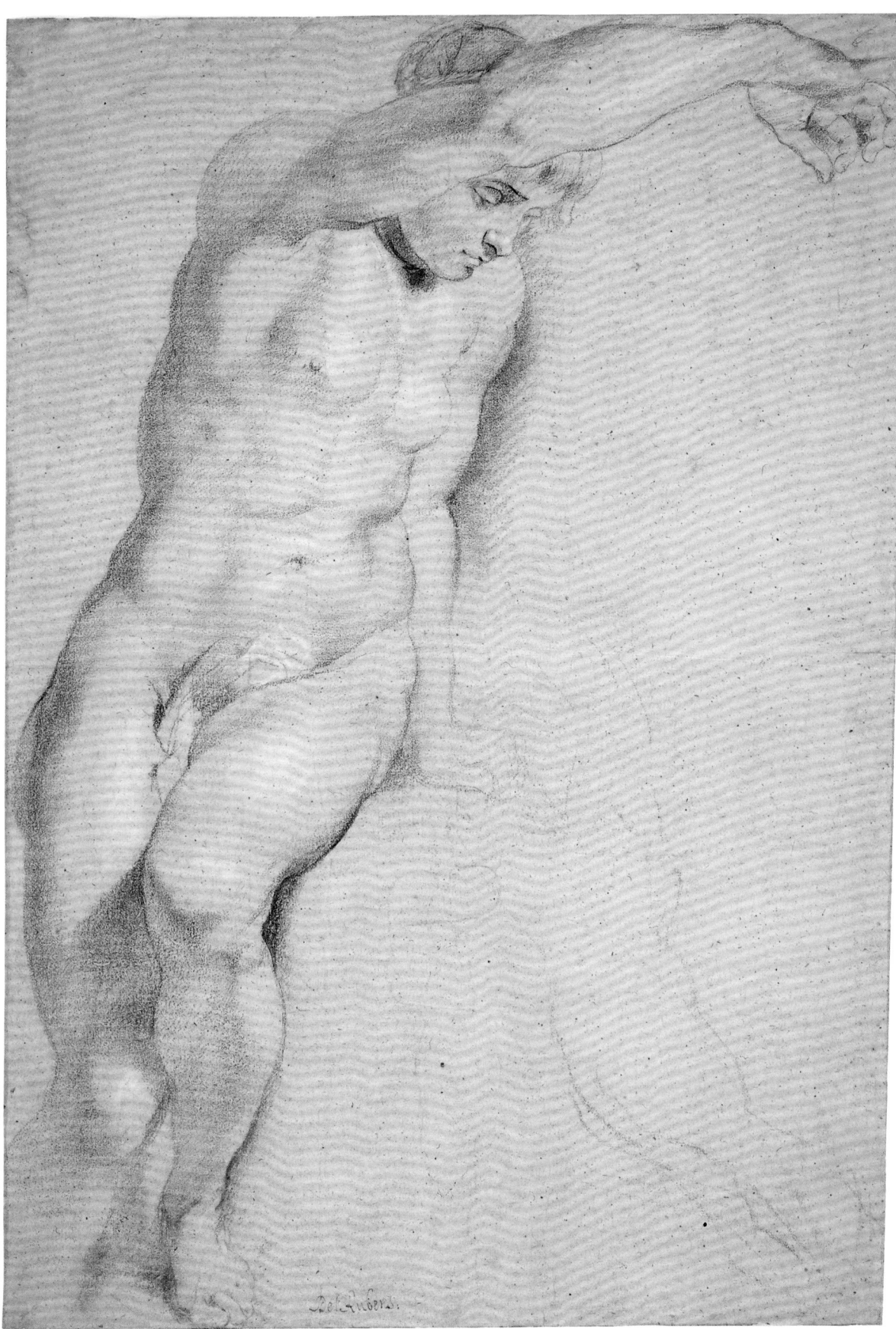

Dutch and Flemish Drawings

*from the Royal Library
Windsor Castle*

Catalogue by Christopher White

North Carolina Museum of Art, Raleigh

1994

Published on the occasion of the exhibition
"Dutch and Flemish Drawings from the
Royal Library, Windsor Castle." The
exhibition and catalogue were funded by
the North Carolina Museum of Art
Foundation

Exhibition Itinerary

The Montreal Museum of Fine Arts
Montreal, Quebec
October 13, 1994 – January 15, 1995

North Carolina Museum of Art
Raleigh, North Carolina
January 28 – April 16, 1995

Indianapolis Museum of Art
Indianapolis, Indiana
April 29 – July 30, 1995

© 1994 by North Carolina Museum of Art
Catalogue introduction and illustrations of
drawings in the exhibition
© Her Majesty Queen Elizabeth II
All rights reserved

Library of Congress Catalogue Number
94–67498
ISBN 0–88259–968–2

The North Carolina Museum of Art is an agency
of the State of North Carolina, James B. Hunt,
Jr., Governor, and the Department of Cultural
Resources, Betty Ray McCain, Secretary.

Designed by James Shurmer

Typesetting by August Filmsetting,
St Helens, UK

Printed by Balding & Mansell,
Cambridgeshire, UK

Front cover: Peter Paul Rubens,
Self-Portrait in Old Age (cat. no. 24)

Back cover: Joris Hoefnagel
View of Windsor Castle from the North
(cat.no.13)

Frontispiece: Peter Paul Rubens,
A Female Nude: Study for Psyche (cat. no. 22)

Contents

Foreword and Acknowledgments

Throughout history drawings have served a variety of functions, both practical and aesthetic. Sketches provided a repository of stock motifs to be utilized by an artist or his students in a variety of compositions. Preliminary studies document a master's first inspirations or conceptions, giving us a look into the artistic process that lies behind the genesis of a painting. Beginning in the sixteenth century, when the first collections of drawings were being formed, drawings were executed as finished works of art. The sixty-four sheets in this exhibition, the first organized by the Royal Library to be devoted exclusively to Dutch and Flemish artists, encompass all of these functions. Viewed together, they offer insight into the artistic achievement of two of the most creative societies in European history.

The trustees and staff of the North Carolina Museum of Art, the Indianapolis Museum of Art, and the Montreal Museum of Fine Arts are grateful to Her Majesty Queen Elizabeth II for graciously permitting this superb selection of drawings to travel to North America. The project was first conceived in 1989 in consequence of Christopher White's work on the complete catalogue of Dutch and Flemish drawings in the Royal Collection at Windsor Castle. We would like to express considerable thanks to the staff of the Royal Library at Windsor Castle, in particular Oliver Everett, Royal Librarian; Jane Roberts, Curator of the Print Room; and Theresa-Mary Morton, Curator of Exhibitions. This project would have been impossible without the central contribution of Professor White, a distinguished scholar of Dutch and Flemish art and the Director of the Ashmolean Museum, Oxford. Working with the staff of the Print Room at Windsor, he selected the drawings for exhibition and wrote catalogue entries for each work.

Richard S. Schneiderman, then Director of the North Carolina Museum of Art, lent the project his immediate and enthusiastic support, and invited the participation of Montreal and Indianapolis. The staff of each of the three participating museums deserve our thanks. However, we wish especially to recognize John W. Coffey, Acting Chief Curator, David Steel, Curator of European Art, and Peggy Jo Kirby, Registrar, at the North Carolina Museum of Art; Martin F. Krause, Curator of Prints, Drawings, and Photographs at the Indianapolis Museum of Art; and Mayo Graham, Chief Curator, and the staff of the Montreal Museum of Fine Arts.

Lawrence J. Wheeler *Director* North Carolina Museum of Art

Pierre Théberge *Director* Montreal Museum of Fine Arts

Bret Waller *Director* Indianapolis Museum of Art

Preface

This catalogue has been produced to accompany the exhibition of drawings by Netherlandish masters in the Royal Collection. Sixty-four drawings have been selected from the 732 drawings by Dutch and Flemish artists of the fifteenth to the early nineteenth centuries preserved in the Royal Library at Windsor Castle. All these drawings are discussed and illustrated in the new comprehensive catalogue, *The Dutch and Flemish Drawings in the Collection of Her Majesty The Queen at Windsor Castle*, by Professor Christopher White and Charlotte Crawley, published by the Cambridge University Press in 1994. We are delighted that Professor White, the principal author of that catalogue, was also able to find the time to write this exhibition catalogue.

Apart from the traveling exhibitions of drawings by Holbein, this is the first exhibition organized by the Royal Library to be devoted to the work of northern artists. The majority of our exhibitions have been concerned with the unparalleled series of drawings by Italian artists that are kept at Windsor. Like the Italian drawings, the majority of the Netherlandish drawings were acquired by King George III over two hundred years ago. Although they are less well-known than the Italian drawings, it is hoped that this exhibition will demonstrate that they are no less impressive.

We are delighted to be working with the North Carolina Museum of Art, the Montreal Museum of Fine Arts, and the Indianapolis Museum of Art on this exhibition. We are particularly grateful to the North Carolina Museum of Art, who has coordinated the arrangements for the American tour and who is the publisher of this catalogue.

Oliver Everett *Librarian* Windsor Castle

Author's Preface and Acknowledgments

The present catalogue is based on *The Dutch and Flemish Drawings in the Collection of Her Majesty The Queen at Windsor Castle*, published by the Cambridge University Press in 1994, which was compiled by myself (fifteenth to seventeenth centuries) and Charlotte Crawley (eighteenth century). I must warmly thank my co-author for providing the basic catalogue information for the eighteenth-century drawings in the exhibition and also the general editor of the series, the Hon. Mrs. Jane Roberts, the Curator of the Print Room, who has been consistently helpful and encouraging throughout the long process of cataloguing the Dutch and Flemish drawings in her charge. The latter's sharp eye and sharp pencil have contributed many essential *addenda et corrigenda* to the final publication. Detailed acknowledgment of the many scholars who helped will be found in the *catalogue raisonné*. In addition I would particularly like to thank Dr. Elizabeth McGrath and Professor Michael Winterbotham. In the preparation of the exhibition Miss Theresa-Mary Morton has given invaluable and efficient support.

All photographs of items in the Royal Collection are reproduced by gracious permission of Her Majesty Queen Elizabeth II. The other comparative illustrations are reproduced with the kind permission of the following: Amsterdam, Rijksmuseum ([25, 64]: Rijksmuseum-Stichting Amsterdam); Amsterdams Historisch Museum ([50]); Berlin, Staatliche Museen, Kupferstichkabinett ([40]: photo Jörg P. Anders); Boston, Museum of Fine Arts ([52]); Brussels, Bibliothèque royale Albert Ier, Cabinet des Estampes ([10]: © Bibliothèque royale Albert Ier); Cambridge, courtesy of the Provost and Scholars of King's College ([2]: photograph H. G. Wayment); Florence, Comune: Musei e Patrimonio Artistico ([3]: Fototeca dei Musei Comunali di Firenze); Hamburg, Kunsthalle ([28]: photo © Elke Walford); London, British Library ([43]: by permission of the British Library); London, British Museum ([4, 5, 7, 16–18, 35, 41]: courtesy of the Trustees of the British Museum); London, Victoria & Albert Museum ([18]: courtesy of the Board of Trustees of the V&A); Munich, Alte Pinakothek ([47]); New York, Cooper-Hewitt Museum ([7]: photograph Ken Pelka; [8]. Both Courtesy of Art Resource, N.Y.); New York, Metropolitan Museum of Art ([24]); New York, Pierpont Morgan Library ([25]); Norfolk, Va., The Chrysler Museum ([26]: Gift of Walter P. Chrysler, Jr. 71.462); Stockholm, Nationalmuseum ([12]: Photo Statens Konstmuseer); Venice, Civici Musei Veneziani d'Arte e di Storia ([1]); Washington, National Gallery of Art ([31]); Vienna, Graphische Sammlung Albertina ([6]); Washington, Private Collection ([35]); Private Collection ([13]: photograph Fitzwilliam Museum, Cambridge; [22]: photograph © Sotheby's). (The figure within square brackets denotes the catalogue entry to which the illustration is related.)

Christopher White

Introduction

At Windsor Castle, overlooking the North Terrace, with views of the River Thames and Eton beyond, a large paneled room, lined with cases of solander boxes, contains one of the most spectacular collections of Old Master drawings in the world. Situated within the old structure of the Castle, the room, which had been one of those used by George III during his later years, was set up as a Print Room by Queen Victoria and Prince Albert in the 1850s. Using his favorite architect, John Thomas, the Prince himself devoted much loving attention to the project, which was realized very shortly before his death. And as an appropriate testimony to his creation, the room is signed and dated twice (once in 1859 and once in 1860) by Albert. Today it happily retains its original character, and the experience of studying in such an atmosphere is a perfect enhancement to that of looking at the drawings themselves.

When regarded from a historical point of view, the collection – now numbering over 35,000 drawings and watercolors – is an idiosyncratic assembly, reflecting the taste of a number of British monarchs and their advisers. It is probably most famed for the approximately six hundred drawings by Leonardo da Vinci and eighty-one portrait drawings, many of which are worked in color, by Hans Holbein the Younger. But Italian Renaissance draughtsmanship at Windsor is also strongly represented by around twenty drawings each by Raphael and Michelangelo, including an outstanding group of the latter's beautifully wrought presentation drawings, as well as fine examples by other fifteenth- and sixteenth-century artists.

The *Seicento* is superbly and richly represented by outstanding examples by Annibale and Agostino Carracci and their cousin Lodovico (over 600 drawings), by Domenichino (1758 sheets, consisting of the bulk of the artist's studio at his death), by Guercino (348), Guido Reni (62), Stefano della Bella (152), Castiglione (over 200, including a group of his rare monotypes), Carlo Maratta (nearly 200), and by that honorary Italian, Nicolas Poussin (68 drawings). The Old Master section of the royal Print Room concludes with an outstanding series of drawings by Venetian eighteenth-century artists, above all by Canaletto (143) and by Giovanni Battista Piazzetta (36).

Balanced against the incredible riches of the collection, there are surprising lacunae; for all the strengths of the seventeenth century, including four superb studies by Rubens, for example, there is not a single sheet by Rembrandt, while the 143 drawings by Canaletto are complemented by not one example by Guardi. You cannot write a history of drawing on the basis of the collection, but you can enjoy the work of certain great artists in unprecedented numbers and, more significantly, in unparalleled quality.

For all that is recorded about the Royal Collection of pictures and other works of art, there is a surprising dearth of information about the history of how the drawings came into the royal possession.[1] Most were originally mounted in albums, and had

---

[1] The most detailed analysis is provided by Blunt, pp. 1–18, but for Charles I, see Roberts (1989), pp. 115–29, and for George III, see Vivian. See also Roberts (1986), pp. 8–15, as well as the introductions to the various catalogues of individual parts of the collection.

these not been later dismembered, much more would have been known about their history. Until recently it has generally been assumed, largely on the basis of what George Vertue and Horace Walpole wrote in the eighteenth century, that the great tradition of collecting Old Master drawings goes back to the reign of Charles I (1625–49) and that the drawings found at Kensington Palace in the early eighteenth century (see below) were largely his acquisitions. Given his remarkable assembly of paintings it would seem entirely appropriate that the King should also have owned such works as the Holbeins and Leonardos which are at Windsor today. But apart from the "great booke" of portrait drawings by Holbein, inherited by Charles I from his brother, Henry, Prince of Wales – but almost immediately afterwards exchanged by the King for Raphael's painting of *St. George and the Dragon*, then owned by the Earl of Pembroke and now in Washington – and the handful of framed drawings described by Abraham van der Doort in his inventories of the Royal Collection drawn up in the 1630s, there is no incontrovertible evidence that the King's taste for pictures was matched by a similar taste and discernment for drawings. Although it is possible that his collection of drawings and prints may never have been included in the various royal inventories, it seems more likely that, unlike his great contemporary, Thomas Howard, Earl of Arundel, whose important collection of drawings, including Holbein's "great booke" (given to *him* by the Earl of Pembroke), is securely documented, works on paper did not greatly appeal to the King. (Another collector far closer in taste to the King, the Duke of Buckingham, also appears to have concentrated on pictures to the virtual exclusion of drawings.)

The earliest reference to the book of Leonardo drawings in the Royal Collection occurs in the diary of Constantin Huyghens, secretary to William III (1689–1702), for 22 January 1690. Although there is no evidence, it seems likely that this volume, with the Holbein "great booke" documented as back in royal possession by 1675, was acquired after the Restoration of the monarchy in 1660 rather than before, and that the credit for purchasing them must go to Charles II (1660–85), who did so much to restore the Royal Collection to the glories of its heyday under his father. However, details concerning the formation (or re-formation) of Charles II's collection are tantalizingly incomplete.

Aside from these references, the first important record of drawings belonging to the Crown occurs in the list, made shortly before 1728, of twenty-three books of drawings and prints, as well as some individual items, discovered by Queen Caroline, the consort of George II (1727–60), in a bureau at Kensington Palace. Apart from the Holbein volume and books of prints by Hollar and Dürer, the drawings are nearly all by sixteenth- and seventeenth-century Italian artists, including such names as Leonardo, Michelangelo, Raphael, Titian, and Parmigianino. No Dutch or Flemish master is mentioned. As with the Holbein and Leonardo albums, it seems more likely that these were also acquired by Charles II rather than by either his father or any of the subsequent monarchs, none of whom had manifested much interest in the visual arts. If much of Charles I's collection of paintings was unrecoverable, his son, it can be surmised, succeeded in giving the Royal Collection a new dimension.

Frederick, Prince of Wales, the eldest son of George II, appears to have been the first Hanoverian to add to the drawings collection by acquiring from Dr. Richard Mead the volume of drawings by Nicolas Poussin, which had previously belonged to Cardinal Camillo Massimi. But it was the Prince's son, George III (1760–1820), who was responsible for the most substantial enrichment of the collection and who, apart from the Holbeins and Leonardos, is largely responsible for its character today. He started his collecting activities when Prince of Wales by purchasing two volumes of flower drawings by Maria Sibylla Merian in 1755, before going on in 1762, far more significantly, to acquire the entire collection of paintings, drawings, and other works of art formed by Joseph Smith, British Consul in Venice, and the large holding of drawings that had been assembled by Cardinal Alessandro Albani in Rome. Although the 10,000 or so drawings involved in these purchases were principally by Italian masters, a large proportion of the drawings by Dutch and Flemish masters in the present Royal Collection were almost certainly acquired during George III's reign. Just under 500 of the 732 drawings by Dutch and Flemish artists now housed at Windsor Castle can be traced in George III's inventory, and he was indisputably the principal collector of these drawings.

The majority of George III's drawings were thus acquired in Italy, principally as part of the block purchases from Consul Smith and Cardinal Albani made in 1762. We know that the King's agents – and chief among them his librarian, Richard Dalton – acquired smaller groups of drawings and even individual items from time to time, but the documentary evidence for these purchases is almost nonexistent. Only one itemized invoice relating to the King's purchase of drawings exists. The main source of the little we do know is the inventory (known as "Inventory A"), which was drawn up around 1800, when the collection was still kept at Buckingham House in London. By that time the various purchases had evidently been sorted and where necessary rebound in new albums, so that the original context and the provenance of individual drawings have been irretrievably lost. Fortunately, however, a detailed typescript list of the contents of George III's albums was made before the drawings were numbered, removed, and mounted separately during the earlier part of this century. It is therefore possible to establish some sort of idea of the arrangement of the drawings between around 1790 and 1930, and occasionally to guess at the earlier arrangement.

Whereas the volumes listed in Inventory A as *Diversi Maestri Antichi* and *Paesi di Claudio Lorenese e Altri* (which included a number of Dutch landscapes) and *Accademie di Diversi Autori* (which possibly included No. 22; this is inscribed "Del Rubens," which suggests an Italian provenance) were evidently acquired in Italy, the contents of the volumes entitled *Rubens, Vandyke, Vischer &c*, (including Nos. 16, 23, 33, 35, 43, and 52), *Dutch Masters* (including Nos. 27–32, 40, 42, 47, and 57), *Dutch Landscapes* (including Nos. 19, 37, and 61) and *Italian Flemish & Dutch Landscapes* (including Nos. 21, 36, 41, 44, 45, 50, 51, 55, 58, 59, and possibly 48) may well have been acquired elsewhere. It is almost certain that two of George III's Rubens drawings[2] and his one autograph Van Dyck drawing (No. 35) are identifiable in the catalogues of auctions held in the Netherlands earlier in the eighteenth century; both Rubens drawings were in a sale in The Hague in 1760, the year of the King's accession, while the Van Dyck was sold in Amsterdam in 1732. By *c.*1800 both of the Rubens studies had been pasted into the *Rubens, Vandyke, Vischer &c* album noted above, while the artist's late self-portrait (No. 24) – for which the early provenance has not been traced – was to be found in "An Unbound Volume (A Portfolio)." The Asselyn view of the Colosseum (No. 41) may likewise be identifiable in an Amsterdam sale of 1757. The only (non-

2 W & C 436 and 441.

royal) collector's mark borne by any of the drawings in this exhibition is that of Jonathan Richardson the Elder on No. 52. This may relate to the sale of Richardson's great collection in 1747. The drawing is certainly identifiable in George III's collection, although the process of acquisition is unrecorded.

George III's holdings of Dutch and Flemish drawings cover the whole range of works now in the Royal Collection, beginning in the late fifteenth century with the *Christ on the Cross* (No. 1), either by or after Hugo van der Goes, and continuing with such striking sixteenth-century works as the large drawings of the *Fall of the Rebel Angels* by Dirck Barendsz. (No. 11) and the *Circumcision* by Jans Soens (No. 15). All three drawings are notable for their high degree of finish, suggesting that they may have been made either as *modelli* or as *ricordi*; indeed, the inscription on the verso of No. 15 proves conclusively that it was the *modello* attached to the artist's contract. Most of the remaining sixteenth-century drawings can be identified as preparatory drawings for engravings produced by such artists as Crispin van den Broeck, Crispin van de Passe, and Marten de Vos (see No. 10). But the richest and most varied group in this part of the collection is by Jan van der Straet (called Stradanus) whose work for engravers is very well illustrated with preparatory studies for such series as the *Life of the Virgin* (see No. 4), the *History of the Medici* (see No. 5), an untitled series on early Roman history (see No. 6), the *Nova Reperta*, a survey of recent inventions (see No. 7), and the *Vermis Sericus* (see No. 8), a history of the silk worm industry under the Medici. Stradanus's preparatory work for his painting is here represented by a preparatory study (see No. 3) for the decorations in the *studiolo* of Francesco I de' Medici in the Palazzo Vecchio in Florence.

There is a relatively small but reasonably representative group of Flemish seventeenth-century drawings, among which the four drawings by Rubens must take pride of place. In addition to the three superb drawings in the exhibition (Nos. 22–24), which very well represent different aspects of the master's draughtsmanship, there is a design for a title-page with the *Temple of Janus*.[3] Rubens's protégé Van Dyck was only represented in George III's collection by one undoubtedly authentic work, the masterly chalk portrait of Nicolaas Rockox (No. 35). (The *Landscape near Genoa* (No. 34) and a portrait of Charles II as Prince of Wales[4] were only added to the collection in this century.) Other notable Flemish drawings of the period include delicately drawn landscapes by Jan Brueghel the Elder (No. 19) and Roelant Savery (No. 21), as well as a varied group of studies by Cornelis de Wael (see No. 33), which were almost certainly executed after the artist had moved to Genoa.

Turning to drawings executed in the northern Netherlands, George III owned a small but representative collection by members of the school of Haarlem at the turn of the seventeenth century. Two typically elaborate drawings by Hendrick Goltzius (Nos. 16 and 17), executed for engraving by his stepson Jacob Matham, are complemented by the large ball scene (No. 20) by the latter. In a collection notable for examples of the finished drawing, it may be that Rembrandt's economy of line did not appeal to the taste of the King and his advisers, which would explain the absence of any examples of his work. His style is, however, reflected in the group of "6 of the School of Rembrandt" in George III's volume of *Dutch Masters*, which includes Lambert

[3] W & C 436.

[4] W & C 355.

Doomer's large copy after Rembrandt (No. 47) and Ferdinand Bol's *Nathan Admonishing Jacob* (No. 42).

Among the Dutch seventeenth-century drawings in George III's collection, the forty-seven drawings by Hendrick Avercamp (including Nos. 27–32) are of outstanding interest. They were included in the *Dutch Masters* volume, but their earlier history is unknown. They comprise the largest single collection in existence, accounting for nearly one third of the artist's drawn *oeuvre*, and include examples of the full range of both the artist's subject matter and technique. In Inventory A the identity of the artist was not known and the drawings were described as by "some Master in the Stile of Breughel." Other examples of genre subjects are found among the group (from the same volume) described as "14 Two of which are by A: Van Ostade, and the others imitators of him." Although these do not include any works accepted as by Van Ostade today, there are lively examples by such pupils as Cornelis Dusart (No. 57). Four characteristic portrait heads by Cornelis Visscher (see No. 52) were, if their detailed description in Inventory A can be so interpreted, highly prized in the King's collection.

A substantial part of the Dutch collection consists of landscapes, especially those by Italianate artists, such as Herman van Swanevelt (No. 36), Jan Asselyn (No. 41), Jan Hackaert (No. 51), and Willem Romeyn (No. 45), as well as a probable Roman view by that inveterate traveler Willem Schellinks (No. 48). Given the King's feelings about the loss of his American colonies, he may have found Nicolaes Berchem's unusual double-sided sheet with an *Allegory on the Discovery of America* (No. 43) a poignant souvenir. The interest in classical landscape continues into the eighteenth century with good examples by Gaspar van Wittel (Nos. 54 and 55), Isaac de Moucheron (Nos. 58 and 59), and others.

There are fewer native landscapes, but George III owned two dated drawings by that rare early seventeenth-century artist Marten de Cock (No. 37), as well as excellent examples by Jan Lievens (No. 38), Jacob van Ruisdael (No. 50), and by Avercamp (No. 32). As with the Italianate landscapes, interest continued into the eighteenth century. Characteristic marine subjects with shipping, by such artists as Reynier Nooms (Zeeman) (No. 46), also formed part of the King's collection.

Compared with his spectacular holdings of Dutch and Flemish paintings, acquisitions of drawings by the future George IV (1820–30) are disappointing as far as they can be determined. He was possibly less attracted by the more cerebral and austere qualities of Old Master drawings than to the more colorful and decorative pieces that he acquired in such vast numbers. According to bills in the Royal Archives dating from 1803 to 1816, the purchases by the Prince of Wales (Prince Regent from 1811) were, with the exception of a very large group of military subjects (a favorite preoccupation of the Prince)[5] by Dirck and Jan Anthonie Langendijk, limited to a scene from a play by Cornelis Troost (No. 60) and a group of watercolors by the younger Langendijk of street scenes and interiors (see Nos. 62 and 63), some of which were acquired immediately after they were made. A more topical subject, *Queen Hortense of Holland Haunted by Napoleon* (No. 64), by Wijnand Esser or the younger Langendijk after Esser, was bought in 1815.

[5] The military subjects by Dirck and Jan Anthonie Langendijk are discussed in A.E. Haswell Miller and N.P. Dawnay, *Military Drawings and Paintings in the Collection of H.M. The Queen*, 2 vols (London, 1970).

Queen Victoria (1837–1901) and the Prince Consort, who enjoyed looking at the collection of drawings in their possession – there are references in the Queen's diaries recording her pleasure in studying drawings by various artists – for the most part reserved their patronage for contemporary artists. However, their purchases included works by Old Masters, such as the portrait of Queen Elizabeth I (No. 18) noted below.

In dynastic collections there is a habitual preoccupation, which continues in the present reign, with the personal history of the royal line, and the collection of Dutch and Flemish drawings at Windsor Castle plays its part in documenting this history from the sixteenth century onwards. A finely wrought posthumous portrait of Queen Elizabeth I by Crispin van de Passe (No. 18) was purchased – as a work by Isaac Oliver – during the reign of another Queen, Victoria, while H.M. Queen Elizabeth II has recently acquired a portrait of Charles I attributed to Hendrick Pot.[6] Among crucial historical events, Charles II's departure from Scheveningen at the time of the Restoration of the Monarchy figures large in the collection and is represented in the exhibition by drawings by both Willem van de Velde the Younger (No. 53) and Pieter Bout (No. 56). The subject of the latter, acquired during the reign of George III, went unrecognized at the time, being described as "an Army going to embark at Scheveling." Topographical views of the royal residences have always been popular and are shown here with Joris Hoefnagel's two studies of Windsor Castle, made for that great sixteenth-century atlas by Braun and Hogenberg, the *Civitates Orbis Terrarum*; the free preparatory study (No. 13), completed with colored washes, was bought by H.M. Queen Elizabeth II, while the final squared-up drawing (No. 14), which also includes a view of Oxford, appears to have been acquired during the reign of Queen Victoria.

The great acquisitive days of George III will almost certainly never return, but the Royal Collection remains a living organism which offers instruction and delectation to the monarch and his or her subjects as well as to the international community.

[6] W & C 421A.

The Catalogue

Catalogue note

The works by each artist have been arranged in approximate
chronological order according to the date of the artist's birth,
and within a single artist's *oeuvre*, the date of execution.
For full bibliographical information, and for further details
concerning the watermarks, the reader is referred to
Christopher White and Charlotte Crawley, *The Dutch and
Flemish Drawings of the Fifteenth to the Early Nineteenth Centuries
in the Collection of Her Majesty The Queen at Windsor Castle*
(Cambridge 1994; abbreviated as w & c). That publication
supersedes the catalogues of the Flemish and Dutch drawings
by Leo van Puyvelde, published respectively in 1942 and
1944, in which many of the drawings were first discussed in
print. In the measurements height precedes width.

Attributed to **Hugo van der Goes**

Active from *c.*1467, died 1482

First recorded as a master of the Ghent Guild in 1467, Van der Goes the following year was called to Bruges with other artists to work on the decorations connected with the marriage of Charles the Bold and Margaret of York. He remained active in Ghent until at least 1475, but around 1476 he entered the monastery of the Roode Klooster near Brussels, where he continued to paint. In later years he suffered from a mental disorder.

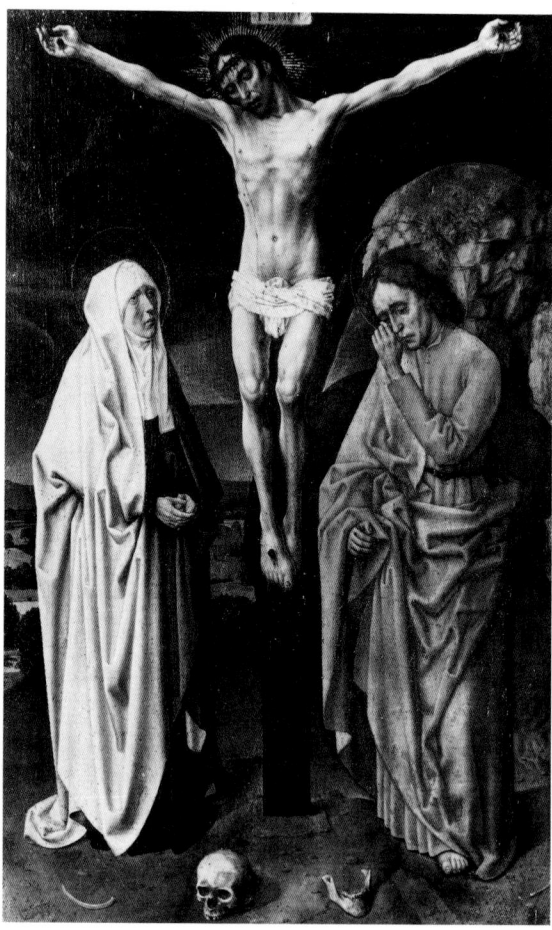

Hugo van der Goes,
Crucifixion
Oil on panel, $16\frac{5}{8} \times 10\frac{11}{16}$ in.
(42×27 cm)
(Venice, Museo Correr:
I, 934)

1 *Christ on the Cross*

$10\frac{1}{8} \times 8\frac{1}{4}$ in. (258×210 mm) (max.)

Pen and brush and brown ink, heightened with white, on slate-gray prepared paper

Watermark: Gothic letter *p*

Coll: possibly George III

Bibl: Popham (1926), no. 13; w & c I (RL 12951)

Apart from some minor differences in the drawing of the knees and the folds of the loincloth, the drawing corresponds with a painting of the *Crucifixion* in the Museo Correr, Venice, sometimes but not invariably accepted as being by Hugo van der Goes.

There is a similar disagreement about whether the present drawing is by the master or is a copy. There are no undisputed drawings by Hugo van

der Goes, but a convincing case can be made for the beautiful drawing of *Jacob and Rachel* at Christ Church, Oxford,[1] which is executed in the same technique and on paper with a preparation of the same color as that used in the present sheet. Although perhaps marginally lower in quality, No. 1 is very close to the Christ Church drawing in style and may with some reservation be attributed to Van der Goes. It can also be compared to a very similar drawing of a *Seated Female Saint with a Book on Her Knees* in the Courtauld Institute Galleries, which has been considered to be an autograph *ricordo* after a figure in a lost painting by Van der Goes.[2] The present drawing may be another example of such procedure.

[1] Byam Shaw, no. 1309, Pl. 772.
[2] Seilern, no. 314, Pls. XXVI-XXVII.

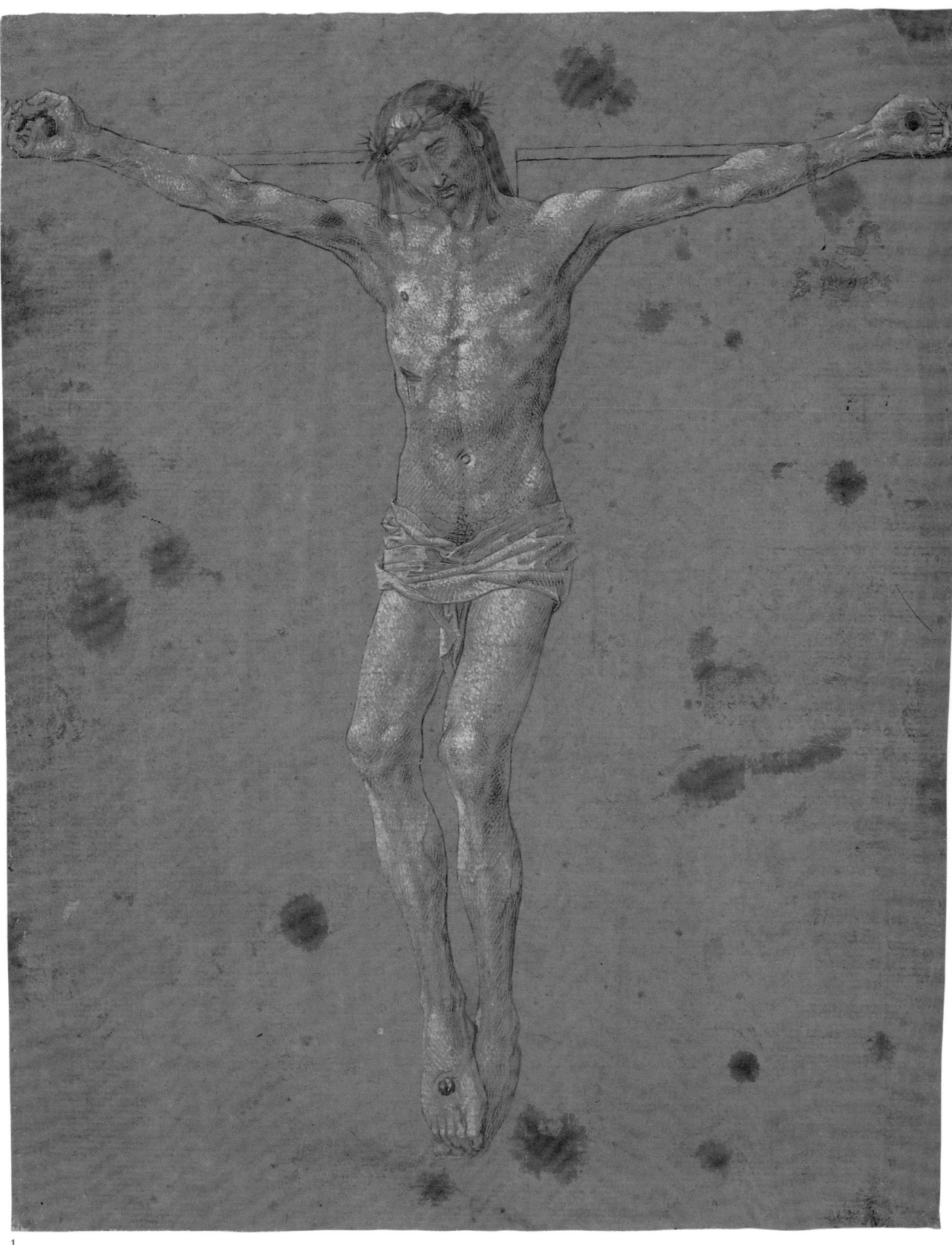

The Master of the Story of Tobit

Active *c*.1480–90

2 *Tobias and the Fish*

$7\frac{3}{16} \times 6\frac{15}{16}$ in. (183×177 mm)

Pen and brown ink

Watermark: Gothic letter *p* surmounted by a four-petalled flower

Bibl: Popham (1928), p.178; W & C 2 (RL 12952)

In the foreground Tobias, watched by the angel Raphael standing behind him, draws the fish out of the water, an event recorded in the apocryphal Book of Tobit, which was a popular source in the art of the Netherlands. The scene in the left background may either represent the return home of Tobias and the angel to Tobit and Anna, or, possibly, the reception of Tobias and the angel by Raguel, his wife Edna, and his daughter Sara in the town of Ecbatana, an event that immediately followed the main incident in the present drawing.

The present drawing and another also with a subject taken from the Book of Tobit provide the basis for a clearly recognizable group of drawings in the style of Hugo van der Goes, all executed in pen and ink with the same careful hatched shading. The existence of a related series of glass roundels illustrating the story of Tobit suggests that the draughtsman was primarily a designer for stained glass, working in the Netherlands near the end of the fifteenth century. The glass roundels were probably executed a little later than the related drawings. A roundel which exactly repeats the composition of the present drawing is now in King's College Chapel, Cambridge.[1]

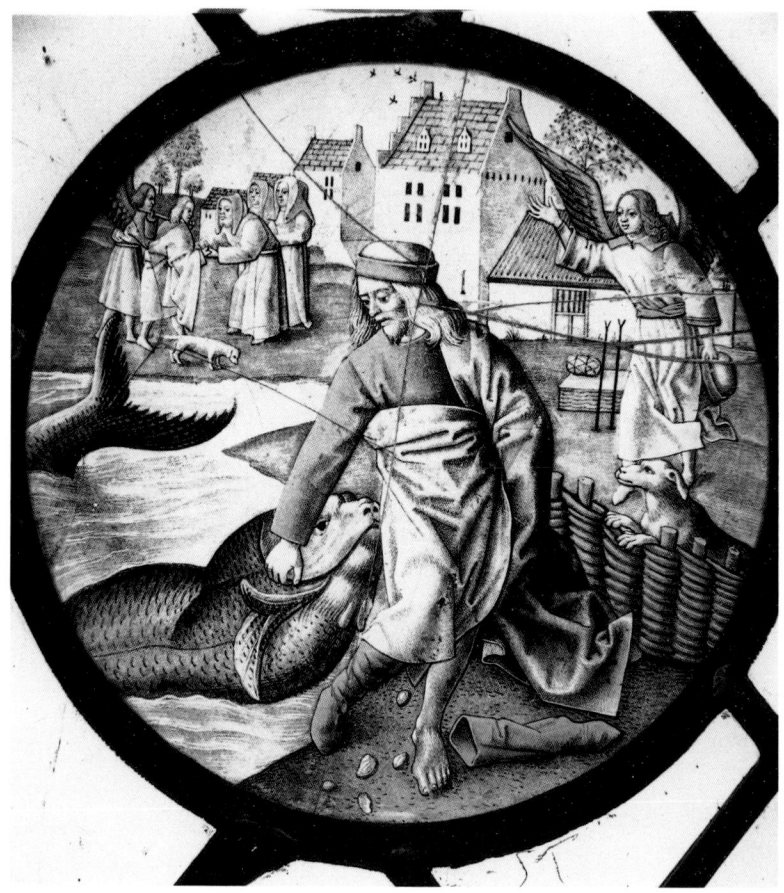

Flemish, *Tobias and the Fish*
Painted glass roundel set in lead, diam. $7\frac{15}{16}$ in. (200 mm)
(Cambridge, King's College Chapel)

[1] Wayment, no. 51c 1.

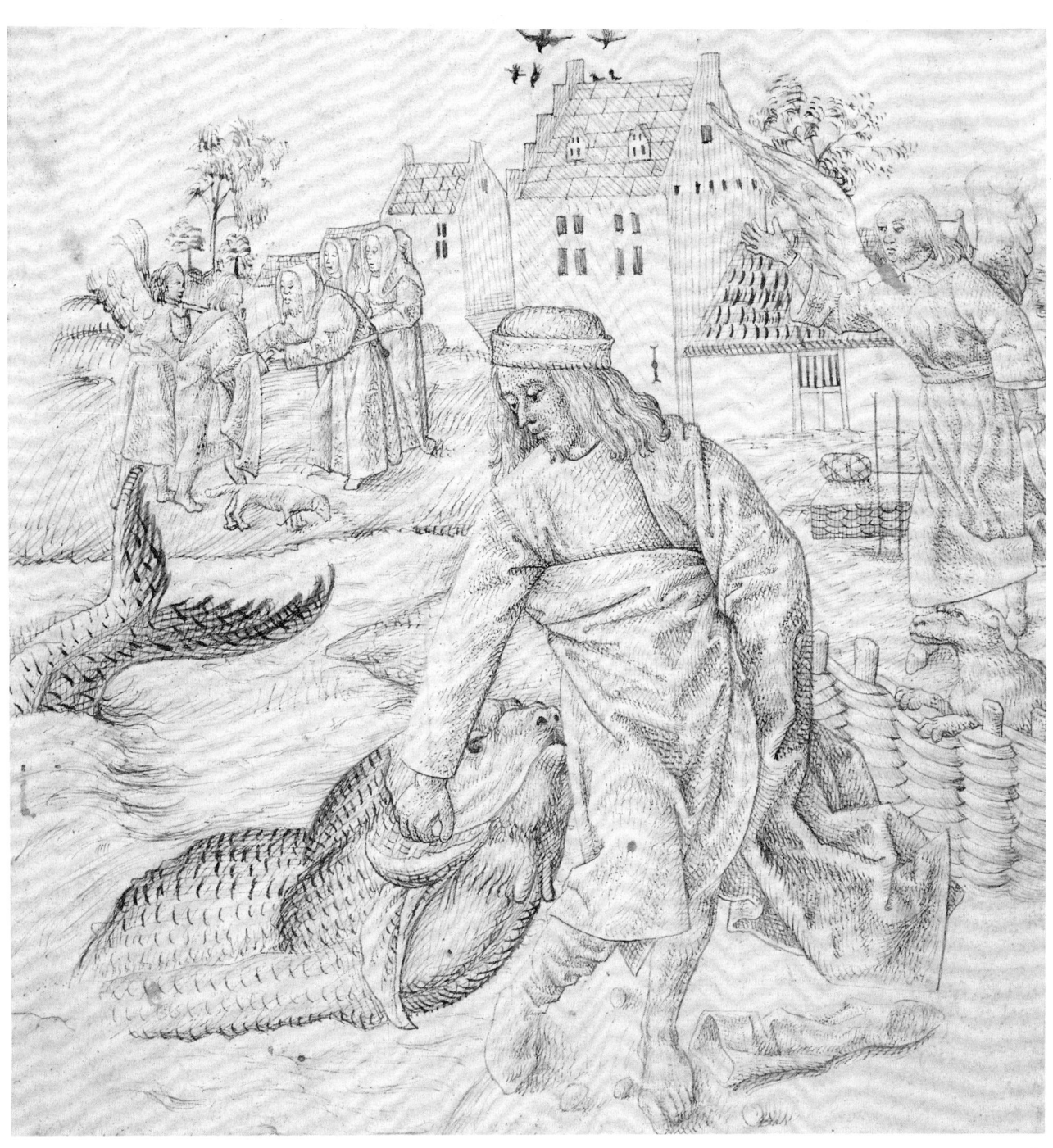

2

Jan van der Straet, called Stradanus

1523–1605

Jan van der Straet, called Stradanus, was born in Bruges and was a pupil of Pieter Aertsen in Antwerp before becoming a master in 1545. He left the Netherlands shortly afterwards, traveling south via Lyon and Venice before reaching Florence. Apart from several years spent in Naples and Flanders in the second half of the 1570s, Stradanus lived for the remainder of his life in Florence, where he carried out many commissions for the Medici family. He made numerous designs for the Medici tapestry factory and was an active participant in a number of large-scale decorative schemes celebrating various events connected with the Grand Dukes of Tuscany, although almost nothing of the latter work has survived.[1] Over the course of his life Stradanus produced a large number of preparatory drawings for prints; for the most part his designs (including Nos. 4, 5, and 7) were engraved in Antwerp. According to Baldinucci, Stradanus only turned to such work after he came back to Florence following his return visit to Antwerp in or shortly after 1578.

3 Ulysses and Circe

11¾ × 8⅝ in. (299 × 220 mm)

Pen and brownish-black ink with brownish-gray wash, heightened with white, over traces of black chalk, on yellow prepared paper

Bibl: Thiem (1958), p. 97; w & c 143 (RL 12969)

In Florence Stradanus joined the circle of artists working with Giorgio Vasari during the second half of the 1550s and the 1560s on the decorations of the apartments of Eleonora of Toledo (the wife of Grand Duke Cosimo de' Medici) as well as other rooms in the Palazzo Vecchio. In 1569 the team

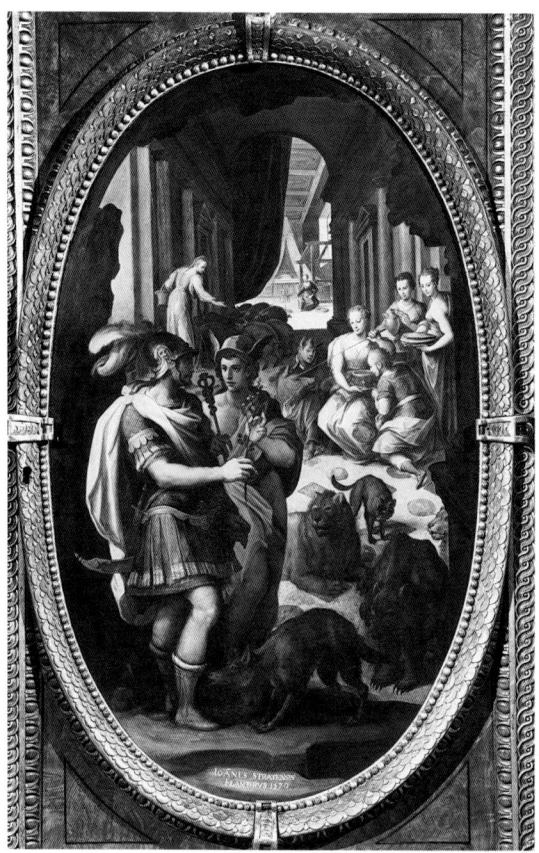

Jan van der Straet, called Stradanus, *Circe Changing the Companions of Ulysses into Animals* Oil on panel, 46 5/16 × 26 15/16 in. (117 × 68 cm) (Florence, Palazzo Vecchio, Studiolo di Francesco I)

under Vasari began work on the *studiolo* of Francesco I de' Medici, a small room adjoining the Salone del Cinquecento on the first floor. Based on an iconographic program drawn up by Vincenzo Borghini, thirty-four paintings were produced which were inserted into the walls; in addition the decoration included eight bronze statues and stuccoes and painted panels on the ceiling. Stradanus was responsible for two paintings, both signed and dated 1570, the oval *Circe Changing the Companions of Ulysses into Animals* and the rectangular *Alchemy*, for both of which preparatory drawings exist at Windsor Castle.[2]

The subject of the present drawing is taken from the *Odyssey*, Book X, lines 302–306, which describes the Greek hero's visit to Circe's island on his way home from the Trojan War. It was Circe's habit to transform travelers into animals by doctoring viands with a magic potion. On the left, Ulysses is led in by Mercury, who gives him the "moly" root to protect him from Circe; they are watched by several of Ulysses's companions who have been changed into animals. Behind, Circe, holding her magic wand and watched by two female companions, administers the magic potion to one of Ulysses's followers, while further back other animals are fed; in the background a woman can be seen spinning in a large chamber. Ulysses subsequently overcame the sorceress and forced her to change his companions back into human form. In order to adapt his design in the drawing to the small painting, which was placed on the left wall of the *studiolo*, Stradanus omitted a number of the animals from the final design.

[1] See Van Sasse van Ysselt.
[2] For the painting of *Alchemy*, see Venturi, IX, part VI, p. 435, Fig. 246, and for the drawing, w & c 142.

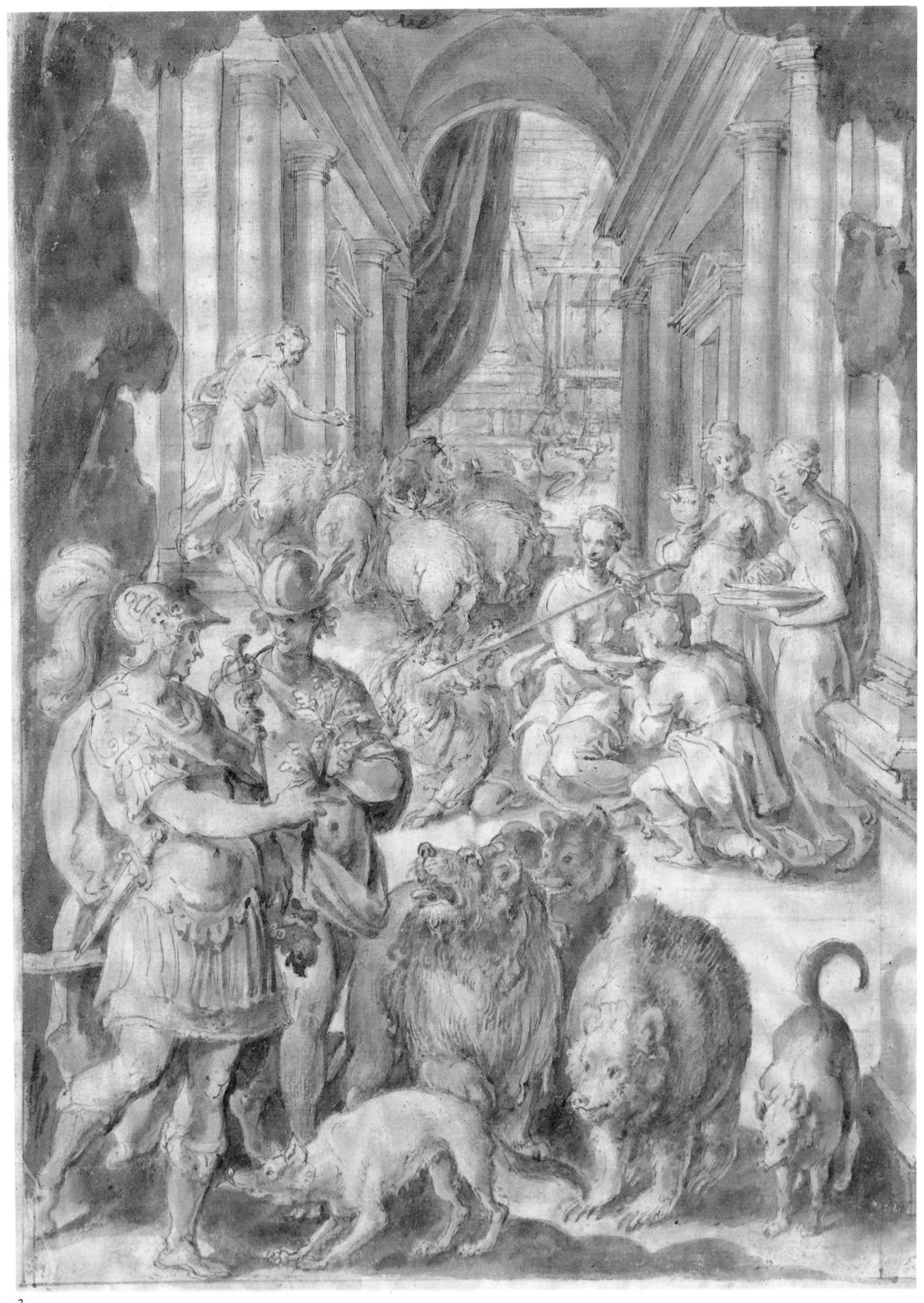

3

4 *The Marriage of the Virgin*

$6\frac{11}{16} \times 5\frac{1}{8}$ in. (170 × 130 mm)

Pen and brown ink with brown wash, heightened with white, on pink prepared paper

Signed lower center on the step: *Io. STRADANVS INVENTOR.*

Coll: George III

Bibl: Thiem (1958), pp. 99–100, 103, and (1959), pp. 156, 160, 165, n.1; w & c 148 (RL 4700)

The present drawing is one of a set of preparatory studies at Windsor for the title page and seventeen illustrations for the *Life of the Virgin*, engraved in reverse to the same scale, and published by Adriaen Collaert in Antwerp.[3] Although the prints are undated, two of the drawings bear an indistinct date which appears to be 1580. The engravings were probably made soon after this date. The composition of the *Circumcision* in the series was copied in a Bruges tapestry dated 1587.[4] (Since the tapestry is in the same direction as the drawing, it appears that the latter rather than Collaert's engraving may have been the source.) The engravings were later used as models for a series of engraved scenes around the Madonna and Child on a silver altar in the Museo degli Argenti in Florence.[5]

The scene shown in No. 4, based on the account in the *Golden Legend*, takes place beneath an elaborate baldacchino with St. Joseph on the left, holding his miraculously flowering rod, which revealed him as the successful suitor, and Mary on the right, supported by her seven virgin companions. To the left of St. Joseph can be seen the unsuccessful suitors, two of whom break their rods over their knees in disgust.

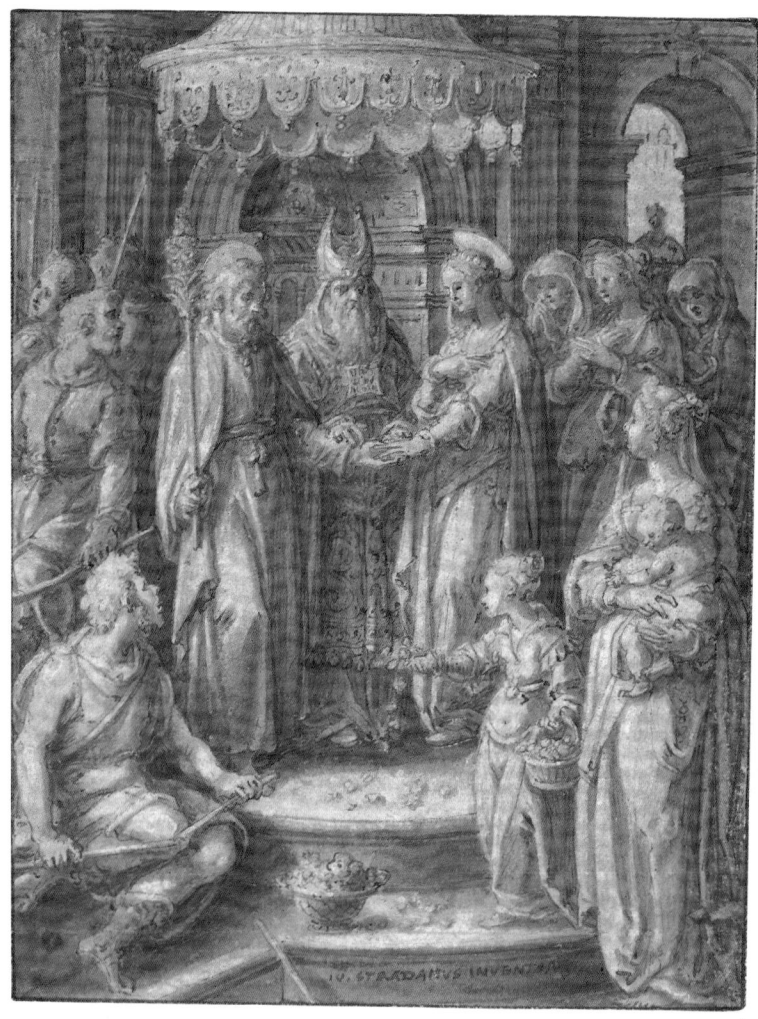

4

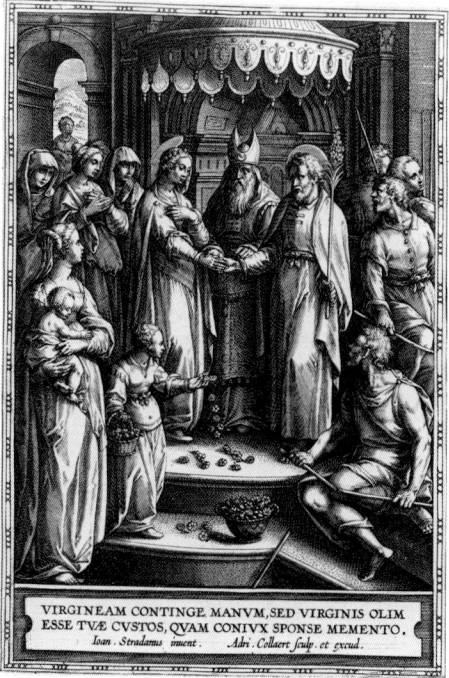

VIRGINEAM CONTINGE MANVM, SED VIRGINIS OLIM
ESSE TVÆ CVSTOS, QVAM CONIVX SPONSE MEMENTO.
Ioan. Stradanus inuent.   Adri. Collaert sculp. et excud.

Adrian Collaert after Stradanus,
The Marriage of the Virgin
Engraving, platemark $7\frac{13}{16} \times 5\frac{1}{2}$ in. (197 × 139 mm)
(London, British Museum, Department of Prints and Drawings)

[3] Hollstein, IV, p. 202, nos. 127–46; for the other drawings, see w & c 144–61.

[4] Bruges, no. 29, repr.

[5] Thiem (1959).

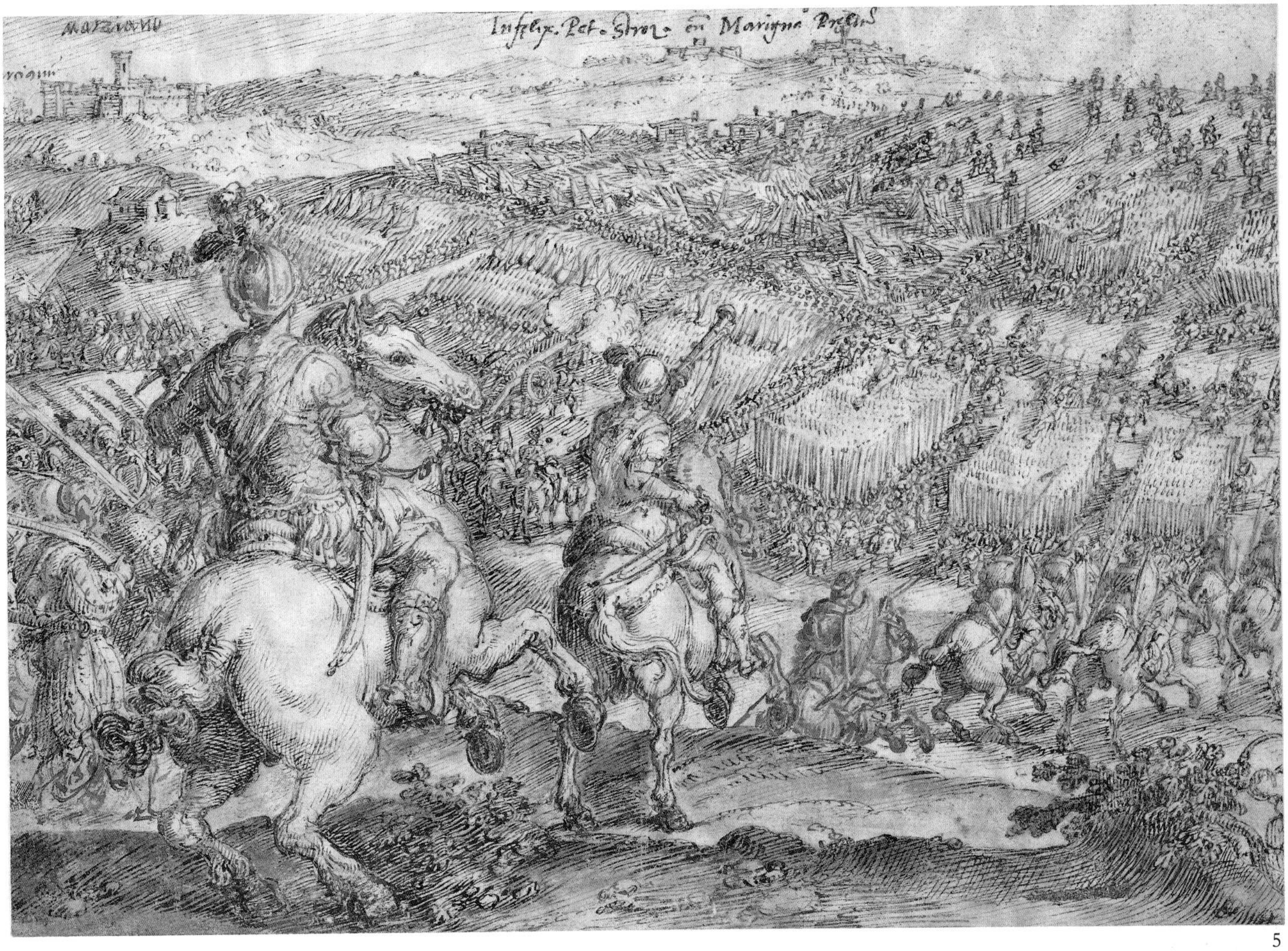

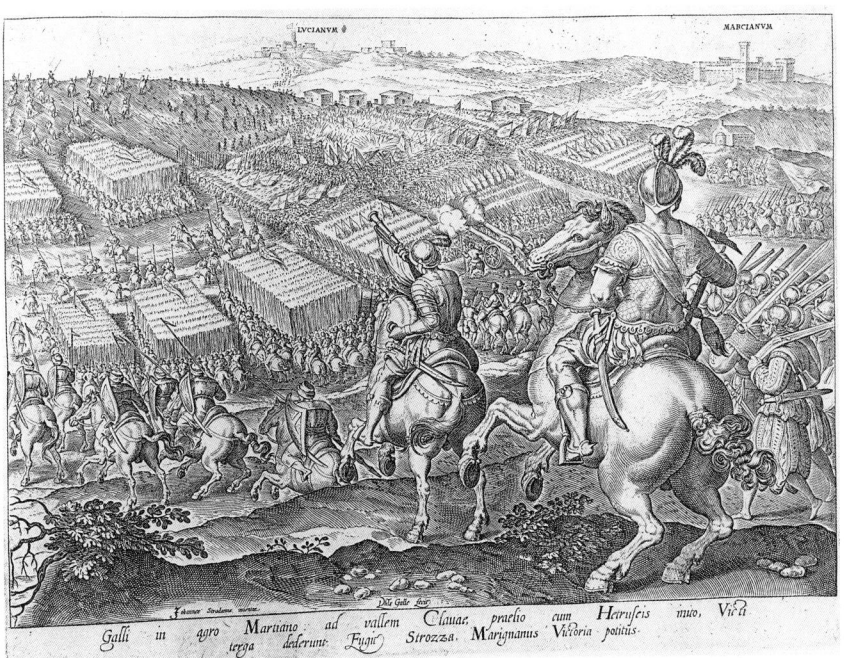

5

5 The Battle of Marciano in 1554

$7\frac{15}{16} \times 11\frac{1}{2}$ in. (202 × 292 mm)

Pen and brown ink with brownish-gray wash, heightened with white, indented for transfer

Inscribed along top: [Ma]*rcianū | Marziano*, and *Infelix. Pet. Stroz. in Marigna Prel* (The unfortunate Piero Strozzi in the battle of Marignano [*sic* for Marciano])

Coll: George III

Bibl: Reznicek (1964), under no. 31; w & c 164 (RL 6339)

This study is one of a group of preparatory drawings, including another at Windsor representing an earlier stage in the same battle,[6] for a series of prints of the *History of the*

[6] w & c 163, listing the other preparatory drawings.

Philippe Galle after Stradanus, *The Battle of Marciano*
Engraving, platemark $8\frac{11}{16} \times 11\frac{1}{2}$ in. (220 × 290 mm)
(London, British Museum, Department of Prints and Drawings)

Medici (*Mediceae Familiae rerum feliciter gestarum victoriae et triumphi*), designed, according to the title page, by Stradanus and engraved by Philip Galle (although five of the twenty-two plates were engraved by Hendrick Goltzius), which was published in Antwerp in 1583.[7] Plate 5, for which this drawing is preparatory, was engraved by Philip Galle. The drawing coincides very closely (in reverse) with the printed image, which is precisely the same size as No. 5.

The present drawing depicts the battle of Marciano, situated southeast of Siena, in which the Sienese forces, under the Florentine exile Piero Strozzi and including French troops, were routed by the Florentine forces commanded by Gian Giacomo de' Medici, Marchese di Marignano, with an army of 24,000 Spanish and Italian troops, on 2 August 1554. In the left foreground, a general on horseback – possibly Gian Giacomo de' Medici – follows cavalry and infantry towards further troops in the valley. The inscription along the top of the sheet refers to Strozzi's troops, seen fleeing on the distant hillside. The town of Marciano is on the left horizon. In the engraving the other hill is identified as Lucignano.

The battle had already been the subject of a painting in the Palazzo Vecchio, Florence, executed for Cosimo de' Medici in 1561. In 1569, fourteen years before the publication of the engravings, Stradanus had designed nine tapestry cartoons with subjects taken from the history of the war with Siena. These were for the use of the Fabbrica degli Arazzi, which had been founded by Cosimo in 1546 and was put under the direction of Vasari in 1557. A version of the present drawing, in the Uffizi, Florence,[8] drawn in pen and wash without hatching, may possibly relate to the tapestry cartoon design of 1569.

6 Cornelia, Mother of the Gracchi, with Female Companions Engaged in Needlework

$7\frac{13}{16} \times 10\frac{13}{16}$ in. (199 × 275 mm)

Pen and brown ink with brown and gray wash, heightened with white

Signed lower right: *Stradanus*
Coll: George III

Bibl: Thiem (1958), pp. 94–95; w & c 165 (RL 4762)

The subject, which largely corresponds to Valerius Maximus IV, 6.1 (on conjugal love) and Plutarch, 2–3 (Tiberius and Gaius Gracchus), is Cornelia, the daughter of Scipio Africanus and the wife of Tiberius Sempronius Gracchus, by whom she had two sons, Tiberius and Gaius, known as "The Gracchi." She was noted for her virtue.

In the foreground, four women seated in a richly decorated room are making embroidery, threads, needlepoint, and lace. The woman seated at the spinning wheel (with a child beside her) is presumably Cornelia; on the right is another woman with a child in front of the fire. The children are presumably intended to be the Gracchi. To the left of the bed, Tiberius Gracchus is shown killing the male snake emerging from a dish, presumably illustrating the tale of how he found two snakes (probably the scene represented through the doorway in the background) and in response to a prophecy killed the male to save the life of his wife (see below).

The drawing is a preparatory study in reverse for the engraving by Theodoor Galle, inscribed: *Ne te fatidicis Tyrrhenus terreat augur/ Graccus ait monitis, Cornelia, non mihi vitae/ Tantus amor, tantae post funera coniugis vnguam/ Ut superesse velim, iugulum sed masculus anguis/ Prebebit prior, immineant vt summa priori/ Fata mihi, vitamque tuis virtutibus aequent* ("'[Titus Sempronius]

Gracchus says: 'let not the Etruscan soothsayer terrify you, Cornelia, with his prophetic warnings. I have not so great a love of life that I should ever wish to survive after the death of so great a wife. But the male snake shall present his throat [to be slit] first, so that the final fate may threaten me first and make [your life equal to your virtues]' "). This forms part of an untitled and undated series of six subjects from early Roman history.[9] Preparatory drawings, shaded with hatching as well as wash, for the remaining five plates are in the Albertina, Vienna.[10] As with No. 7, the fact that Theodoor Galle was only born in 1571 suggests that the engravings could not have been made much before c.1590.

The composition of the present subject is a reworking of an earlier version by Stradanus, which is known from the engraving of 1576 by P. D. Furnius as part of a set of six plates depicting celebrated Roman women.[11]

[7] Hollstein, VII, p. 80, nos. 462–83.
[8] Reznicek (1964), no. 31, Fig. 30.
[9] Hollstein, VII, p. 86, nos. 390–95.
[10] Benesch (1928), nos. 171–75, Pls. 46–47.
[11] Hollstein, VII, p. 44, no. 19. Although the *mise-en-scène* is similar, none of the figures is identical. As the inscription emphasizes, greater prominence is given in this version to the incident of Tiberius Gracchus killing the snake. The engraving was presumably based on a now-lost drawing by Stradanus.

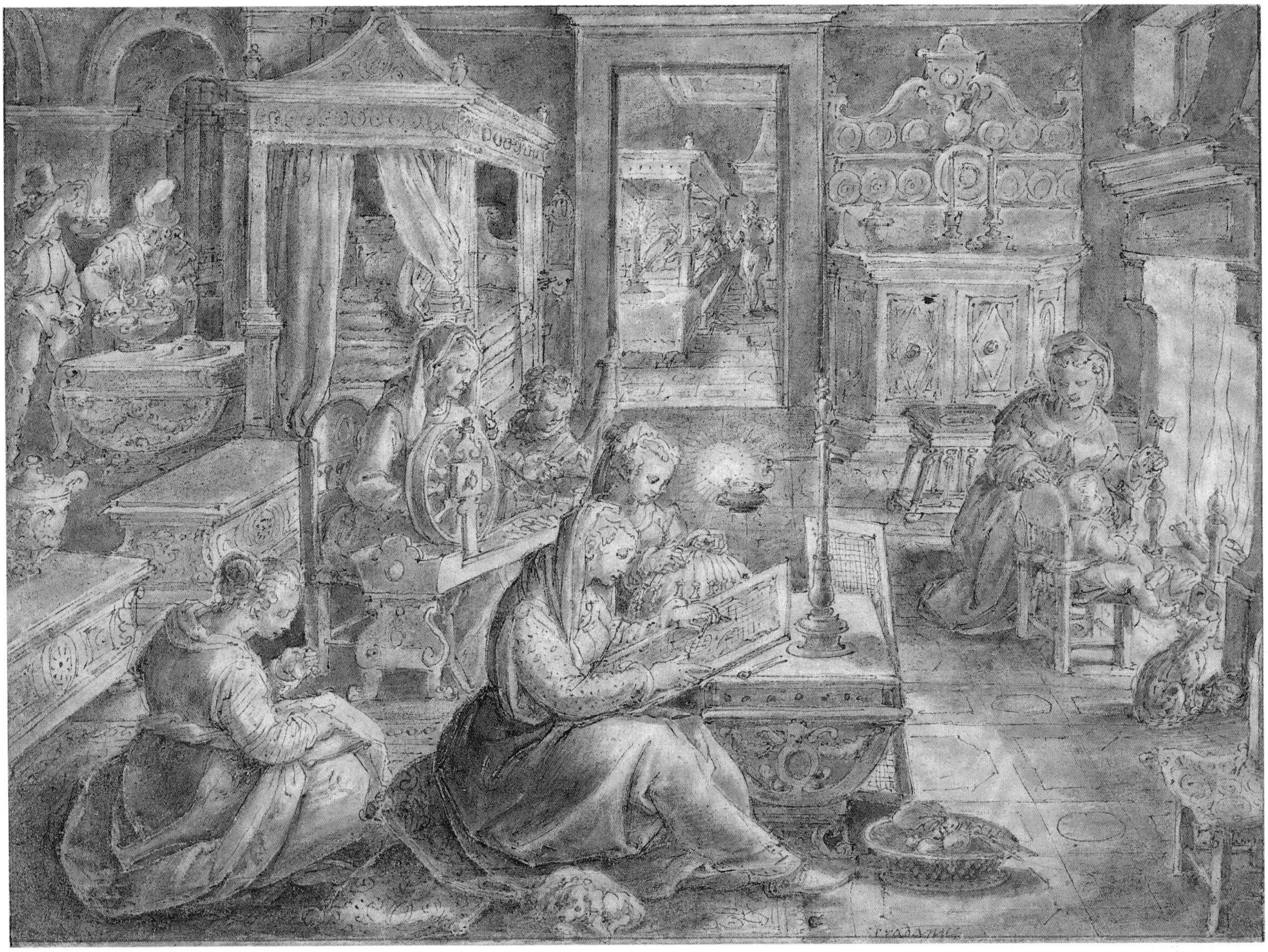

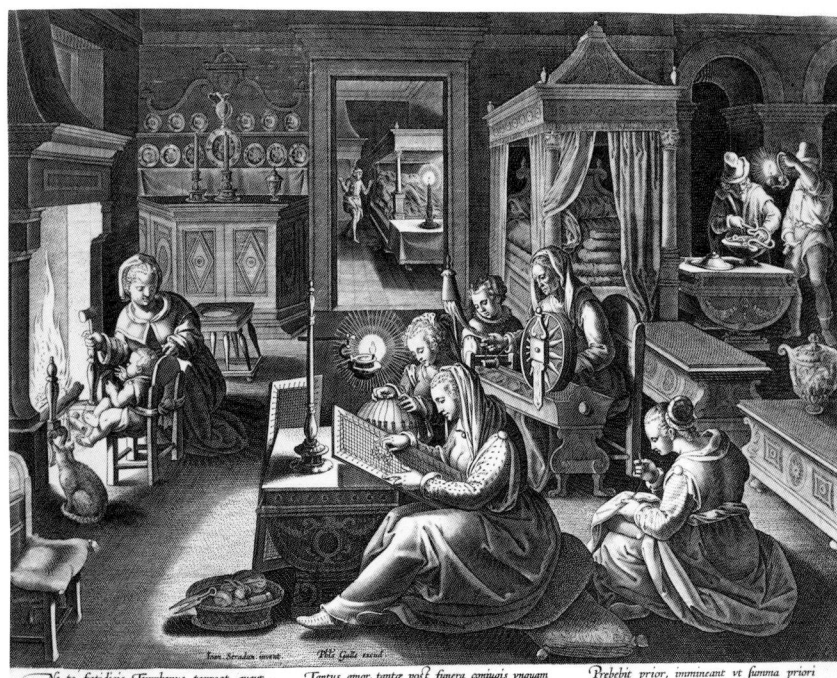

6

Theodoor Galle after Stradanus,
*Cornelia, Mother of the Gracchi, and Her Female
Companions*
Engraving, 8½ × 11 in. (215 × 280 mm)
(cut within platemark; Vienna, Graphische
Sammlung Albertina)

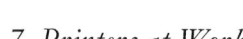

7 Printers at Work

$7\frac{5}{16} \times 11\frac{5}{16}$ in. (186 × 289 mm) (max.)

The figure of the seated compositor lower right is drawn on another piece of paper and inserted.

Pen and brown ink with brown wash over traces of black chalk, with touches of red chalk, heightened with white

Signed lower center: *Ioannes Stradan.*
Inscribed upper left on capital: *Io: Guttem/bergius | Argenti/nensis* (Johannes Gutenberg of Strasburg) and *Moguntie* (Mainz) | *1440*; and on the soffit of the arch: *Sigilla fumus atra paginae imprimens/ Librum dat usque mille milliũ agmina* (The smoke, as it prints little black figures on the page, produces a book up to a thousand thousand columns long); the date *1440* is repeated in the spandrel. On the *verso* there is a long inscription by the artist about the invention of printing; see below.

Coll: George III

Bibl: Thiem (1958), p. 91; Gerhardt, pp. 44–49; Roberts (1986), no. 57; w & c 167 (RL 4761)

With a preliminary sketch in the Cooper-Hewitt Museum, New York,[12] the present drawing is a preparatory study for the engraving by Hans Collaert entitled *Impressio Librorum* (the printing of books). The composition was reversed in the process of printing. The scale of No. 7 is precisely that of the printed image. *Impressio Librorum* is part of the series, entitled *Nova Reperta* (new findings), consisting of twenty engravings (ten by Collaert and ten by Theodoor Galle), which were published, without date, by Philip Galle in Antwerp.[13] The prints illustrate a wide variety of

[12] Benisovich, p. 250.
[13] Hollstein, IV, p. 213, nos. 129–48 and VII, p. 87, nos. 410–30.

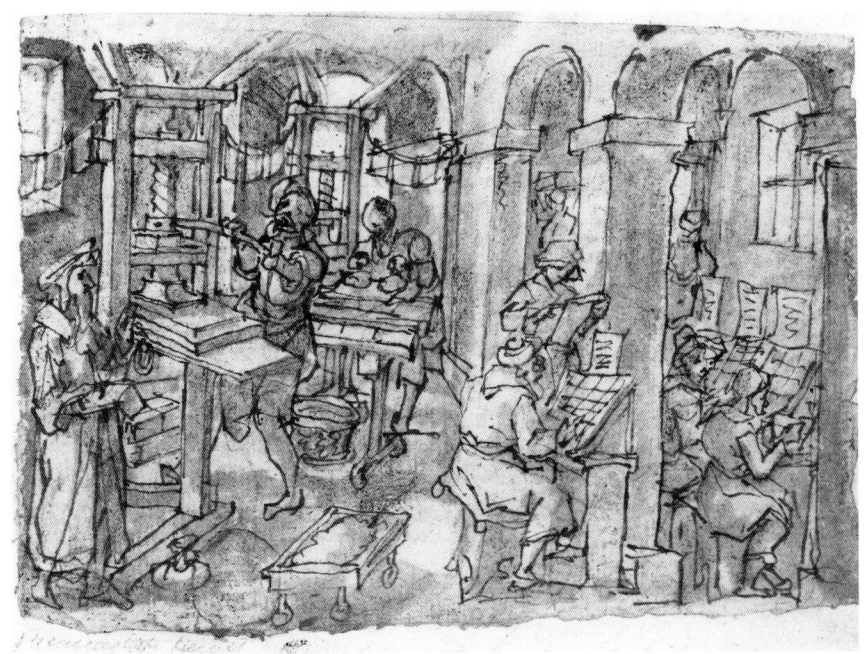

Jan van der Straet, called Stradanus, *The Printing of Books*
Pen and brown ink with gray wash, $4\frac{5}{16} \times 6$ in. (108×151 mm) (New York,
Cooper-Hewitt Museum, Friends of the Museum Fund: 1901–39–301)

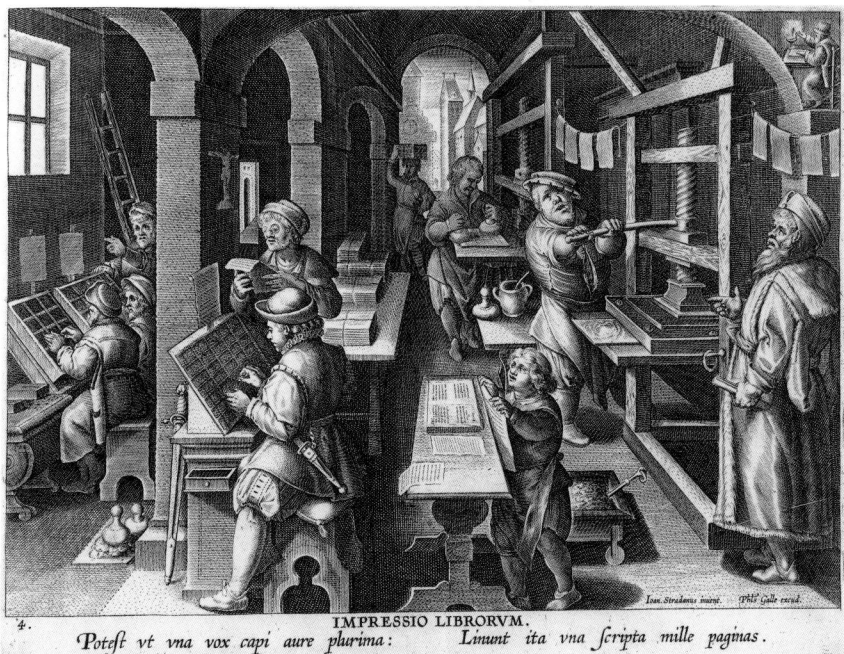

Hans Collaert after Stradanus, *Impressio Librorum*
Engraving, platemark $7\frac{15}{16} \times 10\frac{7}{16}$ in. (200×264 mm) (London, British Museum,
Department of Prints and Drawings)

inventions and discoveries. Another connected drawing, *Engravers at Work*, is also in the Royal Collection.[14]

Owing to a misreading of the date upper left as 1550 instead of 1440, Thiem had placed Stradanus's work on the *Nova Reperta* series at the very beginning of the artist's career. Theodoor Galle, who engraved half the plates, was only born in 1571. Moreover, Guicciardini's *Descrizzione di tutti i paesi bassi* (which is referred to in the artist's inscription on the *verso*) was only published in 1567, and André Thevet's *Pourtraits et vies des hommes illustres* (the probable source of the portrait of Gutenberg) only in 1584. The probable date of the *Nova Reperta* is more likely to be *c.*1590.

The subject represents a printer's shop, with the master printer on the left looking on. Above his head, sheets of paper are hung out to dry. In front of him, a man pulls a screw press (soon to be replaced by roller presses) while behind the latter the form is being inked. In the center foreground, a young apprentice lays out newly printed proofs, while behind him stacks of paper are being carried in and piled on the table. On the right the compositors are setting the type of the printer's copy displayed above their type-cases, while another man reads proofs. In the upper left spandrel, Johannes Gutenberg is shown at work inventing printing.

Traditionally, printing was believed to have been invented in Mainz in 1440, but by the 1560s this was disputed, among others, by Guicciardini, who is quoted in the long inscription on the *verso* as stating that the town of Haarlem was the first center. The uncertainty which, according to the inscription, Stradanus left to the publisher or engraver to resolve, may well have been the reason for the omission of the inscriptions below the figure of Gütenberg in the related engraving.

[14] w & c 166.

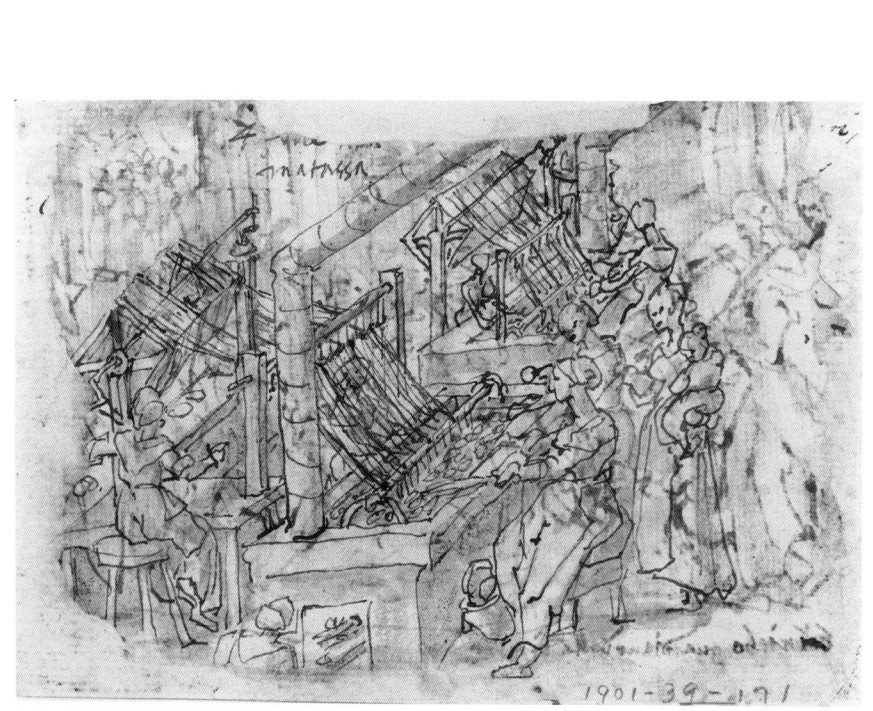

8

(*Left*) Jan van der Straet, called Stradanus, *Unwinding the Cocoons*
Pen and brown ink, $3\frac{15}{16} \times 5\frac{9}{16}$ in. (99 × 141 mm) (New York, Cooper-Hewitt Museum, Friends of the Museum Fund: 1901–39–171 recto)

(*Right*) Karel de Mallery after Stradanus, *Winding Silk*
Engraving, 8 × $10\frac{3}{4}$ in. (202 × 272 mm) (Royal Collection: Windsor Castle, Royal Library)

8 Winding Silk

7 × 10$\frac{9}{16}$ in. (178 × 269 mm)

Pen and brown ink with brown and gray wash over traces of black chalk, heightened with white, indented for transfer

Signed lower left: [J]*oannes* / [S]*trada* (cut at left)

Coll: George III

Bibl: Thiem (1958), p. 92; w & c 172 (RL 4766)

The drawing is a preparatory study, in reverse, for the last of the six plates engraved by Karel de Mallery for the series entitled *Vermis Sericus* (*The Silkworm*), which was published by Philip Galle, without details of either date or place of publication.[15] Finished drawings for plates 2–5 are also at Windsor Castle[16]; all are to the same scale as the engravings. There are also four sheets with preliminary sketches (on a smaller scale) in the Cooper-Hewitt Museum, New York, including one for the present drawing.[17] The series is in the same style and of the same size as the *Nova Reperta* (see No. 7) and was therefore probably also executed around 1590.[18]

The series illustrates the history of the silkworm and silk spinning, and

was dedicated to Constantia Alamannia, the wife of Raffaello de' Medici (died 1628), in Florence. She may be the sister of the Luigi Alemanni (or Alamanni) whose name occurs on the versos of two other drawings by Stradanus.[19] One of the most important industries in Florence since mediaeval times, the silk culture was revived and developed in the sixteenth century by Grand Duke Cosimo I de' Medici (1520–1574). It reached its peak under his son, Francesco I (1541–1587), so that in the year before his death, there were no less than 114 workshops in Florence.

The present drawing represents the process of silk winding, which was usually carried out by women. The engraving is inscribed *Hinc vermium permulta saepe millia* / *Simul legunt parantque telas feminae* (Here women often collect very many thousands of worms and at the same time prepare the threads). The cocoons kept in warm baths are unraveled by women and wound around winders. A woman with a child in her arms carries a basket of cocoons. In the background the cocoons are shown drying on the ground.

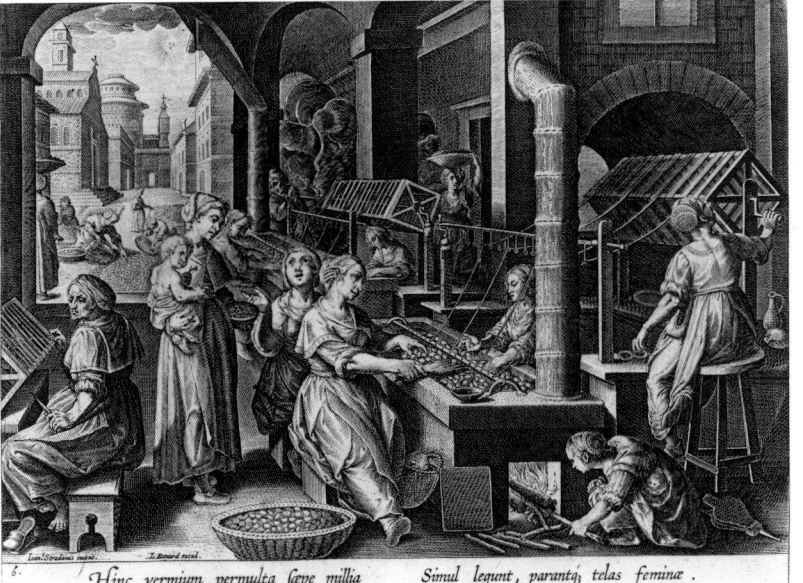

[15] Hollstein, XI, p. 160, nos. 115–20.

[16] w & c 168–71.

[17] Benisovich p. 251, Figs. 2b–f.

[18] Plate 8 of *Nova Reperta* is indeed devoted to the culture of silk; it is entitled *Ser, Sive Sericus Vermis*. Owing to a misreading of the date on one of the *Nova Reperta* drawings (no. 7), Thiem, *loc. cit.*, had placed both series at the beginning of the artist's career.

[19] The drawing of *Printers at Work*, at Windsor (No. 7, inscribed Allemari) and *Christ Preaching in a Ship*, in the Cooper-Hewitt Museum, New York (1901–39–134; inscribed: *Louigiallemane*). Constantia is described as "Costanza di Pietro Alamanni," while Luigi Alamanni (1558–1603) was the son of Piero. Raffaello de' Medici was a descendant of Giovenco de' Medici and was therefore only distantly related to the ruling branch of the family. (See w & c 167.)

Crispin van den Broeck

1524–1591

A painter and draughtsman, Van den Broeck was born in Malines. In around 1550 he became a pupil of Frans Floris in Antwerp, where, apart from a stay in Middelburg in 1584 and a possible journey to Italy, he spent the remainder of his life. He was active producing drawings for the engraver, above all for the Plantin Press, for which he produced his first design in 1566. Many of his drawings were engraved by the Wierix brothers.

9 The Last Supper

$11\frac{9}{16} \times 7\frac{3}{4}$ in. (294 × 198 mm)

Pen and brown ink with gray wash, indented for transfer.

There are the remnants of a cut inscription in the lower left corner: *C v . . .*[?]

Coll: George III

Bibl: W & C 41 (RL 4752)

Christ is seated in the center with St. John on his left; the other apostles are seated around him, with Judas Iscariot holding a purse lower right. With another drawing at Windsor of *The Saints in Glory*,[1] which can also be reasonably attributed to Van den Broeck, No. 9 is probably a design for an engraving, perhaps for a *Passion* series, which was either never executed or does not exist today. It is one of thirty-eight drawings at Windsor associated with Van den Broeck. All but four of the drawings are related to the engravings (by J. Sadeler the Elder) in L. Hillesemius, *Sacrarum Antiquitatum* (Antwerp, 1577). No. 9 is considerably larger in scale than Van den Broeck's designs for the latter publication.

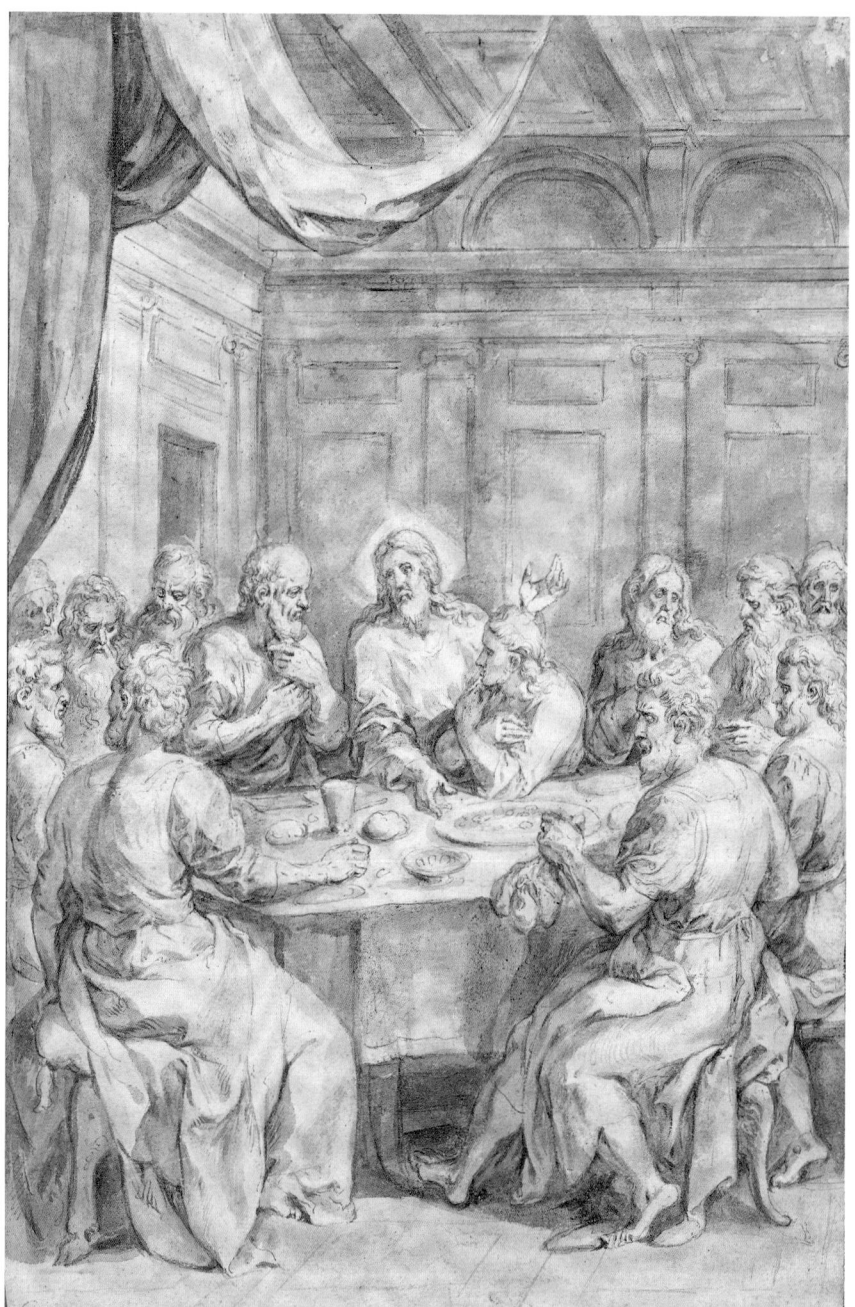

9

[1] W & C 40.

Marten de Vos

1532–1603

De Vos was born in Antwerp. After visiting Italy, where he worked under Tintoretto in Venice, he established himself as an artist in his hometown in 1558. In 1570, following the death of his master, Frans Floris, De Vos became the leading painter in the city. In 1572 he was one of the founding members of the confraternity of Romanists, which was composed of artists who had been to Italy. He produced a large number of drawings, many of which were engraved. His drawings were also much sought after by connoisseurs and artists.

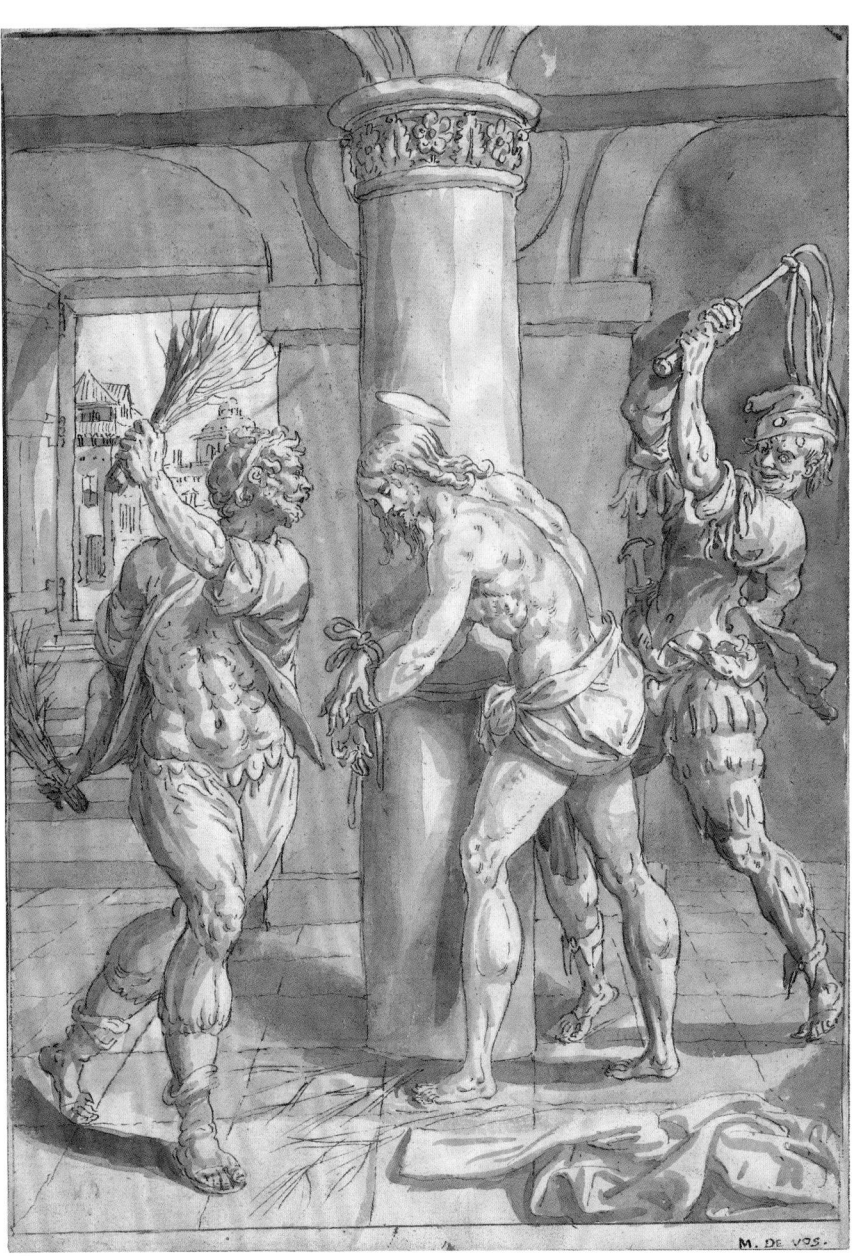

10

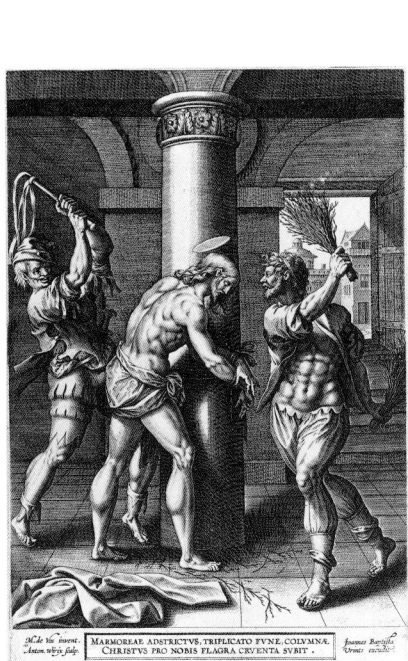

Anthonie Wierix after Marten de Vos, *The Scourging of Christ* Engraving, platemark $11\frac{3}{16} \times 7\frac{3}{4}$ in. (282 × 196 mm) (Brussels, Bibliothèque royale Albert Ier, Cabinet des Estampes)

10 *The Scourging of Christ*

$10\frac{13}{16} \times 7\frac{11}{16}$ in. (276 × 196 mm)

Pen and brown ink with brown wash, over black chalk, heightened with white

Signed (?) lower right: *M. DE VOS*

Coll: George III

Bibl: W & C 197 (RL 4751)

Executed in the artist's usual combination of fine penwork and wash, the drawing is an actual-size preparatory study, in reverse, for the engraving by Anthonie Wierix, which was published by the Antwerp engraver and publisher, J. B. Vrints.[1]

[1] Mauquoy-Hendrickx (1978), no. 294, pl. 35.

Dirck Barendsz.

1534–1592

Barendsz. was born in Amsterdam. As a young man he traveled to Italy and spent about five years in the studio of Titian in Venice (*c.*1555–60) before returning home. The reworked signature in No. 11 uses Barendsz.'s alternative name, Theodorus Bernardus of Amsterdam.

11 *The Fall of the Rebel Angels*

$20\frac{11}{16} \times 12\frac{15}{16}$ in. (527 × 330 mm) (arched at the top)

Pen and brown ink with brown and gray wash, with touches of white bodycolor, indented for transfer

Signed bottom center: *THEODORVS.*/ *BER. AMSTELODA* (?) (altered in black lead to *DENTEROSSA* (?))/*MVF:F*

Verso inscribed in black lead (largely illegible): *Dirck Barendt . . .*/*Van Amsterdam*/ . . . / . . .

Watermark: fleur-de-lys surmounted by a four-petalled flower, with lettering (NIVELLE) below

Coll: presumably George III

Bibl: Judson, no. 55; *Kunst voor de beeldenstorm*, no. 250; W & C 3 (RL 7786)

In his life of the artist, Van Mander describes among "several beautiful altarpieces" by Barendsz. commissioned by an Amsterdam shooting company "a fall of Lucifer . . . with many nudes, most excellently done,"[1] which was largely destroyed in the iconoclastic riots of 1566. Of the three existing shooting companies, the most likely commissioners of the altarpiece are the Kloveniers or arquebusiers. It was probably executed for their guild altar in the Oude Kerk, which suffered particularly severely during the iconoclastic riots. Given the inclusion of the figure of the marksman (lower right) and the prominence of the nude figures, it is reasonable to associate the drawing with the painting, which would have been executed sometime between Barendsz.'s return from Italy in 1562 and the date of its destruction in 1566. (Van Mander speaks of it as the artist's first altarpiece.) The drawing is unusually highly finished for a preparatory study and may have been executed as a *modello* to submit to the patrons. Although the outlines are indented with a stylus, no print after the composition is known.

The subject is taken from Revelation 12: 7–9 and shows God the Father hurling a thunderbolt while seated on a globe and surrounded by saints and angels. Below him, St. Michael accompanied by other angels drives down the rebel angels, here represented in the nude, who are attacked by lions and snakes. The inclusion of a rebel angel as a marksman can probably be read as a symbol of the evil in taking up arms against a divine power.[2] The unusual representation of St. Michael and Lucifer accompanied by supporters rather than depicted alone clearly reflects the well-known painting of the same subject painted by Frans Floris in 1554 for the Swordsmen's Guild in Antwerp.[3] Barendsz. could have seen the picture on his return journey from Italy in 1562.

[1] Van Mander, f.259v.

[2] See *Kunst voor de beeldenstorm*.

[3] Judson, Fig. 106.

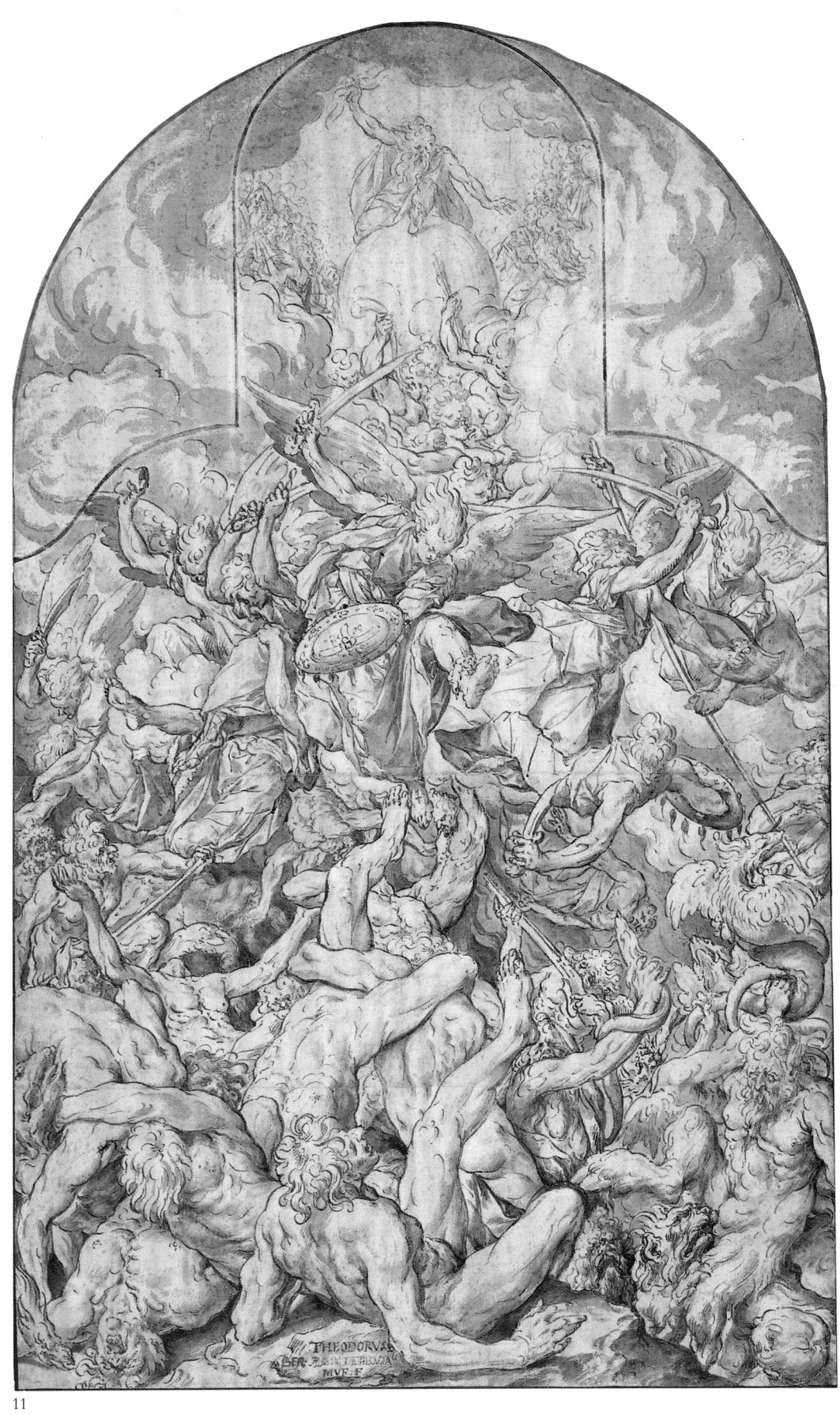

11

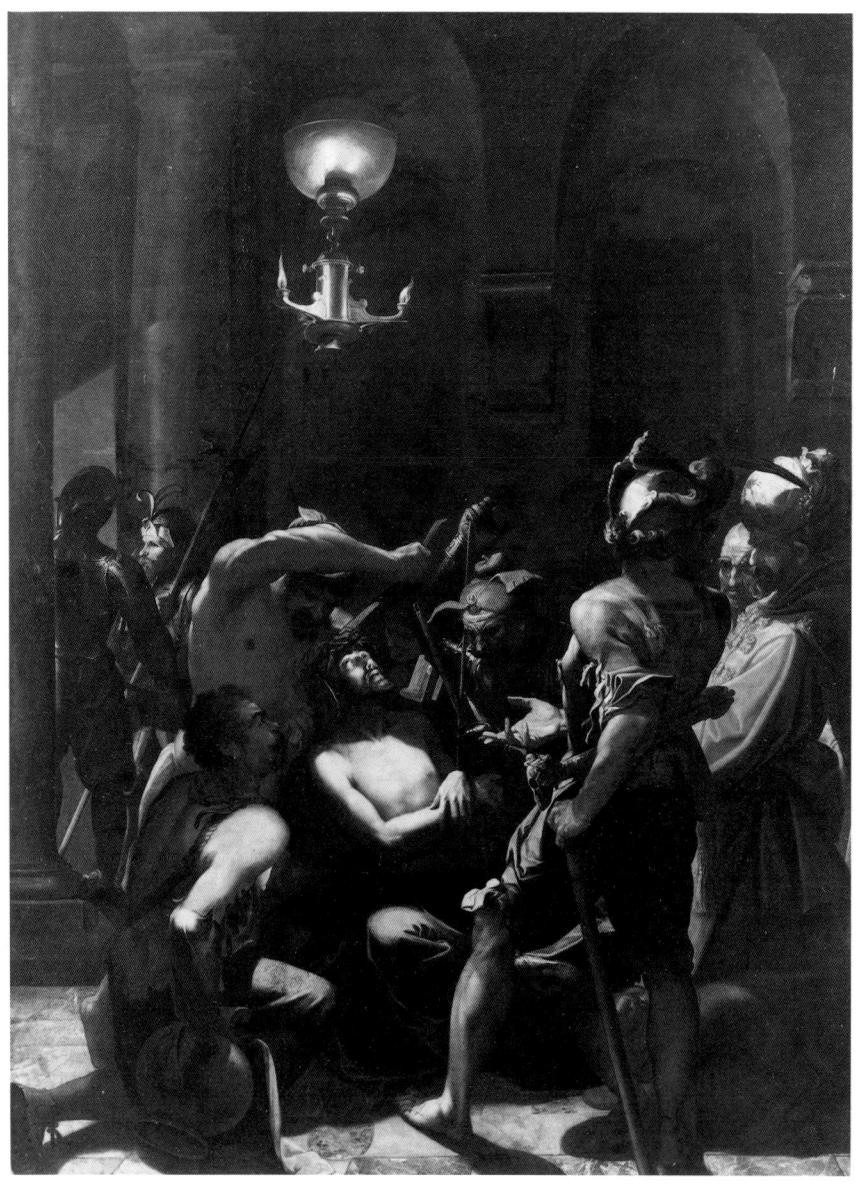

Arnout Mytens, *The Mocking of Christ*
Oil on canvas, $122\frac{3}{4} \times 90\frac{1}{4}$ in. (310×228 cm)
(Stockholm, Nationalmuseum: NM 755)

Arnout Mytens

1541–1602

Arnout Mytens was born in Brussels, but spent much of his life in Italy. He lived in Naples between 1581 and 1594, and died in Rome. Few details of his life, or paintings from his hand, have survived.

12 *The Mocking of Christ*

$21\frac{1}{16} \times 15\frac{15}{16}$ in. (536×405 mm)

Pen and brown ink and brown wash over black chalk on pink-tinted paper, heightened with white

Bibl: Benesch (1951), pp. 351–52;
W & C 58 (RL 01221)

This drawing is the preparatory study for Mytens's large painting now in the Nationalmuseum, Stockholm.[1] The painting, which was praised by Van Mander,[2] was begun in Naples, where the artist lived from 1581 to 1594; Mytens took the painting with him to Aquila in the Abruzzi and finally completed it in Rome. It was taken back to Amsterdam, where it belonged to Mytens's son-in-law, Bernard van Somer, who was also a painter.

There are a number of differences between the drawing and the painting, which are particularly noticeable in the background architecture. In the painting the monumentality is increased at the expense of the intensity of expression found in the drawing. Of the painting Van Mander wrote that "it is painted in an admirably grand style and in a different manner than is usual among Netherlanders – a proof that he was an excellent master, to whom we are indebted, if he succeeds in persuading the Italians to assert less frequently that the Netherlanders are incapable of painting good figures. He has given them sufficient reason to be silent on that point or at any rate to speak of it with more reserve." The strong contrast of light and shade, intensified in the painting, is one of the earliest examples of the Caravaggesque style in Flemish painting. But given the place and date when the picture was started, it would appear to have been conceived in a parallel style with that of Caravaggio, unless it was much transformed during its completion in Rome.

[1] Benesch, Fig. 26. There is a small identical version of the painting on copper (probably a copy) in the Fogg Art Museum, Cambridge (Bowron, p. 122, Fig. 176).

[2] Van Mander, f. 264.

34

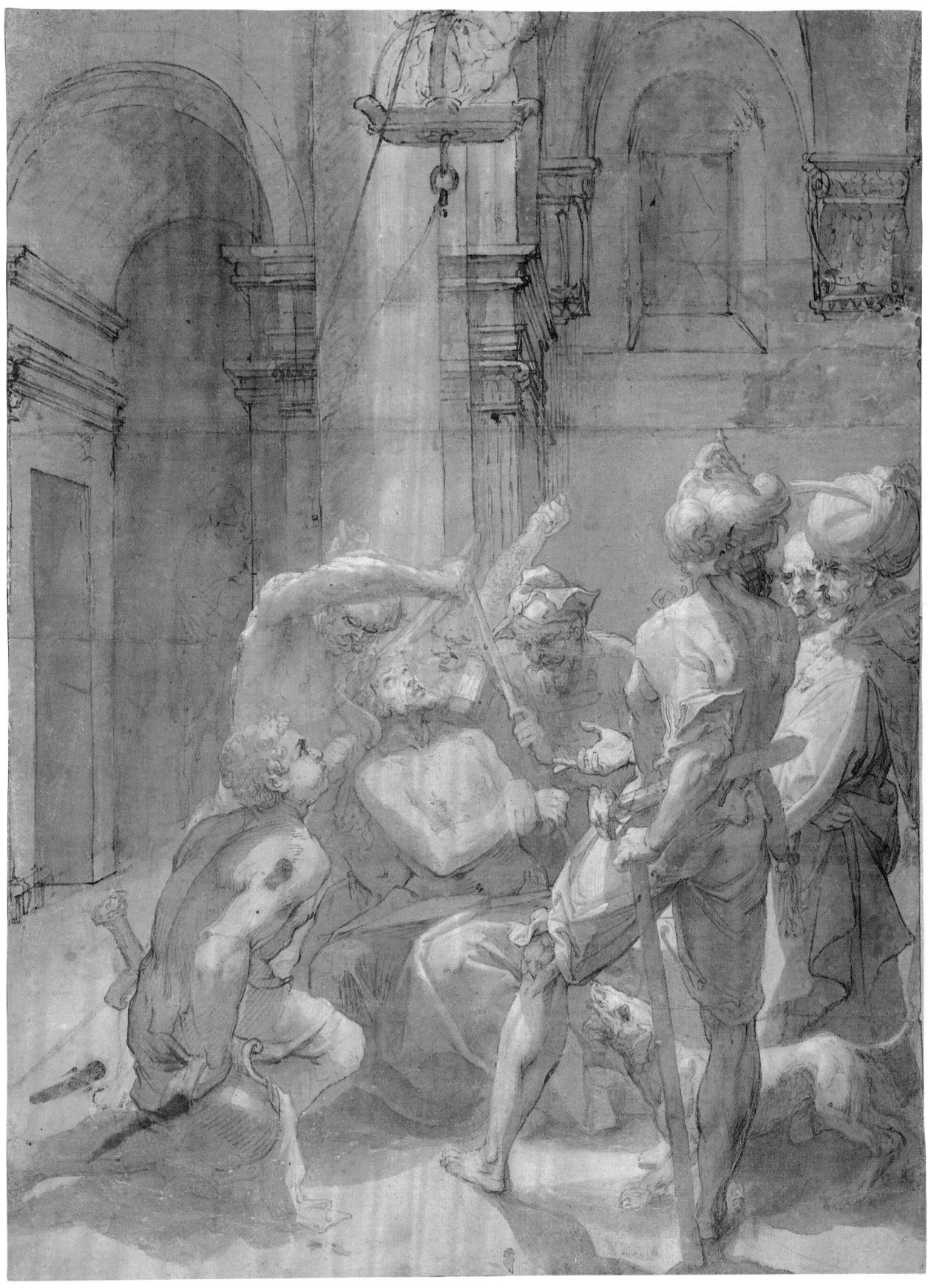

12

Joris Hoefnagel

1542–1601

Joris (or Georg) Hoefnagel was the son of a wealthy Antwerp merchant, part of a cosmopolitan family established in many of the major cities of Europe. After a humanistic education, he traveled to France and Spain, where he made studies of exotic plants and animals as well as landscapes, before going to England. His stay in England may well have provided the stimulus to his outstanding work as a miniaturist. Hoefnagel later became court painter to Duke Albert V of Bavaria and subsequently entered the service of Emperor Rudolf II.

13 *View of Windsor Castle from the North*

$10\frac{3}{8} \times 16\frac{5}{16}$ in. (264 × 415 mm)

Pen and brown ink with brown and blue wash

Inscribed upper right: *Vindesorium celeberrimum Anglie castrum locus | amoenissimus aedificia magnifica: Artificiosa Regum | sepulchra: & illustris Garetteriorū equitum Societas | memorabile reddunt* (Windsor the most celebrated Castle in England is made memorable by its most delightful setting, its magnificent buildings, the finely wrought burial place of kings, and the illustrious Order of the Knights of the Garter); above the Keep: *Winchester tour*; at the left: *oriens* (the east); at the right: *occidens* (the west); at the bottom: *Septentrio* (the north). Inscribed on the *verso: Giorgio Hoefnagel*

Watermark: circle topped by five-armed cross and *M8* (?) with three-lobed flower above

Coll: H. Bier; Francis Springell (sale 1986, when purchased for the Royal Collection)

Bibl: Schilling, pp. 233–34; W & C 53 (RL 12936)

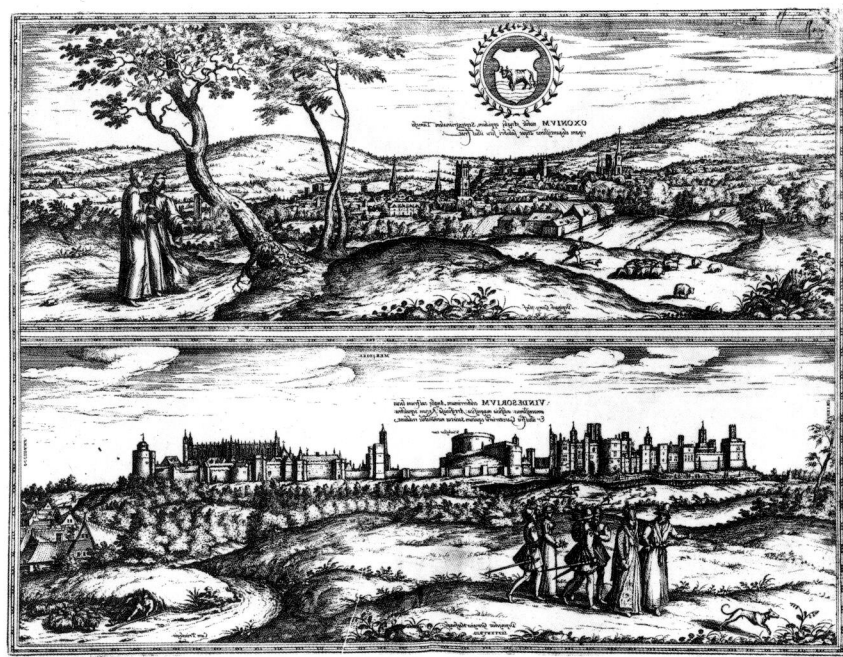

Joris Hoefnagel, *View of Windsor Castle from the North*, from G. Braun and F. Hogenberg, *Civitates Orbis Terrarum*, II, No. 2 Engraving, platemark $14\frac{5}{16} \times 19\frac{3}{16}$ in. (362 × 485 mm) (Private Collection)

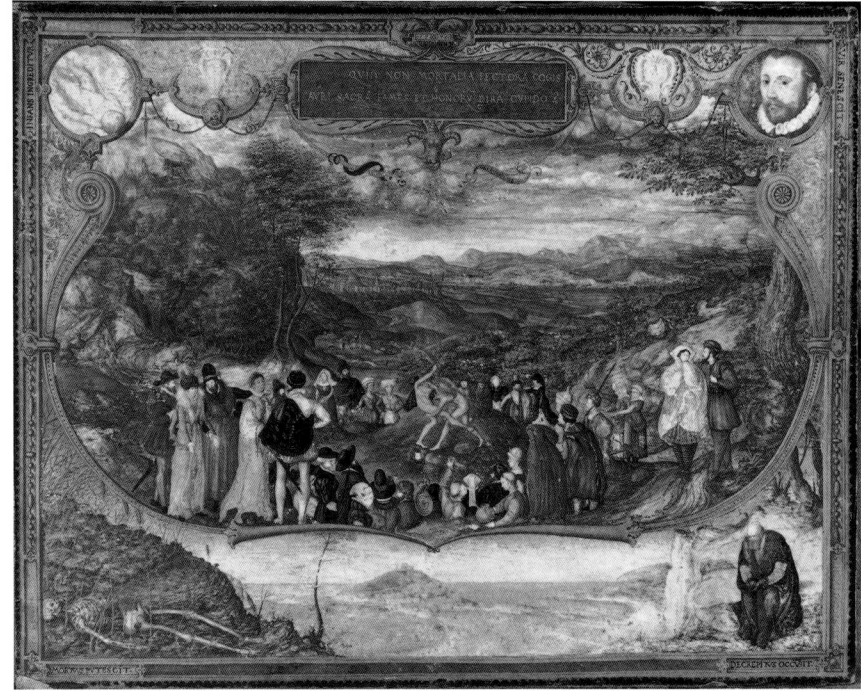

Joris Hoefnagel, *Allegorical Scene* Tempera on vellum, $6\frac{3}{8} \times 8\frac{3}{16}$ in. (157 × 208 mm) (on loan to the Fitzwilliam Museum, Cambridge)

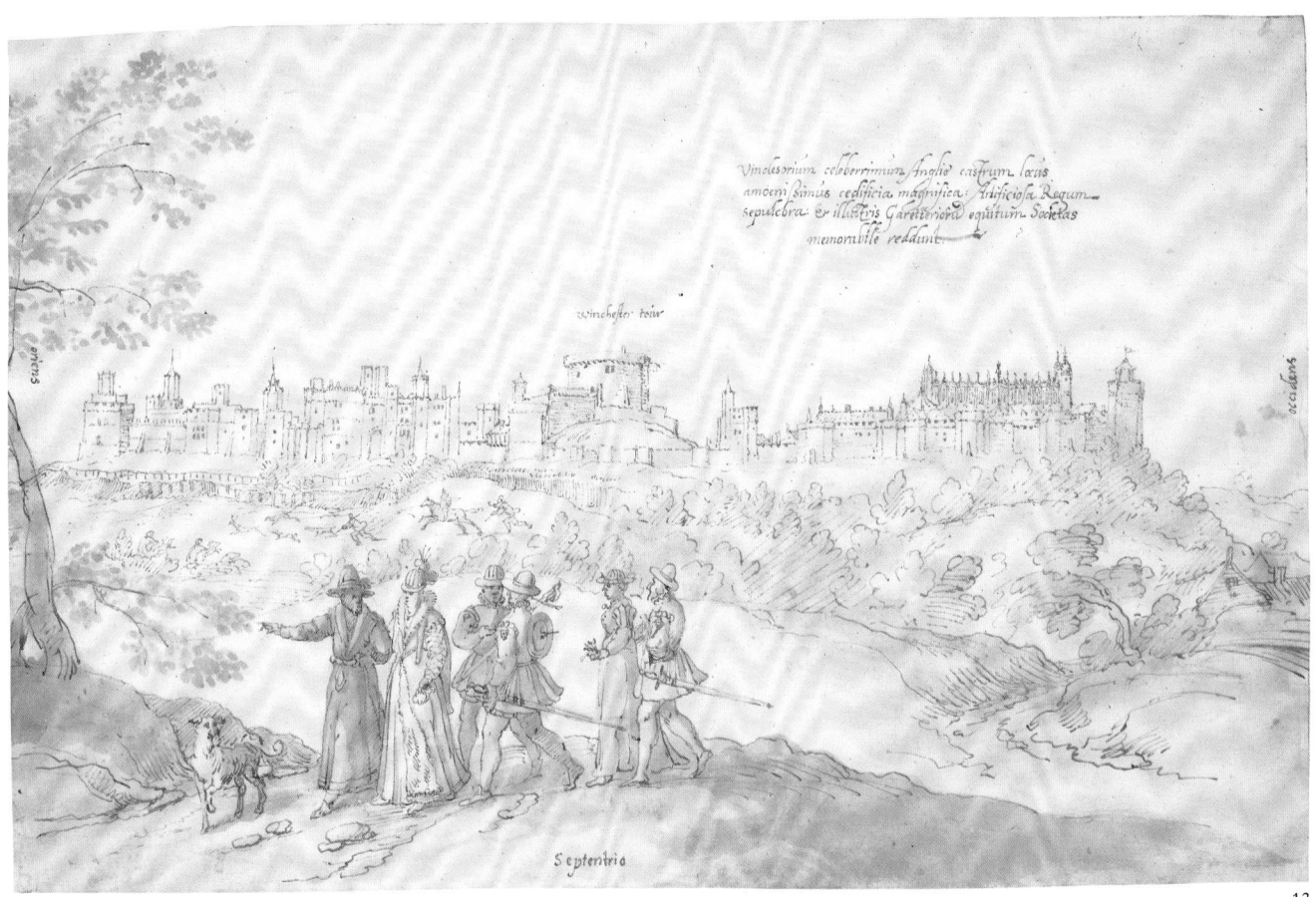

13

The drawing, which is one of the earliest known views of Windsor Castle, shows, from left to right, the North-East Tower, the King's Lodgings, the "Keepe" or Round Tower (wrongly identified as the Winchester Tower), the Winchester Tower, St. George's Chapel, and the Bell Tower or "Clewer." The imaginary foreground, which in reality would show the River Thames, includes six elegantly dressed figures, accompanied by a dog, walking along a road, while a stag is hunted in the middle distance.

It can be deduced from a drawing of Nonsuch Palace, signed and dated 1568,[1] and a set of emblematic drawings entitled *Patientia*,[2] signed and dated in London in 1569, that Hoefnagel was active in England during these two years. He presumably made the present drawing at the same time, but in view of the imaginary foreground, it is questionable whether he drew it on the spot.

Apart from using No. 13 as a preliminary study for the engraving in *Civitates Orbis Terrarum* (see No. 14), Hoefnagel introduced the same view of Windsor Castle in the background of a miniature of an allegorical subject, signed and dated in Antwerp in 1571.[3]

[1] In the British Museum. Stainton, no. 1, Pl. 1.

[2] In the Bibliothèque Municipale, Rouen; coll. MS Leber, 2616 (Antwerp, no. 127, repr.).

[3] Now on loan to the Fitzwilliam Museum, Cambridge (Norman, pp. 321–25, Pl. XLIV).

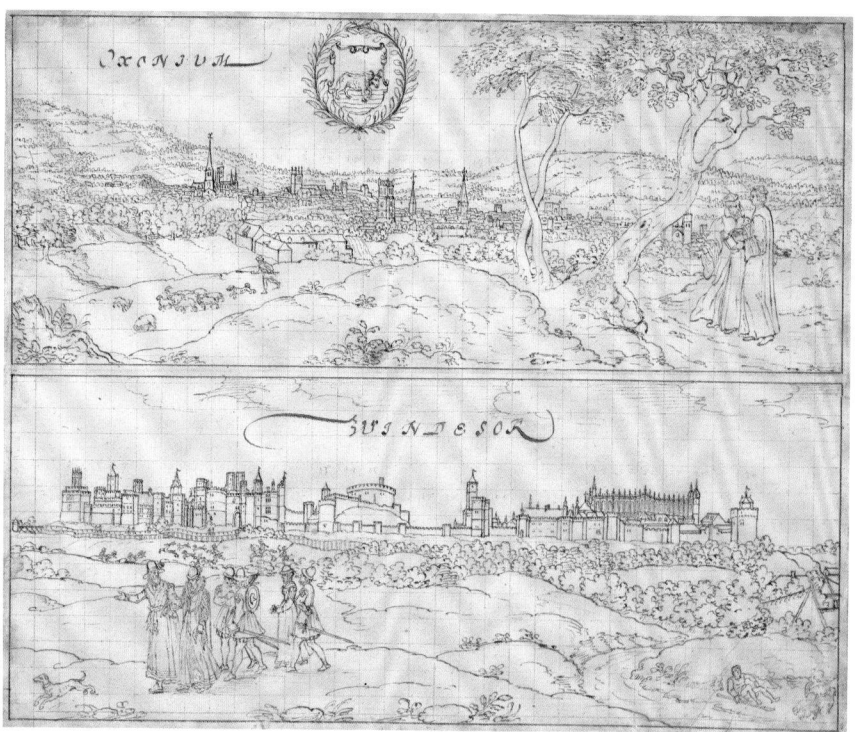

14

14 *Views of Oxford from the East* (above) *and Windsor Castle from the North* (below)

$8\frac{7}{8} \times 10\frac{3}{4}$ in. (226 × 274 mm)

Pen and brown ink over faint traces of black chalk, squared for transfer with numbers inscribed in squaring above skyline in both subjects

Inscribed above: *OXONIUM* (Oxford), and below: *WINDESOR* (Windsor)

Coll: probably acquired shortly before 1901

Bibl: Schilling, p. 234; w & c 54 (RL 13261)

The view of Oxford shows, from left to right, Christ Church Cathedral, Merton College, Magdalen Tower, the spires of All Saints (which had a spire in the sixteenth century), and St. Mary's, and between the tree and the two figures on the extreme right, Holywell Manor; in the left foreground, houses in St. Clement's (?); and above, the coat of arms of the city of Oxford. The view of Windsor shows the same buildings as in No. 13.

Apart from the omission of a narrow vertical strip at either side and of all the inscriptions except for the place names, this drawing corresponds exactly with plate 2 in the second volume of G. Braun and F. Hogenberg, *Civitates Orbis Terrarum* (*Cities of the World*), published in Cologne in 1575. The views of Oxford and Windsor were included on the same plate, one above the other, as here. Delineated in outline only and squared up for enlargement, No. 14 can be considered as the artist's final drawing, for the lower half of which No. 13 served as the preliminary study. Both Nos. 13 and 14 are drawn in the same sense as the related engraving.

It is, however, a curious fact that whereas No. 13 (which carries the same inscriptions as the engraving) is approximately the same size as the lower half of the engraving, the present drawing is considerably smaller. This indicates that the artist reduced the scale of his first study in his final working drawing, which then had to be enlarged on the copper plate. Another example of this unusual procedure exists in the two known working drawings for the view of Cadiz in *Civitates Orbis Terrarum*.[4]

The *Civitates Orbis Terrarum*, published in six volumes in Cologne between 1572 and 1618, is probably the greatest sixteenth-century atlas, on which Hoefnagel continued to work for the remainder of his life. In all he produced sixty-three drawings of various European cities for the series.

[4] The outline drawing is in the Österreichische Nationalbibliothek, Vienna, and the preliminary study is in the Albertina, Vienna (Nuti, Figs. 11 and 12 respectively).

Jan Soens (Giovanni da Parma)

1547/48–1611

Soens was born in s'Hertogenbosch and was a pupil of Gillis Mostaert in Antwerp. By 1575 he was working for the Farnese family in Rome. He subsequently moved to the north of Italy and worked in both Piacenza and Parma, where he died.

15 *The Circumcision*

$16\frac{1}{2} \times 11\frac{1}{8}$ in. (420 × 283 mm)

Pen and brown ink with brown and gray wash, heightened with white, over black chalk; squared for transfer

Inscribed on the old mount: *GIOVANNI DA PARMA*, and on the *verso*, now laid down: *Io Leo' Lazaro Saller Castelano di piacenza faccio fede | si come il a dietro designato è il disegno della Tavola che | si è obligato a fare per il Sig. Girolamo Zamberti [?Lamberti] il Sig.: gio sons per il prezzo di ducatoni sessanta.* [Monogram] (I Leonardo Lazaro Saller, Castellano of Piacenza, hereby declare that the drawing on the other side of this page is the design for the panel painting that Signor Girolamo Zamberti has commissioned from Giovanni Soens for the sum of sixty ducats.)

Coll: George III

Bibl: Béguin, pp. 275–79; w & c 139 (RL 6787)

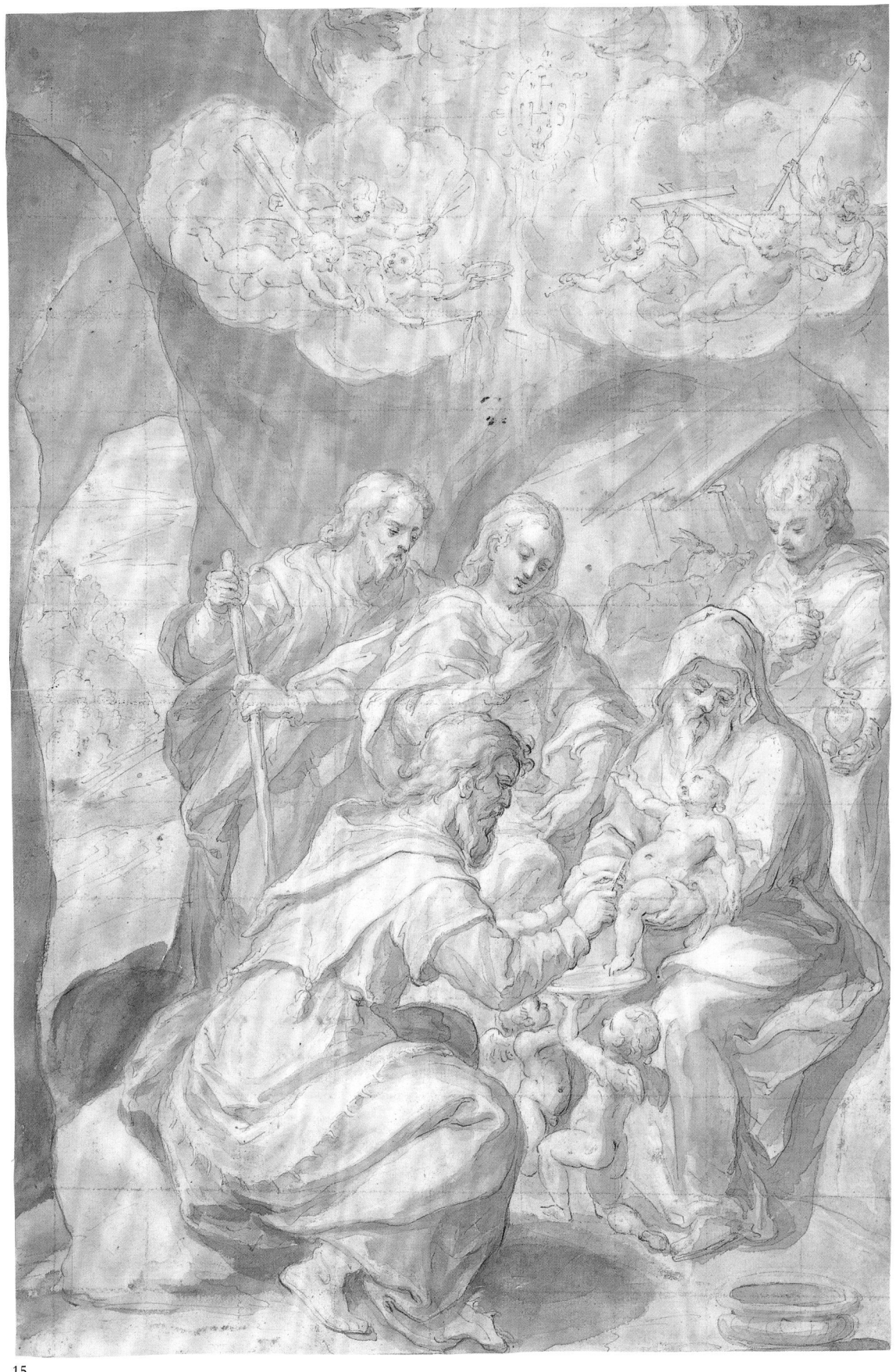

15

The inscription on the *verso* tallies with a recently discovered document recording the first installment of a payment of sixty ducats by a certain Girolamo Lamberti to the artist in December 1604. It can therefore be established that the drawing is the approved *modello* for a lost altarpiece executed for the chapel of the Jesuit College (now the Biblioteca Passerini-Landi), which forms an annex to the church of the Order of S. Pietro in Piacenza. The artist was active in that city in the first decade of the seventeenth century. The painting was last recorded in 1842 and may have been removed during the suppression of churches and monasteries.

The scene takes place in front of a cave at Bethlehem, with the donkey and ox visible in the right background. The upper part of the composition is occupied by the sacred monogram (IHS) flanked by groups of angels with instruments of the Passion. The treatment of the subject is unusual, and both the setting and the inclusion of the monogram IHS associate the composition with the Counter-Reformation iconography favored by the Jesuits. Although as a figure painter he was influenced by Correggio and the Carracci, Soens retained the Flemish style in his landscapes, as can be seen here.

Hendrick Goltzius

1558–1617

Born in Mühlbracht near Venlo, Goltzius moved with his family to Duisburg, where he studied under his father, a glass painter. In order to learn engraving, he was apprenticed around 1575 to the Haarlem artist Dirck Coornhert, who was in exile at Xanten in Cleves. Around 1576/77, Goltzius moved with Coornhert to Haarlem, where he settled. In Italy, from 1590 to 1591, he visited Venice, Rome, Naples, and Florence.

16 *Perseus and Andromeda*

$10\frac{5}{16} \times 14\frac{3}{4}$ in. (263 × 376 mm)

Pen and brown ink with brown wash, the flesh modeled with red chalk and red wash, heightened with white, indented for transfer, on buff paper

Signed lower center: *HG* (in monogram), and dated on the rock behind Andromeda: *A°. 1597*

Coll: George III

Bibl: Reznicek (1961) no. 106; W & C 366 (RL 6438)

The subject is taken from Ovid's *Metamorphoses*, Book IV. Andromeda, naked, is chained to a rock in the center; she is surrounded by numerous spectators, including her parents, Cassiopeia and Cepheus, who are seen to the right of the rock. In the sky on the left, Perseus, with his sword held aloft and mounted on Pegasus, flies down towards the monster advancing in the narrow rocky inlet. The drawing departs from Ovid's account by depicting Perseus mounted on Pegasus rather than carried by his own wings. But it appears to be the earliest representation in the Netherlands to include Andromeda's parents and other spectators as described by Ovid, unlike the artist's earlier engraving of the subject after Blocklandt, dated 1583.[1]

The drawing was engraved in reverse by Goltzius's stepson, Jacob Matham (see No. 20), in the same year.[2] The engraving corresponds very closely indeed to the drawing, and is precisely the same size. No. 16 is among the earliest of the colored preparatory drawings made by Goltzius for other engravers.

[1] Hollstein, VIII, p. 34, no. 157.
[2] *Ibid.*, XI, p. 228, no. 212.

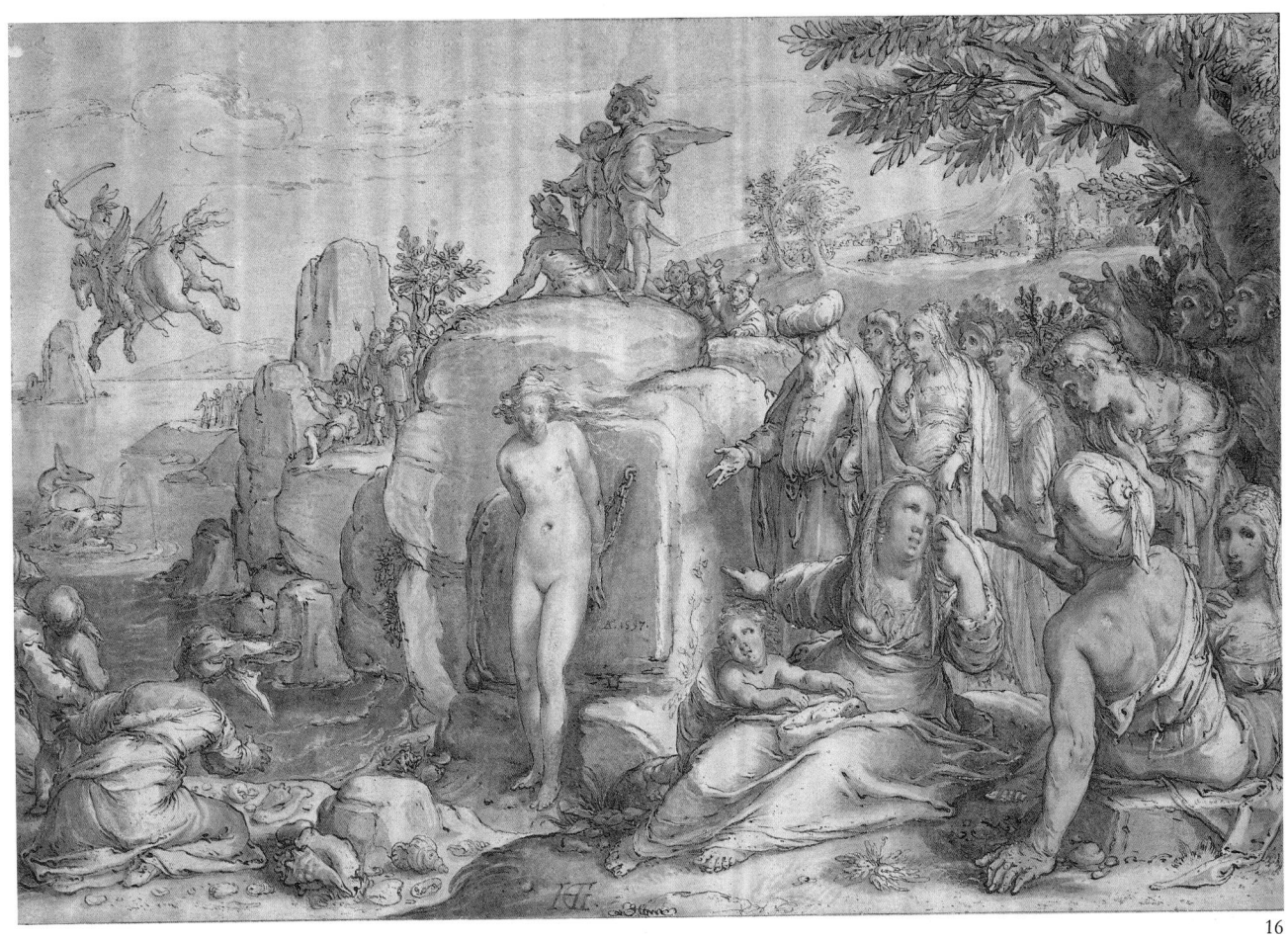

16

Jacob Matham after Hendrick Goltzius,
Perseus and Andromeda
Engraving, $10\frac{11}{16} \times 14\frac{3}{4}$ in. (270 × 372 mm)
(cut within platemark; London, British
Museum, Department of Prints and
Drawings)

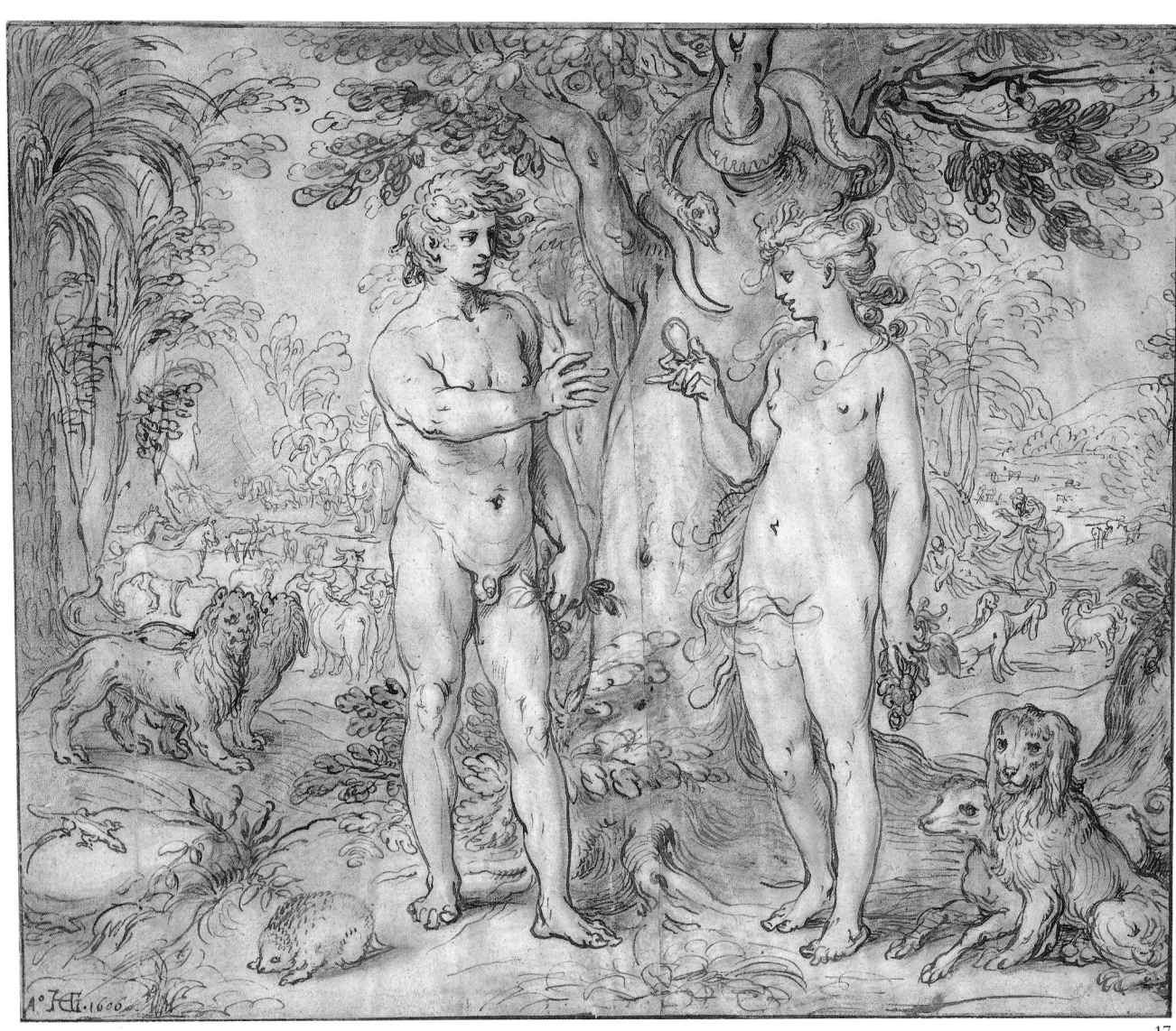

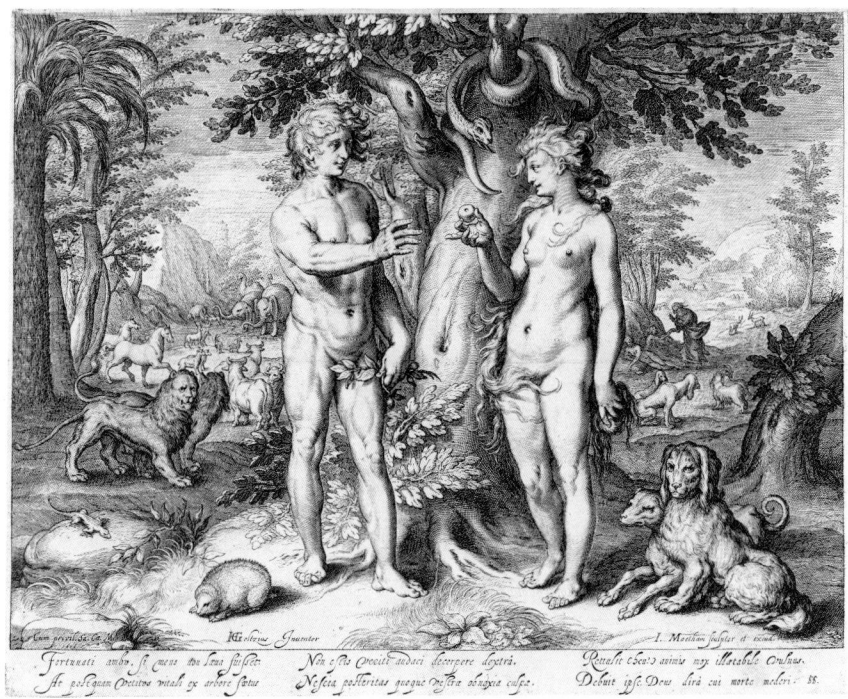

Jacob Matham after Hendrick Goltzius, *The Fall of Man*
Engraving, 12 × 15¼ in. (306 × 387 mm) (cut within platemark; London, British Museum, Department of Prints and Drawings)

17 The Fall of Man

11¼ × 13⅞ in. (287 × 342 mm) (on two pieces of paper)

Pen and ink (two shades) over graphite underdrawing, with red chalk, charcoal (?), and wash, heightened with white

Signed and dated lower left: *Aº HG* (in monogram) *1606*

Coll: (?) Ploos van Amstel (sale 1800); George III

Bibl: Reznicek (1961) no. 9; w & c 367 (RL 4758)

In the center, Eve proffers a fruit to Adam. They stand on either side of the tree of knowledge, with the serpent entwined around its trunk. In the foreground are a lizard, a hedgehog, and a pair of dogs. In the background, the garden of Eden is filled with numerous animals and, on the right, is the scene of the Creation of Eve.

The composition, with a few small changes, was engraved by Jacob Matham in the same year.[3] No. 17 is in the same sense (and on the same scale) as the engraving. The drawing is the latest in the series of drawings made by Goltzius for other engravers; thereafter, he largely devoted his attention to painting. Whereas the animals are still in the tradition of Bartholomäus Spranger, the two nudes are drawn in the style of the early seventeenth century.

[3] Hollstein, XI, p. 215, no. 1.

Crispin van de Passe the Elder

1564–1637

Crispin van de Passe, a pupil of Dirck Coornhert, became a member of the Antwerp guild in 1585. He was very active as an engraver in both the Northern and Southern Netherlands, as well as abroad; he is not recorded as having visited England. Two volumes at Windsor contain seventy-eight drawings by Van de Passe for the illustrated *Ovid* published in Cologne in 1602 and 1607.[1]

18 Queen Elizabeth I

11¹¹⁄₁₆ × 8³⁄₁₆ in. (297 × 208 mm)

Pen and brown and black ink with gray wash; the coarser washes on the cloak and shadow lower right probably by a later hand; indented for transfer

Coll: Dr. Richard Mead (sale 1755); Earl of Hardwicke (sale 1888)

Bibl: Hind, pp. 266, 283; Strong, p. 152, Post. 3; w & c 138 (RL 17018)

Queen Elizabeth I (1558–1603) is seen full-length, wearing a crown set with pearls and a pearl-embroidered dress; she holds the scepter in her left hand and the orb in her right. Despite the nineteenth-century tradition that she is shown in the dress worn by her at the Thanksgiving Service at St. Paul's after the Spanish Armada in 1588, she is probably portrayed in the robe embroidered with pearls that she usually wore at the opening of Parliament.

The drawing is the preparatory study used by Van de Passe for his engraving,[2] where the image is naturally reversed. Various accompanying details, such as the Bible, sword, and table on the right and the curtain on the left were added in the engraving. Although undated, the text below the image establishes

[1] w & c 59–137.
[2] Hind, pp. 282–83, no. 1; see Strong, Post. 4.

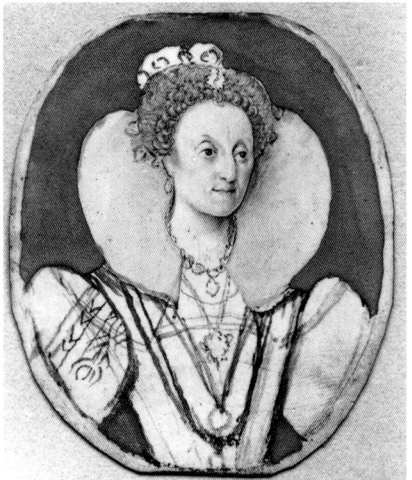

(*Right*)
Crispin van de Passe,
Queen Elizabeth I
(Hind 1)
Engraving, $13\frac{5}{16} \times 8\frac{7}{8}$ in.
(347 × 226 mm)
(cut within platemark;
Royal Collection: Windsor
Castle, Royal Library)

(*Far right*)
Isaac Oliver,
Queen Elizabeth I
Miniature painting on
vellum, $2\frac{7}{16} \times 2\frac{1}{16}$ in. (62 × 53 mm)
(London, Victoria & Albert
Museum)

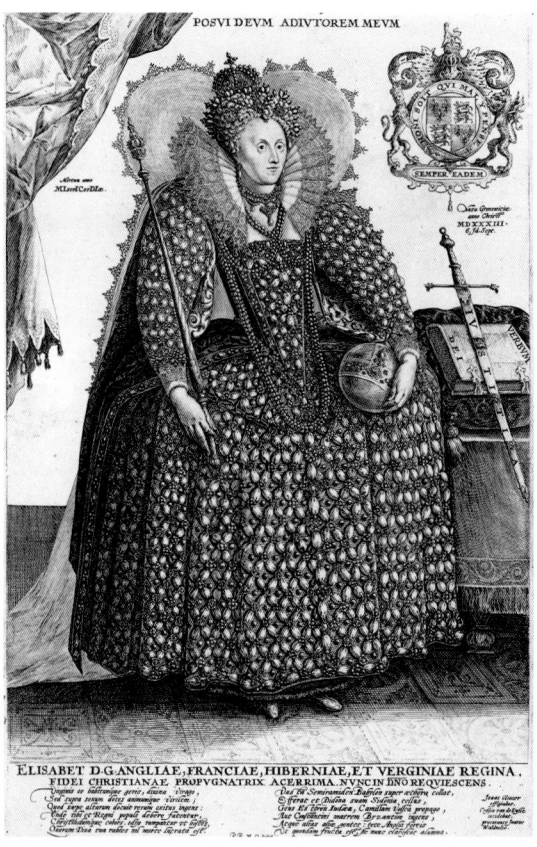

William Rogers,
Queen Elizabeth I
Engraving, $15\frac{1}{4} \times 10\frac{1}{4}$ in.
(387 × 261 mm)
(London, British Museum,
Department of Prints and
Drawings)

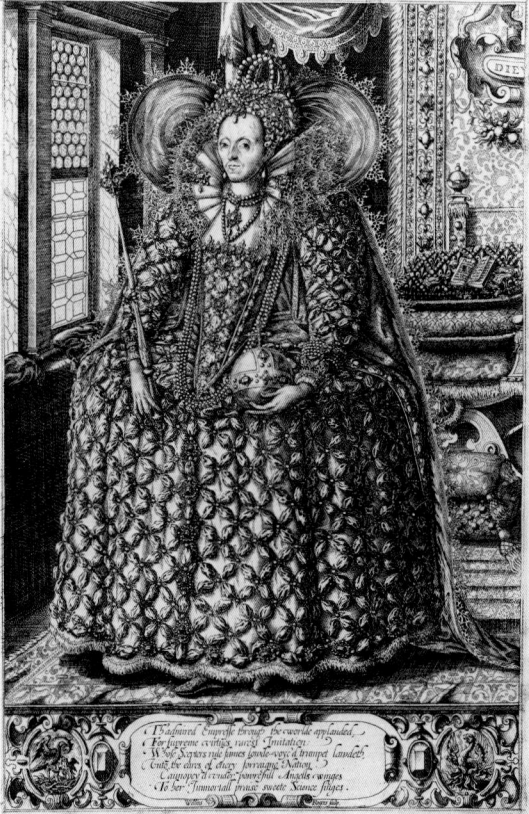

that the print was made after the Queen's death in 1603. The present drawing was long thought to be by Isaac Oliver (*c*.1560–1617). It is, however, quite unlike the latter's drawings and was convincingly attributed to Van de Passe himself by Roy Strong.

The engraving is inscribed *Isaac Oliuier effigiebat* (Isaac Oliver took the likeness), lower right. Although the Queen's facial features accord well (in reverse) with those in Oliver's "pattern miniature" *c*.1592 in the Victoria and Albert Museum, London,[3] it is possible that a (lost) full-length portrait of the Queen by Oliver was the model for No. 18. In the absence of such a portrait, it has been claimed that Van de Passe's posthumous image of the Queen was based on the engraving by William Rogers of *c*.1592.[4] No. 18 is drawn in the same sense as Rogers's engraving, but the figure is smaller in scale. Although the drawing is very similar to Rogers's print, in details (such as the jewels and the lace) it varies considerably. No acknowledgment to Oliver is noted by Rogers, although – at the very least – the Queen's likeness in his print must also be based on Oliver's.

[3] Strong, M. 12.
[4] Strong, E. 30.

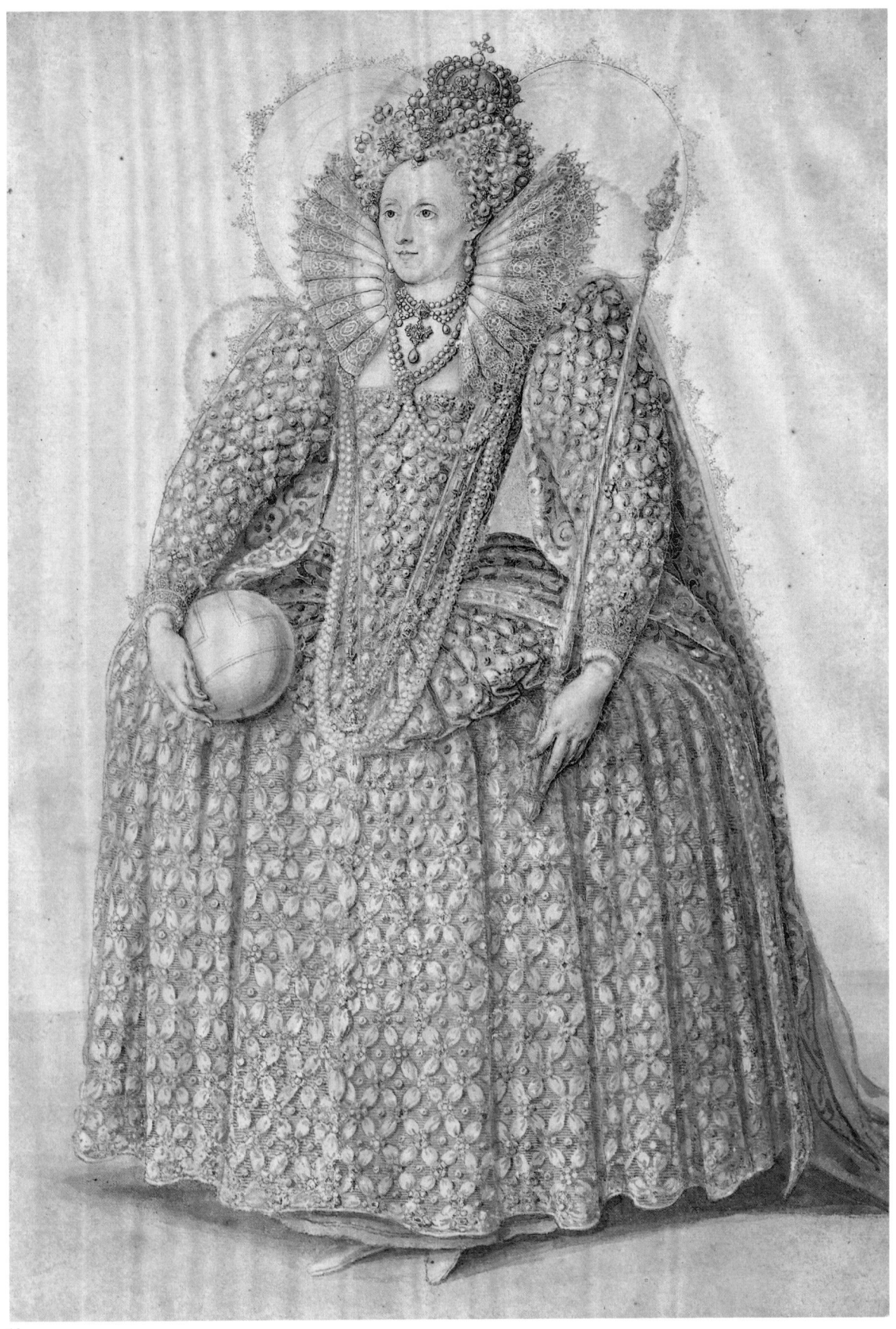

18

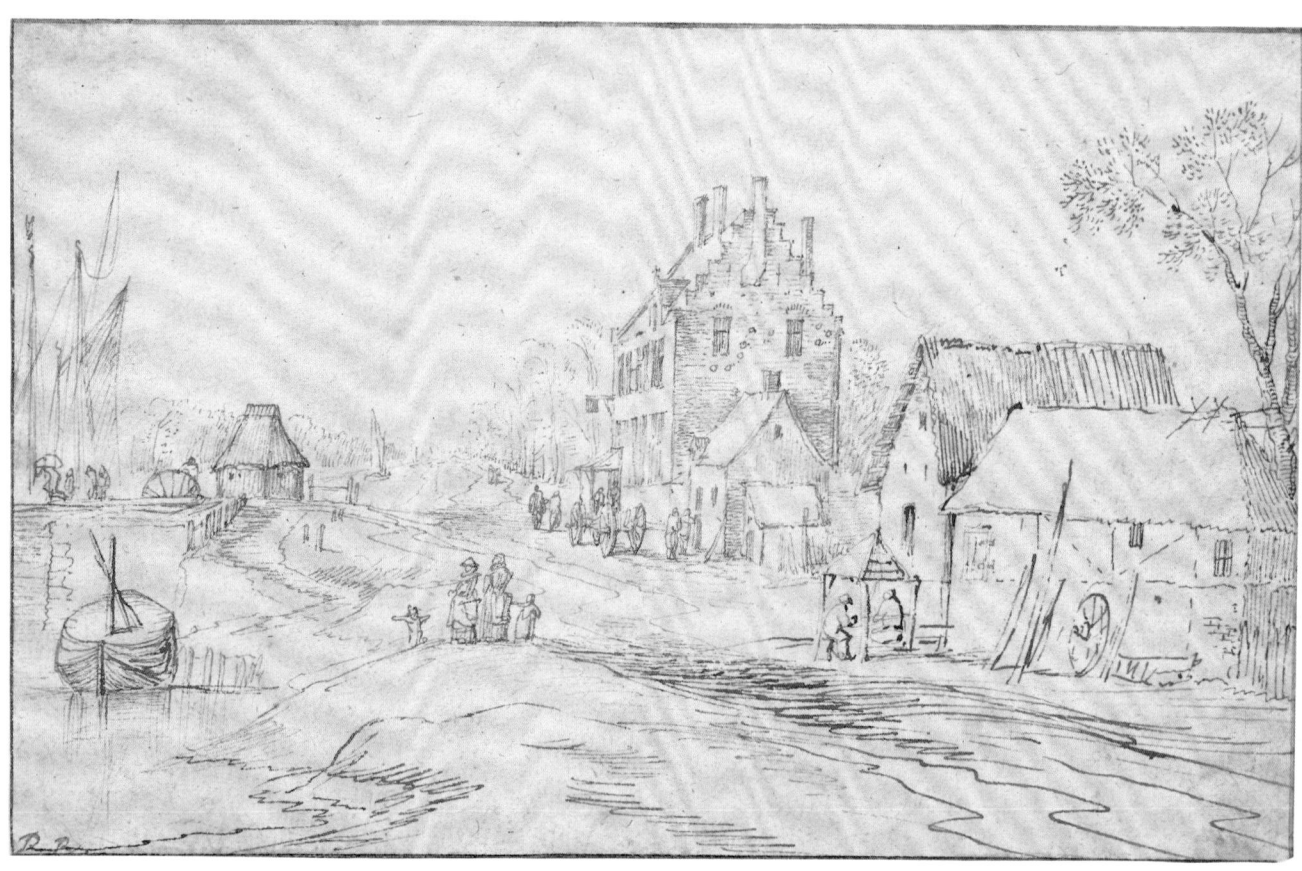

Jan Brueghel the Elder

1568–1625

Jan Brueghel was born in Brussels, the second son of Peter Brueghel the Elder. According to Van Mander he was a pupil of Pieter Goetkind in Antwerp. Around 1589 he went to Italy, stopping in Cologne *en route*. From Naples he went to Rome and then Milan, before returning in 1596 to Antwerp, where he became one of the leading artists. He visited Prague in 1604 and Nuremberg in 1606, when he was also appointed one of the non-resident court painters to the Archduke Albert and the Archduchess Isabella in Brussels. He was a close friend of and collaborator with Rubens.

19 *A Village Street*

$4\frac{7}{16} \times 7$ in. (112 × 178 mm)

Pen and brown ink

Inscribed lower left: *P. B.*(?)

Verso: a very faint and slight landscape sketch in black chalk. Inscribed: *Wittebroek Door P: Breugel*

Coll: George III

Bibl: W & C 330 (RL 6234)

If the location inscribed on the *verso* is correct, the drawing shows the village of Wittebroek, near Boom, in the province of Antwerp, with the Wittebroek canal (built 1550–61 to connect Brussels with the River Rupel) visible on the left. The artist made a large number of delicately executed landscape drawings both of local scenery and that seen on his various travels in Italy and central Europe. He was already celebrated as a landscape artist in his own lifetime.

The same or a very similar inn, seen from the opposite direction, appears in the painting of the *Entrance to a Village with a Windmill*, in the Knecht collection, Zurich.[1]

[1] Ertz, Fig. 29.

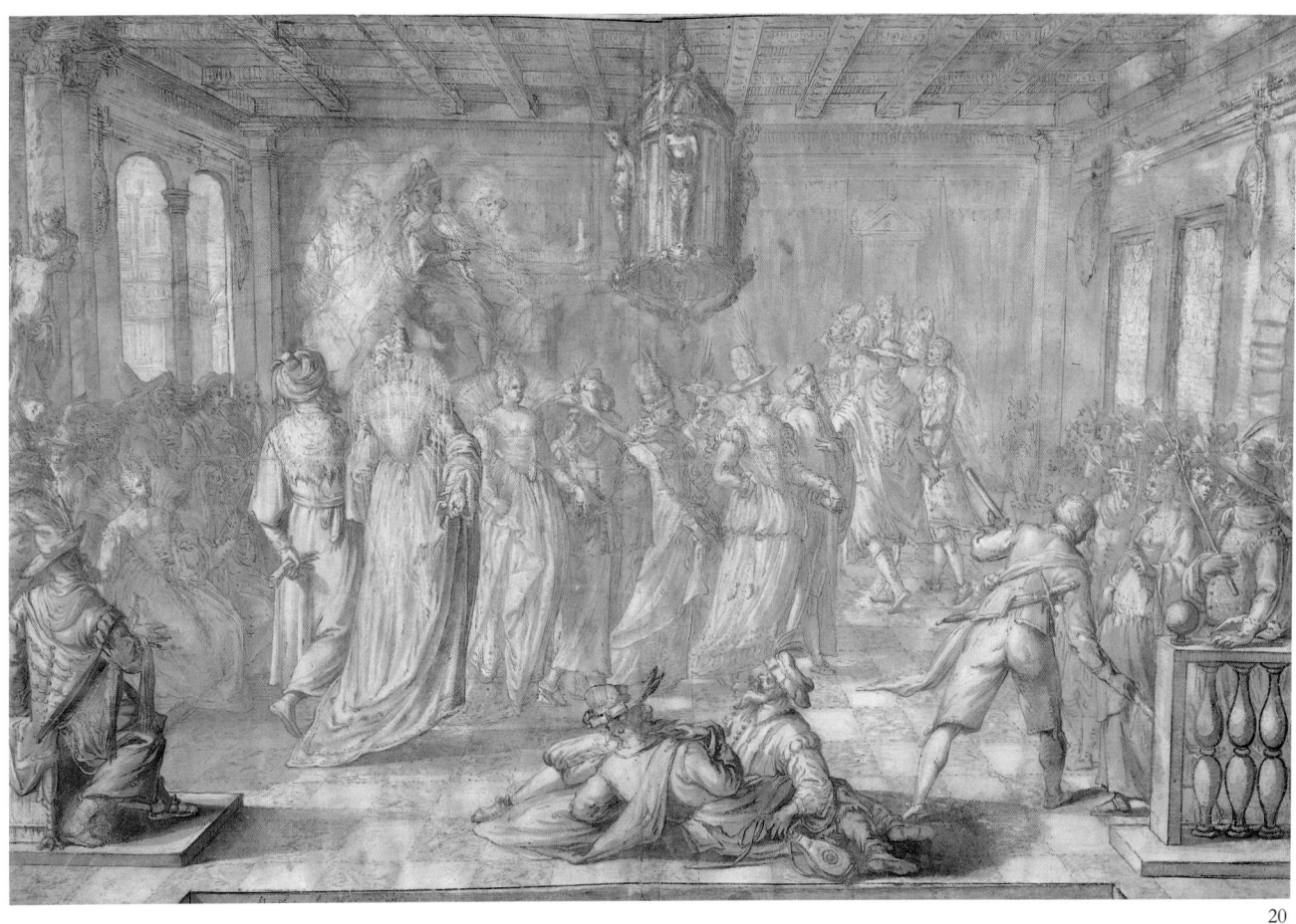

Jacob Matham

1571–1631

Born in Haarlem, Matham was trained by Hendrick Goltzius, who became the second husband of Matham's mother. After a visit to Italy in the second half of the 1590s, which included a stay in Rome, he became a very prolific engraver, producing many prints after designs by Goltzius, including Nos. 16 and 17. On the evidence of No. 20, Matham appears to have visited Venice in 1605.

20 *A Ball Scene*

$17\frac{11}{16} \times 26\frac{9}{16}$ in. (450 × 672 mm)

Pen and brown ink, with brown and gray wash, and touches of red chalk, heightened with white

Signed and dated lower left: *Matham Aᵒ. 1605. vinetia*

Coll: George III

Bibl: W & C 391 (RL 12838)

In the center of a Renaissance room, several couples are dancing to music made by string players on a raised platform on the left. There are numerous spectators on either side of the room, and, in the center foreground, a couple are seated on the floor. An elaborate chandelier, decorated with sculpted figures, is suspended from the ceiling.

There are a number of puzzling features about this drawing. Apart from the fact that Matham usually, if not invariably, signed his name with his initial, there is no other record of his having made a second journey to Italy. Moreover, the pictorial style differs from his usual carefully finished engraver's manner of drawing.

Roelant Savery

1578–1639

Savery was a pupil of his elder
brother, Jacob, and subsequently of
Hans Bol. Early in Roelant's life his
family moved from Courtrai to the
Northern Netherlands for religious
reasons. At first he lived in Haarlem,
but by 1591 he was in Amsterdam.
From 1604 until 1613 (shortly after the
death of Rudolf II), he worked as
court landscape painter for the
imperial court in Prague, during
which time he made a journey through
the Tyrol, producing drawings of the
scenery and of the flora and fauna. His
Alpine landscapes exerted considerable
influence over his contemporaries. He
died in Utrecht.

21 A Windmill

$9 \times 6\frac{7}{8}$ in. (229×175 mm)

The sheet has been made up at the top
left and right on two additional pieces of
paper; the drawing in pen and gray ink
is probably by another hand.

Pen and brown ink with brown and
pink wash over graphite, on eight pieces
of paper

Inscribed lower left: *R. Savarye.*

Coll: George III

Bibl: Ghent, no. 118, repr.; Spicer,
no. C107; W & C 448 (RL 6601)

This delicately executed study, typical
of Savery's fine draughtsmanship, was
presumably done from nature. It
probably dates from the decade
following the artist's return to the
Netherlands from Prague. The
drawing does not appear to have been
used in any of the artist's paintings.
Spicer has commented that "the sheet
was assembled from eight separate
pieces of paper before the drawing
was begun; this is an extreme effort of
paper conservation even for Savery."

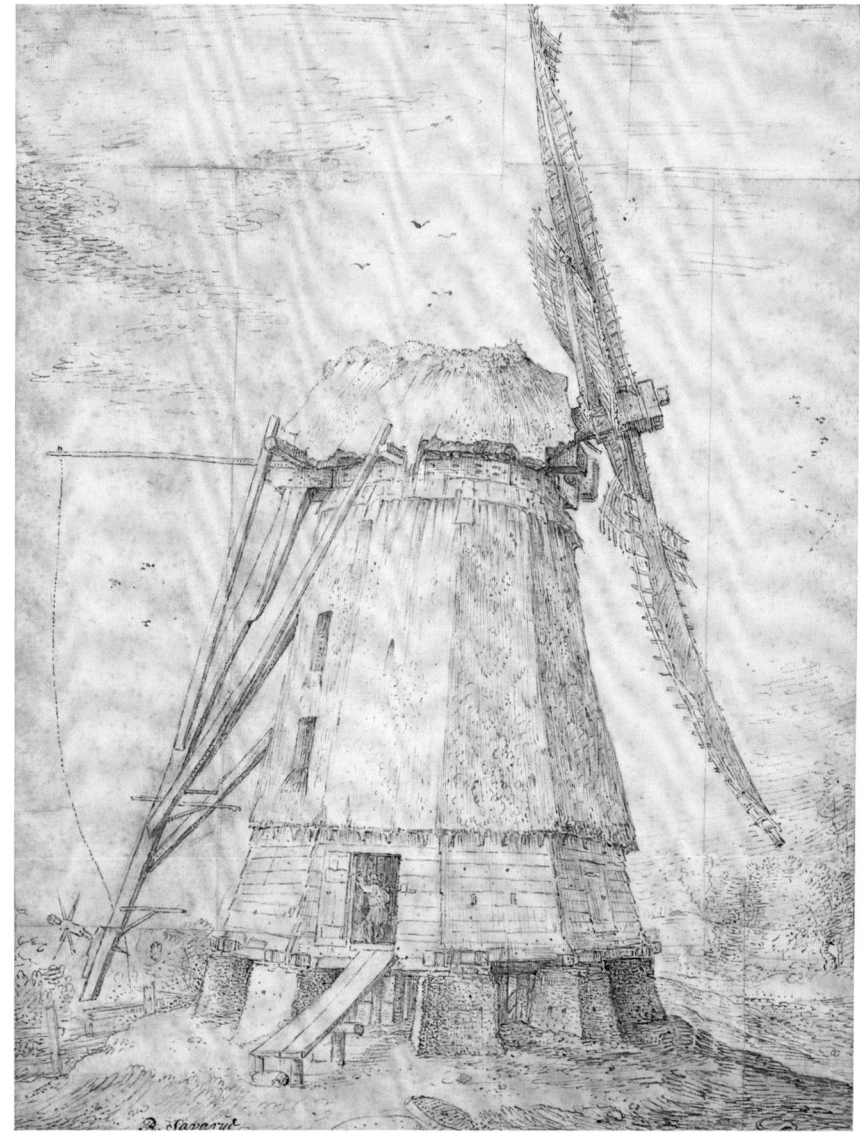

21

48

Peter Paul Rubens

1577–1640

Rubens was born in Siegen in Germany, from where his family moved to Cologne in 1578. In 1587 his widowed mother took her children back to the parents' native city of Antwerp. After studying under Tobias Verhaecht, Adam van Noort, and Otto van Veen, Rubens became a master in the Antwerp Guild of St. Luke in 1598. From 1600 to 1608 he was in Italy, where he was in the service of Vincenzo Gonzaga, the Duke of Mantua. He also spent some time in Rome, Genoa, and Venice and made a visit to Spain. Back home he was appointed a non-resident court painter to the Archdukes Albert and Isabella (and subsequently to the Cardinal-Infante Ferdinand). Rubens very rapidly became the leading painter of Antwerp, and – especially after 1620 – one of the most sought after painters in Europe, executing major commissions for the French, English, and Spanish monarchies. He paid three visits to Paris in the first half of the 1620s and undertook a number of diplomatic journeys, the most important of which were his visits to Madrid and London in 1628/29. He was married twice, and after 1635 spent much time at the Castle of Steen near Malines. He was also a distinguished scholar and an avid collector.

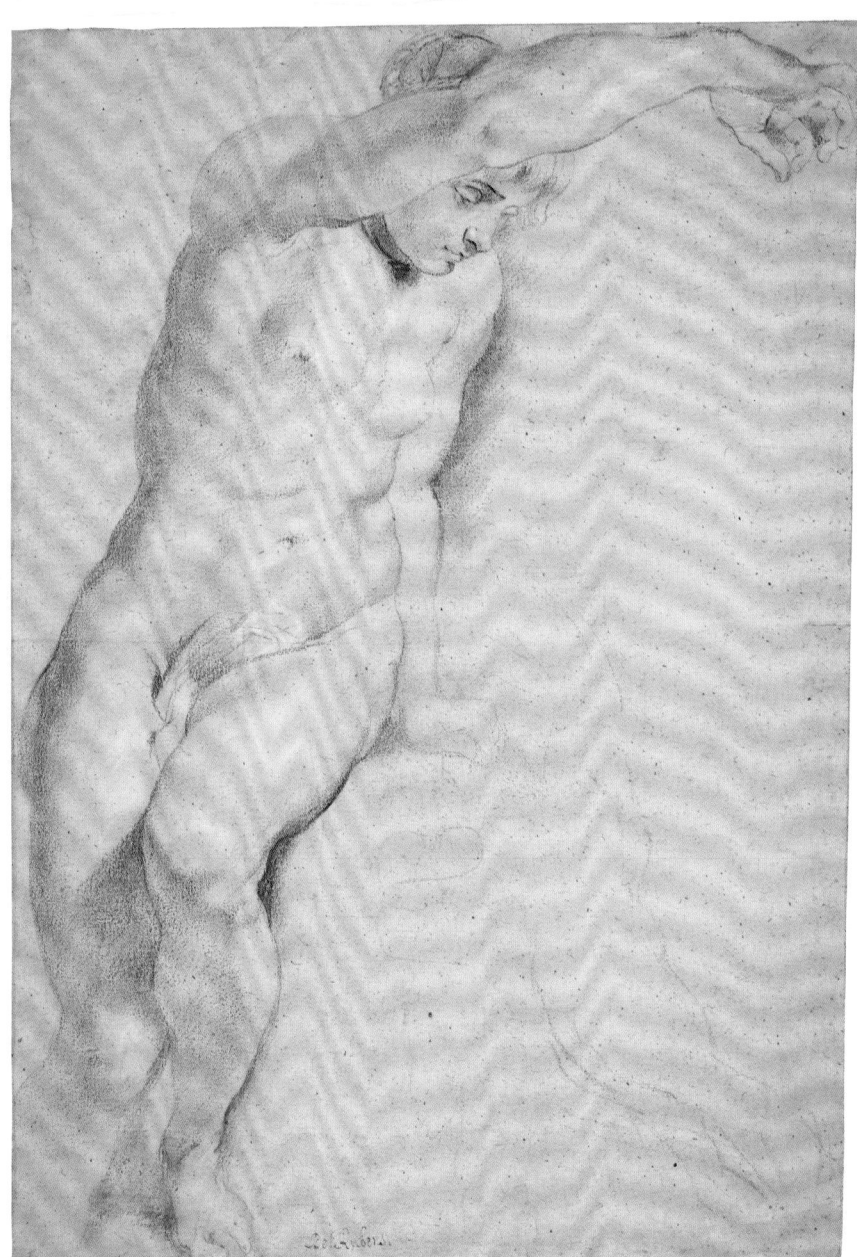

22

22 A Female Nude: Study for Psyche

22 13/16 × 16 3/16 in. (581 × 412 mm)

Black chalk, heightened with white, on buff paper

Inscribed lower center: *Del Rubens*

Watermark: monogram MB

Coll: George III

Bibl: Held (1959), I, p. 28; (1986), p. 31; Burchard and d'Hulst no. 65; w & c 434 (RL 6412)

Peter Paul Rubens,
Cupid and Psyche
Oil on canvas,
$46\frac{1}{4} \times 36\frac{3}{8}$ in.
(117.5×92.5 cm)
(Private Collection)

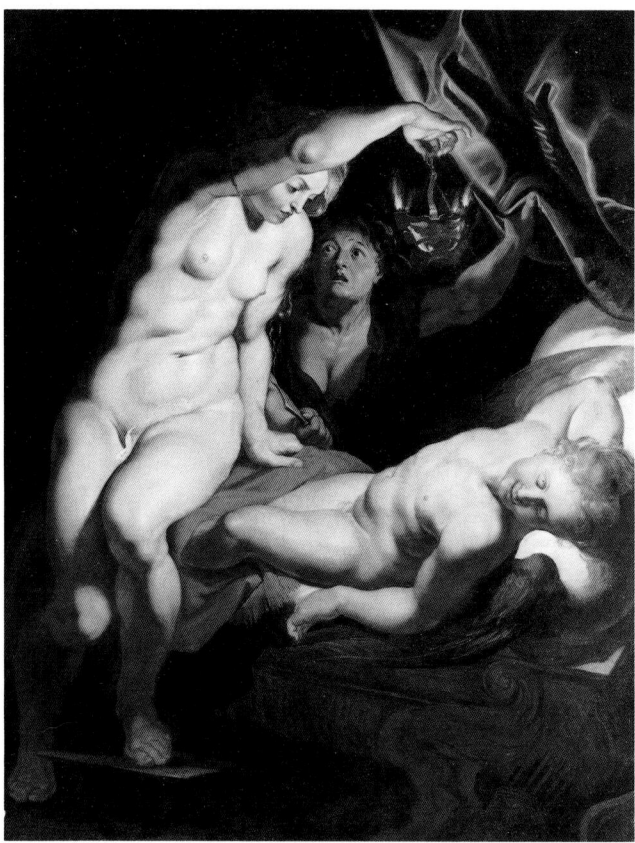

23 *Silenus and Aegle with Other Studies*

$11\frac{1}{16} \times 19\frac{15}{16}$ (281×508 mm)

Pen and brown ink with brown wash

Inscribed by the artist top center: *Vitula* (calf) *gaud[ium]*. (The first word has also been read as *Vetula* [an old woman].)

Verso: Various Figure Studies

Pen and grayish brown ink with gray wash

Watermark: an elephant

Coll: George III

Bibl: Held (1959), no. 29; (1986), nos. 81–82; Burchard and d'Hulst, no. 51; Logan (1977), pp. 412–13; w & c 435 (RL 6417)

This sheet contains a brilliant series of studies, which were probably carried out a few years after Rubens's return from Italy, possibly 1612–14. The principal study (on the left) is that of the sleeping Silenus surprised by the water nymph Aegle, who with blood-red mulberries rubs the brow of the god, bound hand and foot, to persuade him to redeem his promise to sing a song. This he promises to do for Aegle's two young companions, Chromis and Mnasyllos. The subject is taken from Virgil's *Bucolics* (Eclogue VI), the spirit of which the drawing catches perfectly. Silenus's head is repeated above and the figure of Aegle to right of the center. The very summary study lower right may represent Silenus being supported by a figure on either side. Unusual in Rubens's *oeuvre*, the composition is not known to have been developed in a painting.

The group upper right shows a girl in profile with her hand on her chin, a seated woman holding a cornucopia, and a seated young man holding a staff. It may represent a first idea for the painting of the *Four Continents*, in the Kunsthistorisches Museum, Vienna, executed about 1615.[5]

The drawing is a carefully worked-up study made from the life, possibly, following the practice of Michelangelo and Raphael, from a male model. A lightly drawn sketch of an arm (?) can be made out lower right.

The drawing was used as a study for the figure of Psyche holding out an oil lamp in the painting of *Cupid and Psyche*, formerly in the collection of Dr. Ralph Stödter, Hamburg,[1] which was probably executed shortly after Rubens returned to Antwerp in 1608.

Psyche's pose largely repeats, in reverse, the figure in the painting of *St. Sebastian* in the Galleria Nazionale d'Arte Antica, Rome, which was probably started in Italy but only completed after the artist's return to Antwerp.[2]

The pose relates to the drawing of a male torso after the antique marble of *The Gaul and His Wife*, which forms part of the large group of copies after Rubens in the Statens Museum for

Kunst, Copenhagen. These were probably made by Willem Panneels when he was left in charge of the master's studio from 1628 to 1630.[3]

Over twenty years after painting *Cupid and Psyche*, Rubens referred again to No. 22 when painting the oil sketch of *Cupid and Psyche* (now in the Musée Bonnat, Bayonne)[4] for the series of decorations in the Torre de la Parada (the royal hunting lodge near Madrid) on which he was engaged at the time of his death.

---

[1] Jaffé, no. 120.

[2] Jaffé, no. 75.

[3] Garff and de la Fuente Pedersen, no. 257, Pl. 260.

[4] Held (1980), Pl. 189.

[5] Jaffé, no. 302, repr.

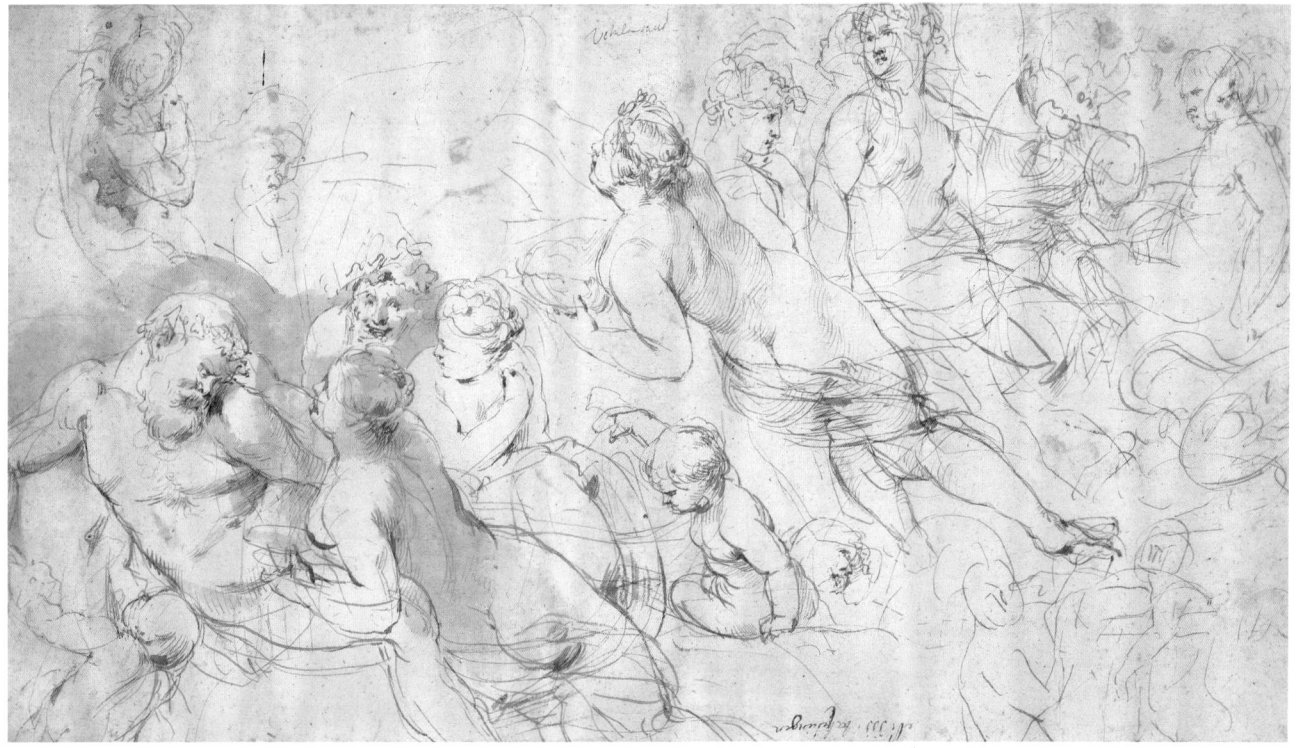

23

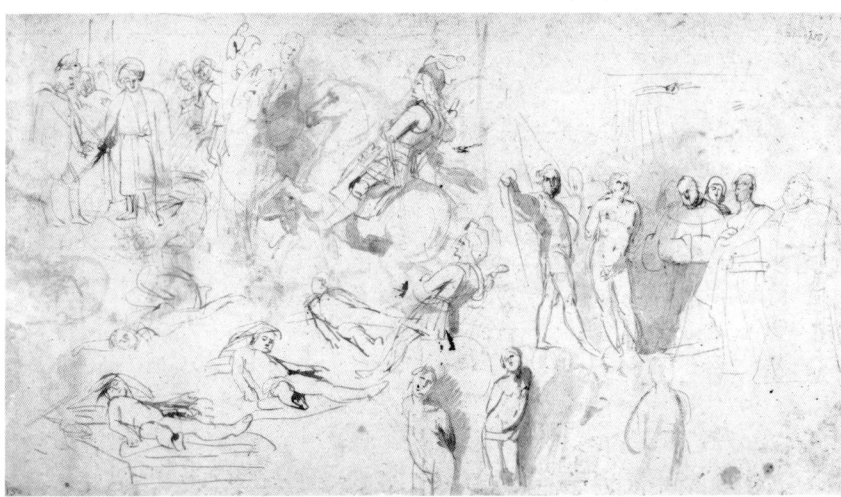

Peter Paul Rubens, *verso* of No. 23. *Various Studies* (inverted)
Pen and grayish brown ink with gray wash

The studies on the *verso*, which were only revealed in 1977, show an unusual combination of different subjects, relating to various works painted by Rubens between about 1614 and possibly as late as 1618. They are executed in a different colored ink and were probably drawn a little later than those on the *recto*. It is possible that the very diverse drawings were added to the *verso* over the course of several years.

24 *Self-Portrait in Old Age*

$7\frac{15}{16} \times 6\frac{5}{16}$ in. (200 × 160 mm)

Black chalk, heightened with white, on oatmeal paper; the remains of other sketches in pen and brown ink

Verso: *A Man and Woman Embracing*

Black chalk

Coll: George III

Bibl: Held (1959), no. 126; (1986), no. 236; Liedtke, I, p. 181; Vlieghe, no. 137[b]; Logan (1987), p. 81, under no. 236; W & C 437 (RL 6411)

The drawing originally formed part of a larger sheet with studies in pen and ink; an arm can be seen upper left, and possibly some drapery lower right. The eyes were drawn twice and are a little higher in the final arrangement.

The study shows the artist during the last years of his life, and in an unusually direct and unflattering portrayal, particularly notable for the careworn expression. It does not obviously relate to any known painted self-portrait, but it has been plausibly connected with the first version of the artist's head (visible in x-radiograph) in the *Self-Portrait with Helena Fourment and Their Son Peter Paul*, in the Metropolitan Museum of Art, New York.[6] Since the younger Peter Paul was only born in 1637, the painting must date from the very end of the artist's life.

The *verso*, which only became visible in 1977, shows a freely executed sketch of a seated couple embracing, possibly to be identified as Jupiter and Callisto, in view of the relationship with the drawing of that subject which occurs on a sheet of studies in the Museum Boymans-van Beuningen, Rotterdam.[7] The female figure closely resembles the nymph on the right of the painting of *Nymphs and Satyrs*, in the Prado, Madrid.

[6] Liedtke, I, p. 181, Fig. 38. This association is disputed by Vlieghe (*loc. cit.*).

[7] Burchard and d'Hulst, no. 194 *recto*, repr.

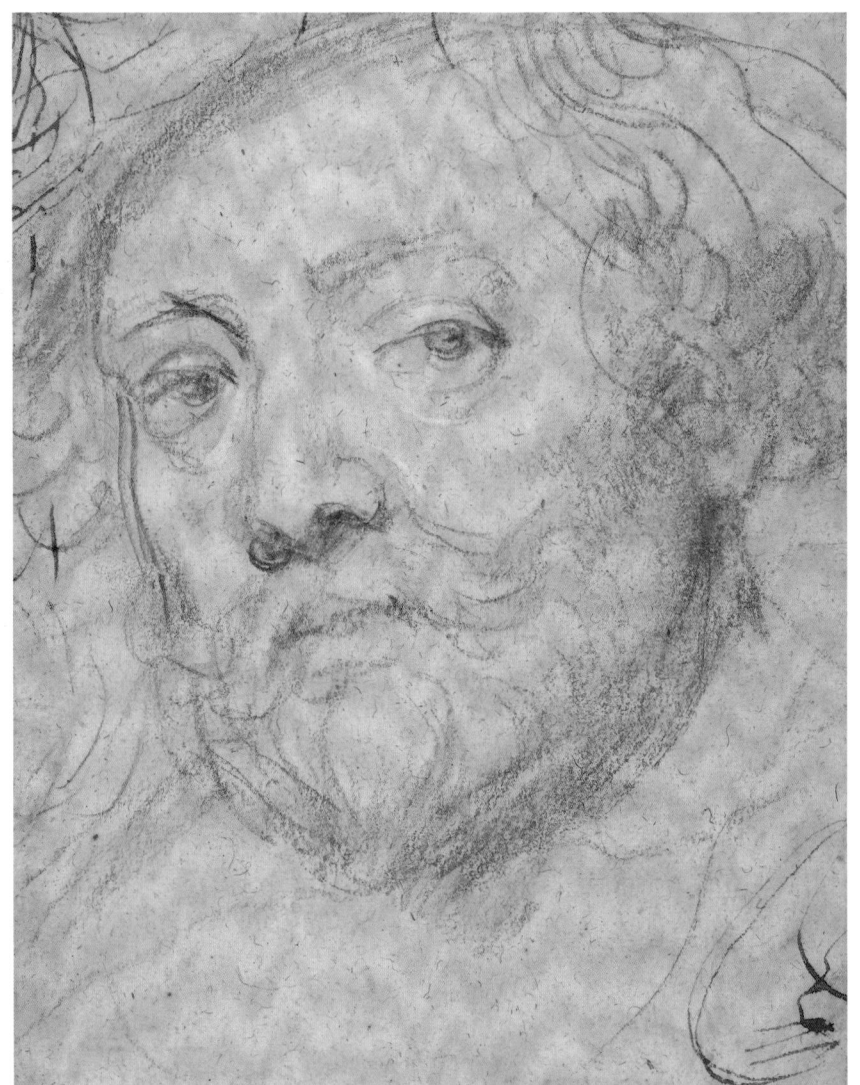

24

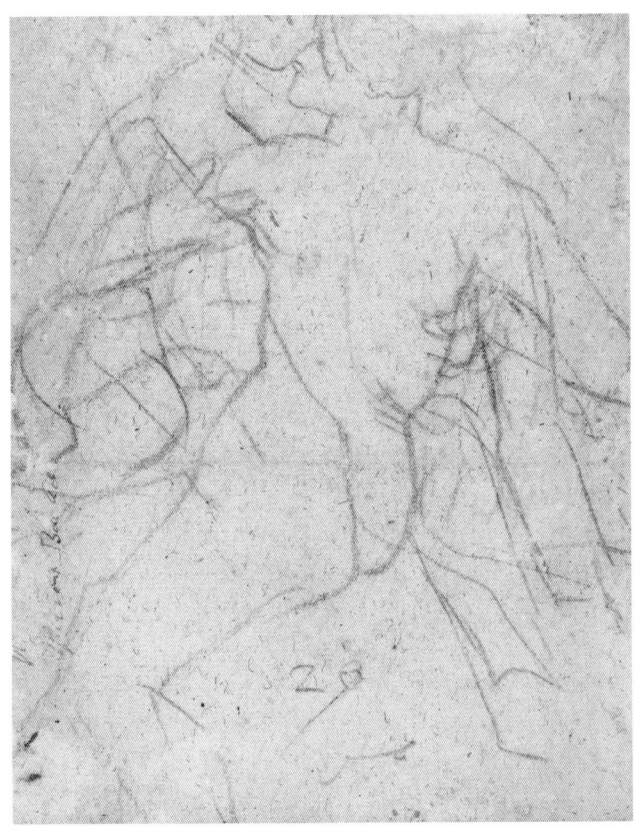

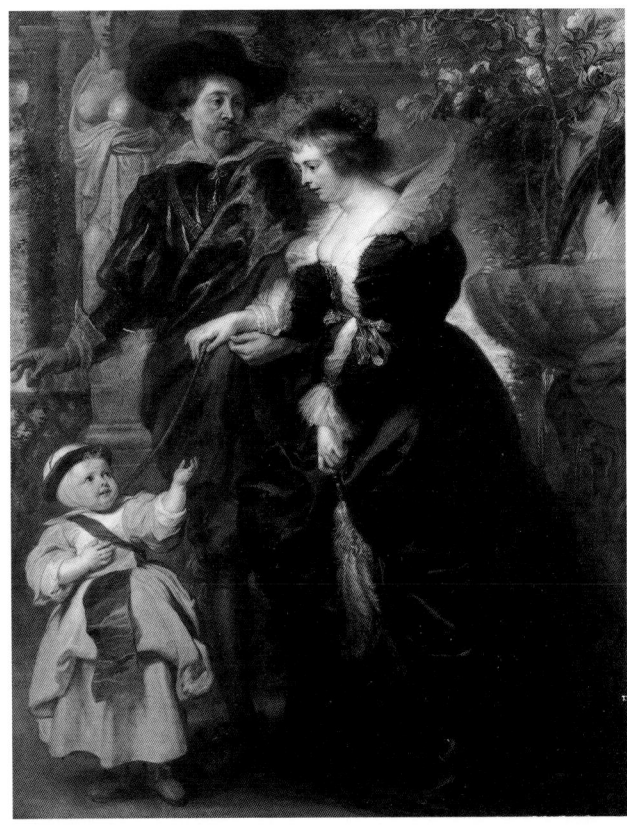

(*Above left*)
Peter Paul Rubens, *verso* of No. 24.
A Man and Woman Embracing
Black chalk

(*Above right*)
Peter Paul Rubens, *Self-Portrait with Helena Fourment and Their Son Paul*
Oil on panel, 8 × 7¼ in. (20.4 × 18.5 cm)
(New York, Metropolitan Museum of Art, Wrightsman bequest)

(*Right*)
Peter Paul Rubens, *Self-Portrait with Helena Fourment and Their Son Paul*: x-radiograph showing the first version of the artist's head

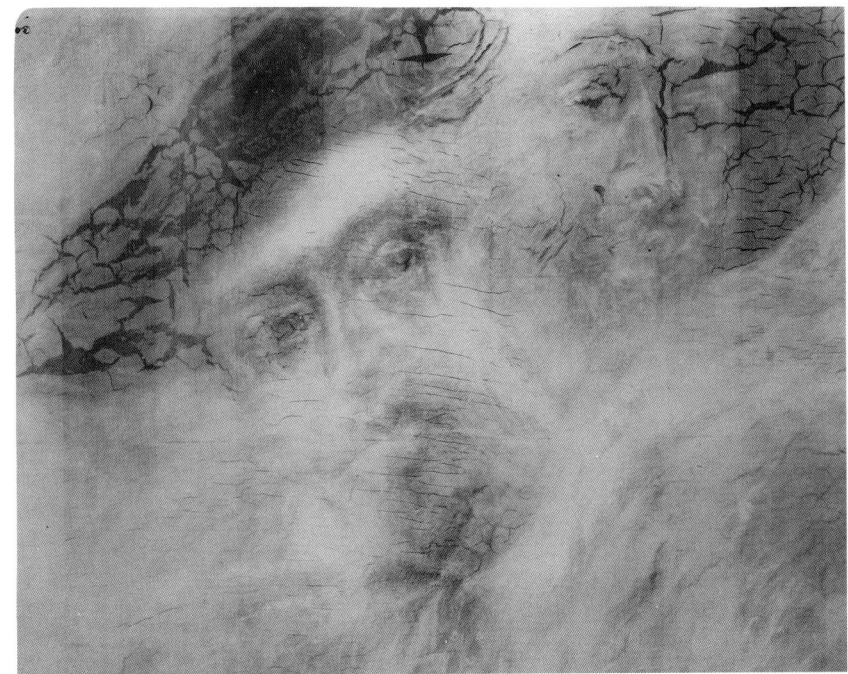

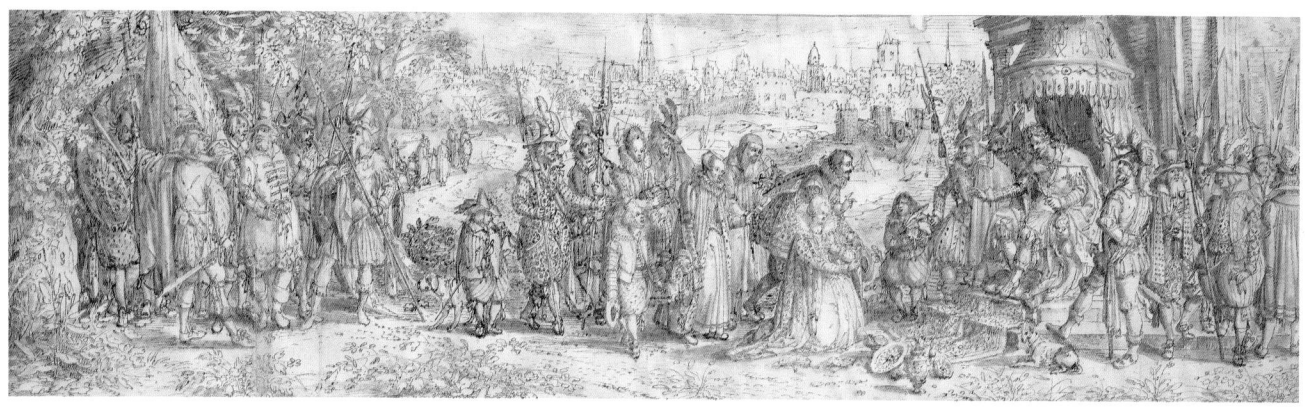

David Vinckeboons

1576–c.1632

Vinckeboons was a pupil of his father, who was also an artist. Father and son emigrated from Flanders to Holland in 1589, later settling in Amsterdam where David died. Remaining faithful to the Flemish landscape tradition, he exerted an influence on Dutch art.

25 The Clemency of Scipio

$7\frac{1}{4} \times 24\frac{3}{4}$ in. (184×630 mm)

On two pieces of paper

Pen and dark brown ink with gray and blue wash, and touches of magenta wash on the left

Bibl: Wegner and Pée, p. 93, no. 47; W & C 493 (RL 12982)

On the right, Scipio, seated on a throne beneath a baldacchino and surrounded by his armed supporters, is in the act of returning the maiden to her fiancé. Behind the maiden are her parents and other companions. The ransom of gold dishes and a ewer are placed on the ground before Scipio, who is about to return them as a wedding gift (the bride's mother is carrying further gifts). On the left, there are more soldiers, one of whom is bearing a standard inscribed, in reverse, *SPQR*. The fortified town of New Carthage can be seen in the background. While Scipio and several soldiers are dressed *all'antica*, the remainder of the figures are shown in

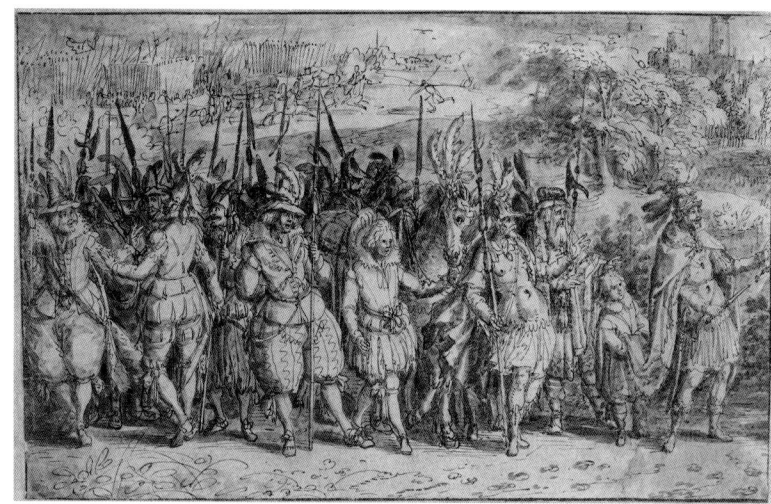

David Vinckeboons, *Meeting of Quintus Fabius Maximus Cunctator with His Son, the Consul* (left part) Pen and brown ink with gray, brown, and blue wash, $7\frac{1}{8} \times 11\frac{3}{8}$ in. (181×289 mm) (New York, Pierpont Morgan Library: 1961.31)

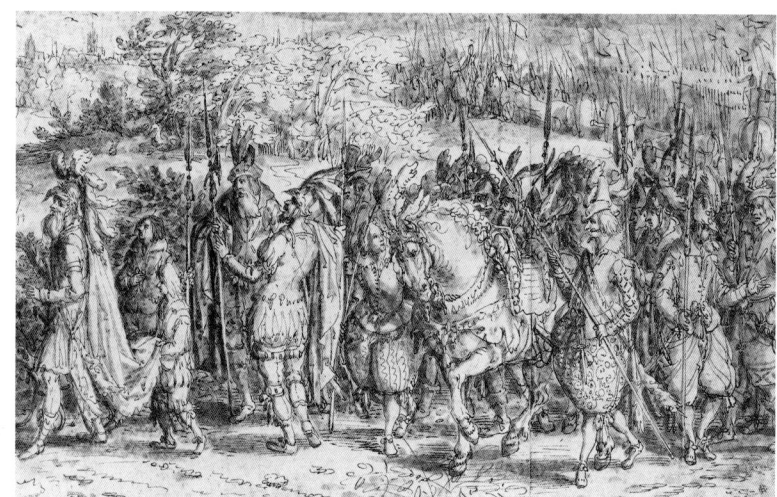

David Vinckeboons, *Meeting of Quintus Fabius Maximus Cunctator with His Son, the Consul* (right part) Pen and brown ink with gray, brown, and blue wash, $7\frac{1}{16} \times 11\frac{3}{16}$ in. (180×284 mm) (Amsterdam, Rijksmuseum, Rijksprentenkabinet)

contemporary costume. The subject is described by both Livy and Petrarch.

This drawing can reasonably be associated with a similarly sized, shaped, and composed drawing of the *Meeting of Quintus Fabius Maximus Cunctator with His Son, the Consul,* which is now in two parts, in the Rijksmuseum, Amsterdam, and in the Pierpont Morgan Library, New York.[1] Both subjects possibly formed part of a series devoted to episodes from Roman history at the time of the Punic Wars, and were probably drawn *c.*1610.

The reversal of the letters *SPQR* on the standard suggests that the drawing – and by association its companion – were intended as preparatory studies for either engravings or tapestries. In view of the extended compositions, with figures crowded into the foreground, the latter purpose is more likely. (A painting by Vinckeboons of *David and Abigail,* with a rather similar composition, served as the source for a tapestry woven by Frans Spierings about 1620.)

[1] Wegner and Pée, p. 99, no. 49, repr.; Stampfle, no. 219.

Pieter Claesz. Soutman

*c.*1580–1657

Born in Haarlem, Soutman moved to Antwerp, where he became a citizen. He may have been a pupil of Rubens. In 1624 he entered the service of the King of Poland, becoming court painter in 1628. By the latter date he had returned to his native city of Haarlem, where he spent the rest of his life. A painter as well as an engraver, he was one of the artists commissioned to paint decorations for the Huis ten Bosch near The Hague in 1648. Cornelis Visscher (see No. 52) may have been one of his pupils.

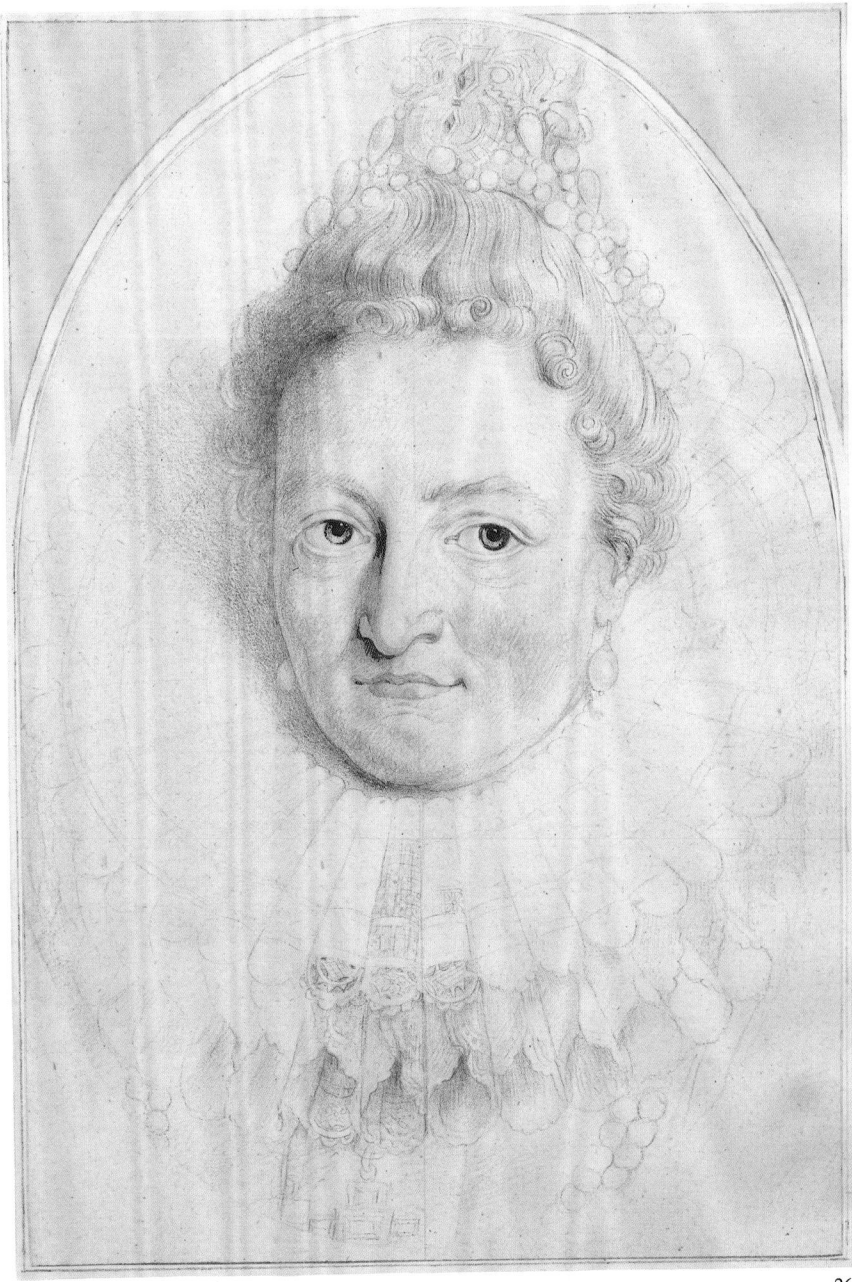

26

26 Infanta Isabella Clara Eugenia

$9\frac{11}{16} \times 6\frac{5}{8}$ in. (247 × 169 mm) (arched at top)

Black and red chalk, touched up with pen and brown ink in the irises, the nose, and the mouth, with a vertical line through the middle of the portrait; indented for transfer

Coll: recorded in the Royal Collection from 1913

Bibl: Burchard and d'Hulst, no. 97; Vlieghe, no. 65a; w & c 451 (RL 12978)

Isabella Clara Eugenia (1566–1633) was the eldest daughter of Philip II of Spain. She was made joint regent of the Southern Netherlands with her husband Albert on their marriage in 1598; after his death in 1621, she was appointed governor. She was portrayed on a number of occasions by Rubens, who had been appointed a court painter in 1609. Sitter and artist were in close contact over political and artistic matters after Albert's death.

The sitter is shown wearing a diadem composed of a jewel with a cluster of pearls, pearl earrings, and a lace cartwheel ruff, with ropes of pearls on her breast. The drawing is probably based on the head in the half-length portrait that Rubens was recorded as painting (with a pendant of Albert) in Brussels in 1616, of which there is a disputed version in The Chrysler Museum, Norfolk, Virginia.[1] Executed in a very precise manner, the drawing was almost certainly made for the engraving[2] of the same size, but in reverse, executed by Jonas Suyderhoef and published by Pieter Soutman as one of a series of ten portraits entitled *FERDINANDUS II^{us} ET III^{us} IMPERATORVM DOMVS AUSTRIACAE.* This series was one of the four parts of an ambitious project comprising fifty-eight engraved portraits, each of which is surrounded by a richly decorated ornamental border. Two parts were devoted to the House of Austria. The other two series were devoted to the Dukes of Burgundy and the Counts of Nassau. Various engravers were involved in this project by Soutman, who provided the drawings and published the set in Haarlem in 1644.

Despite the fact that the inscription on the engraving related to No. 26 states that it was based on a drawing by Soutman after Rubens's painting, it has sometimes been claimed that the drawing was made by Rubens himself (as he undoubtedly did on other occasions) for the engraver.[3] But in addition to the evidence of the inscription, the drawing is executed in a very similar manner to other preparatory drawings for the engraver by Soutman. In 1615/16 the latter had been a pupil of and collaborator with Rubens, many of whose works he later engraved, thus successfully establishing his own reputation while also promoting knowledge of his master's work.

[1] Vlieghe, no. 65, Pl. 14.
[2] Hollstein, XXVIII, p. 221, no. 43.
[3] See, for example, Burchard and d'Hulst, *loc. cit.*

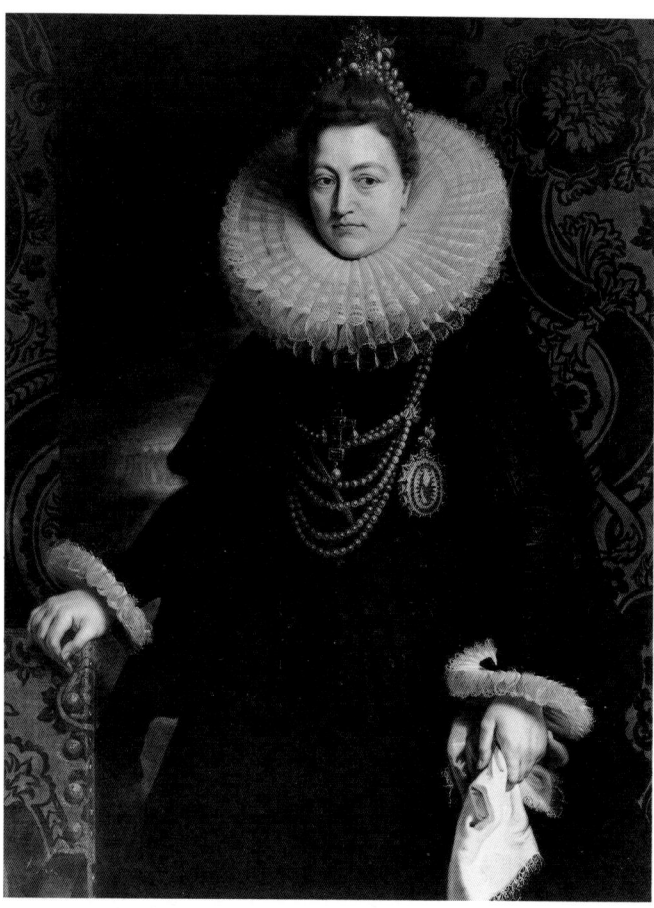

Peter Paul Rubens, *Infanta Isabella Clara Eugenia*
Oil on canvas, 47½ × 38 in. (120.7 × 96.5 cm) (The Chrysler Museum, Norfolk, Virginia, gift of Walter Chrysler, Jr.: 71.462)

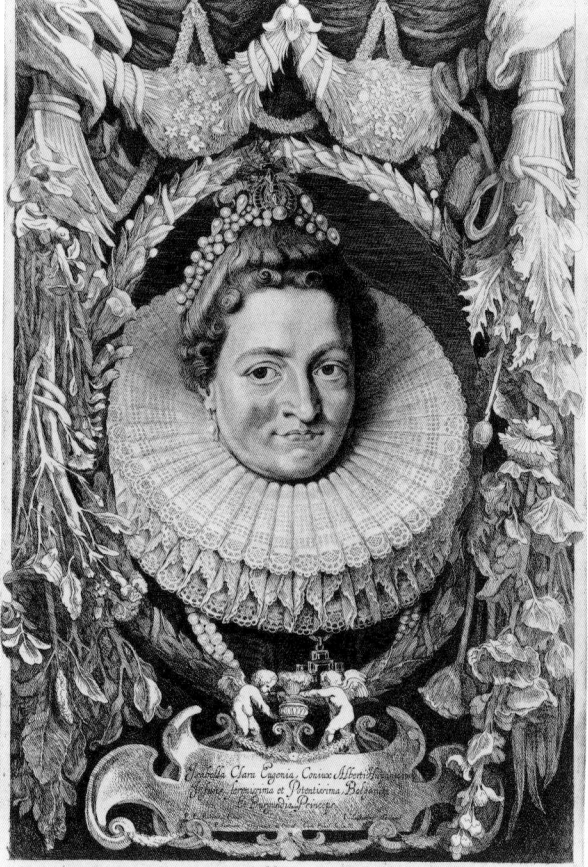

Jonas Suyderhoef after Pieter Claesz. Soutman, *Infanta Isabella Clara Eugenia*
Etching and engraving, 16 5/16 × 11 in. (415 × 280 mm) (Royal Collection: Windsor Castle, Royal Library)

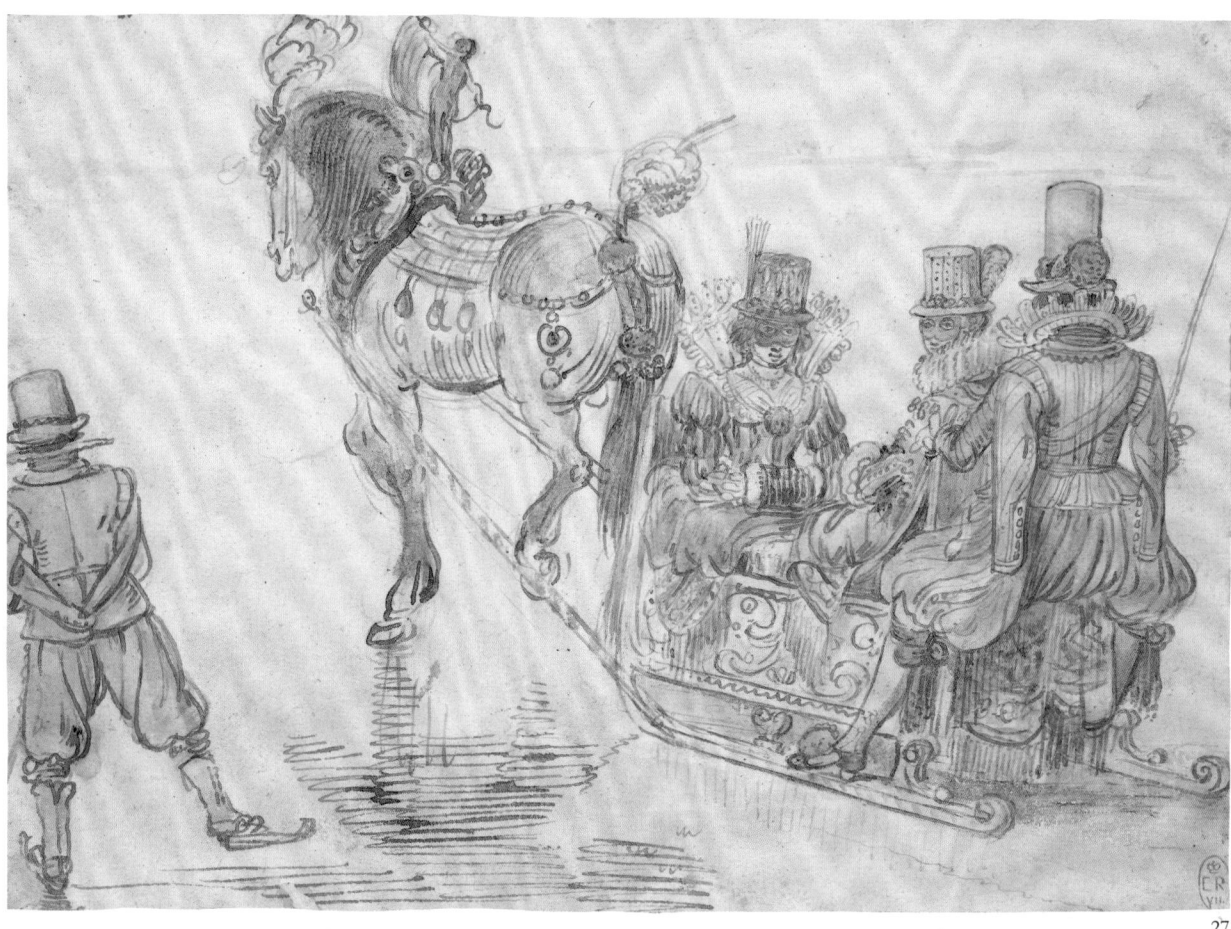

27

Hendrick Avercamp

1585–1634

Although brought up in Kampen, Avercamp may have been trained as an artist under Pieter Isaacsz. in Amsterdam, where he remained until 1613. After his return to Kampen, there are no records of any further journeys. He was a prolific painter and draughtsman, largely concerned with highly populated winter scenes with the figures painted in bright colors. In his drawings he often used a mixture of watercolor and bodycolor. As there are very few dated paintings or drawings, it is difficult to establish a chronology for his *oeuvre*.

27 Two Ladies and a Gentleman on a Horse-drawn Sleigh

$5\frac{7}{16} \times 7\frac{11}{16}$ in. (139 × 196 mm)

Pen and brown ink with brown wash and watercolor over graphite

Coll: George III

Bibl: Welcker, no. T139; w & c 243 (RL 6469)

The forty-seven studies by Avercamp at Windsor Castle amount to nearly one third of his known drawings and represent the largest holding in a single collection. They cover all the categories of his drawn *oeuvre* – studies of single figures and groups, genre scenes, and landscapes – and illustrate the considerable variety in the artist's finish and technique. It is clear that although single figures sometimes recur in his paintings, Avercamp did not regularly make preparatory

drawings. Most of his drawings appear to have been made for their own sake, and, in the case of the more finished colored sheets, were probably sold. The remainder served as a vocabulary of human behavior typically seen in the provincial town of Kampen, which appears in the background of a number of drawings. The style of the costume in many of the Windsor drawings suggests a date of around 1620 and not later than 1625.

The figures in the present drawing have been said to represent the King and Queen of Bohemia, who visited Kampen in 1626. However, the identification remains without foundation and the models should probably be regarded as patrician members of Kampen society.

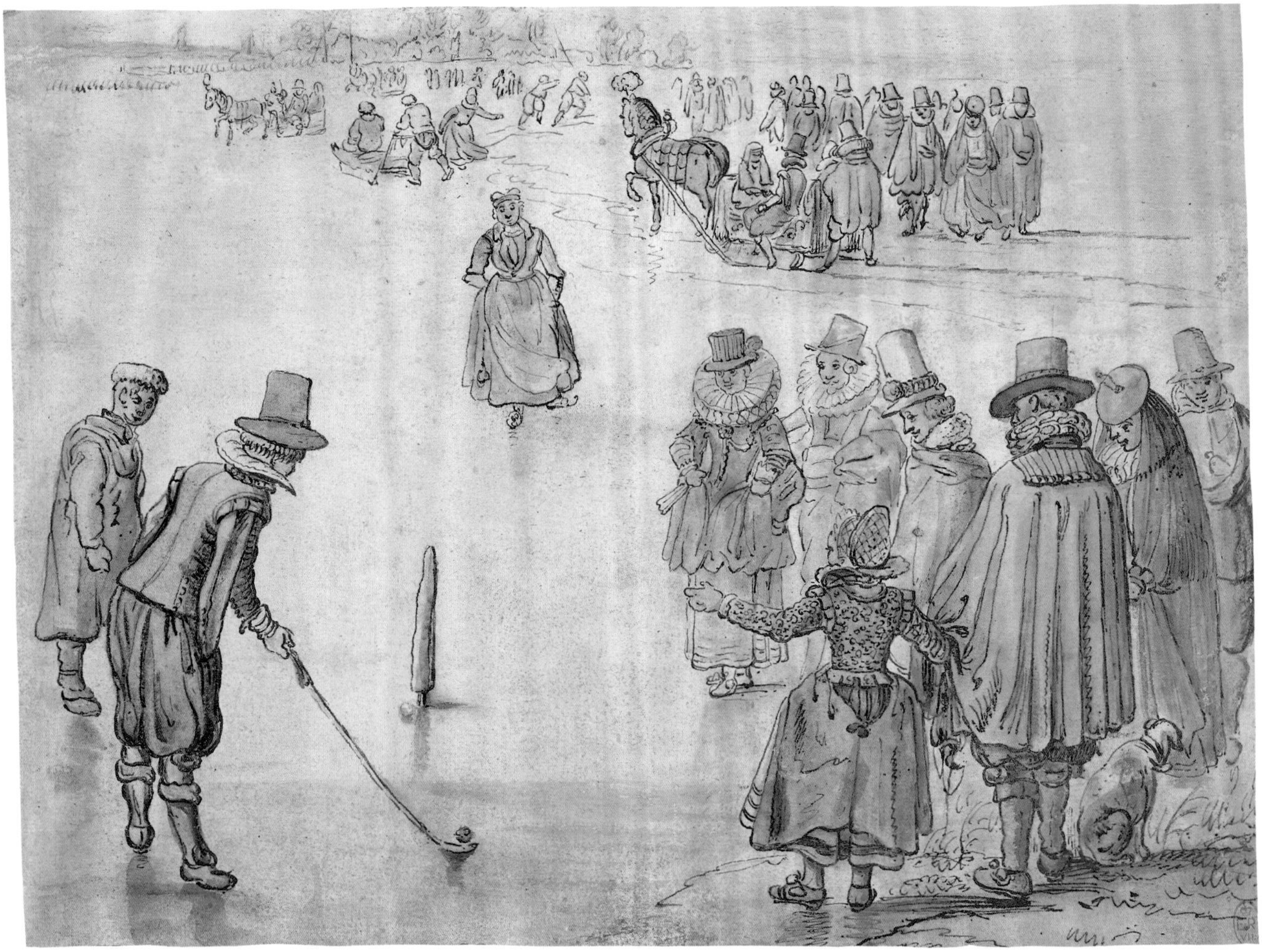

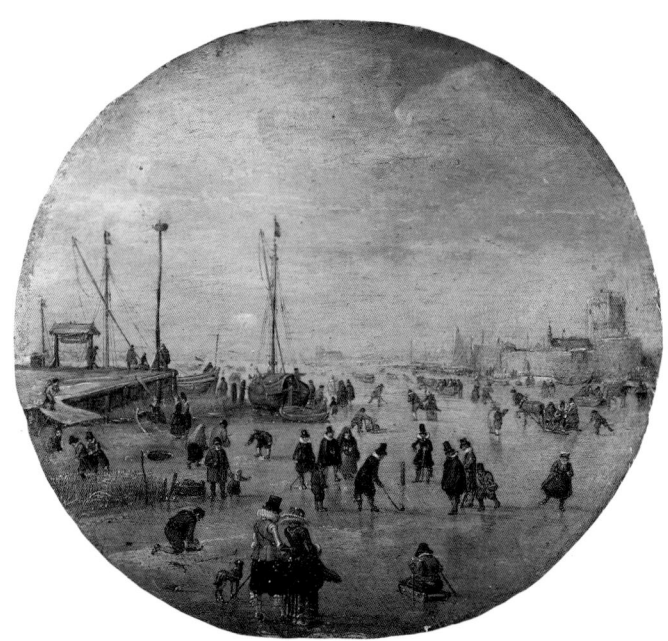

28 *A Game of* Kolf *on the Ice*

$6\frac{15}{16} \times 9\frac{3}{8}$ in. (176 × 238 mm)

Pen and brown ink with brown wash,
watercolor, red chalk, and bodycolor
over traces of graphite

Coll: George III

Bibl: Welcker, no. T140; W & C 244
(RL 6470)

The game of *kolf*, which was popular
in the Netherlands, is more like ice-
hockey than golf. The figure of the
man in a high-crowned hat about to
putt the ball and the horse-drawn
sleigh in the background recur in the
center of Avercamp's circular picture
Winter Landscape, in the Kunsthalle,
Hamburg.[1]

[1] Welcker, no. S51, Fig. XIX.

Hendrick Avercamp, *Winter Landscape*
Oil on panel, diameter $7\frac{1}{4}$ in. (18.5 cm) (Hamburg, Kunsthalle: 3)

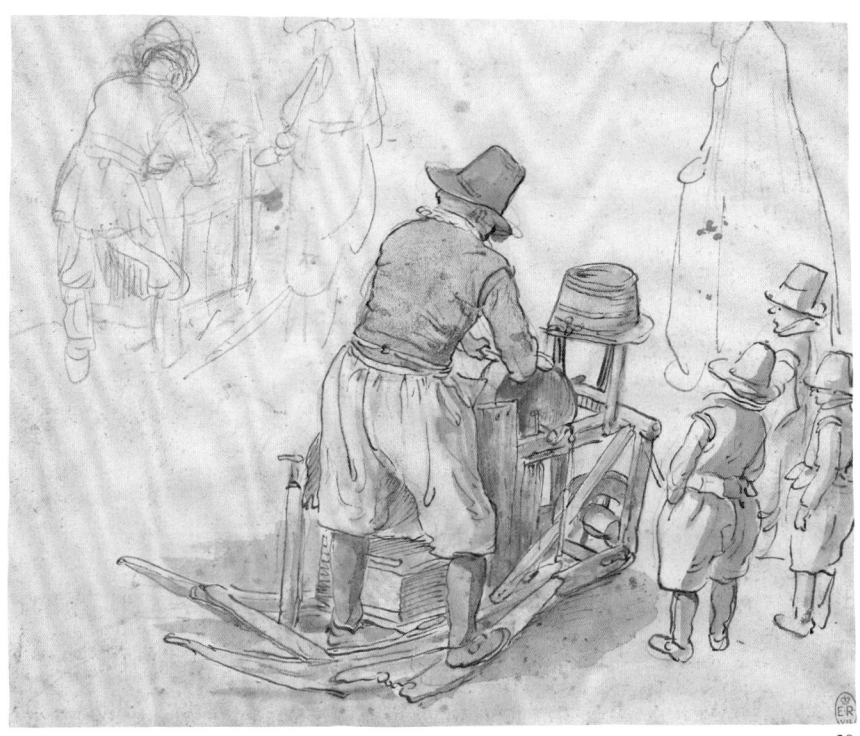

29 Two Studies of a Knife-Grinder

$6\frac{1}{2} \times 7\frac{15}{16}$ in. (165 × 202 mm)

Graphite, pen, and brown ink with brown wash and watercolor

Coll: George III

Bibl: Welcker, no. T141; W & C 245 (RL 6471)

The knife-grinder is seen from behind, holding the blade of a knife against the grinding wheel, which is rotated by means of a pedal activated by the right leg of the knife-grinder. The wheel is cooled by water dripping from the barrel-like container to the right.

This is an unusual drawing showing the preliminary study in graphite as well as the more finished version in pen and watercolor, to which three young spectators have been added.

30 A Scene on the Ice outside a Town

$7\frac{1}{4} \times 7\frac{13}{16}$ in. (185 × 199 mm)

A separate piece of paper has been attached lower left (see below).

Pen and brown ink with brown wash and watercolor over graphite

Coll: George III

Bibl: Welcker, no. T142; W & C 246 (RL 6472)

On the left, an elegantly dressed couple – he wearing a round-topped high-crowned hat and she a *huik* and *borst* (stomacher) – look at the silhouetted figure of a small boy with a warming (?) box on his lap (the additional piece of paper covers part of the original drawing and was clearly added afterwards by the artist or someone else). Behind to the right two gentlemen in cloaks are watching another man kneeling on the ground and tying the shoe of a lady in a ruff, who holds her muff to her face. In the background are numerous figures and horses before a town or village.

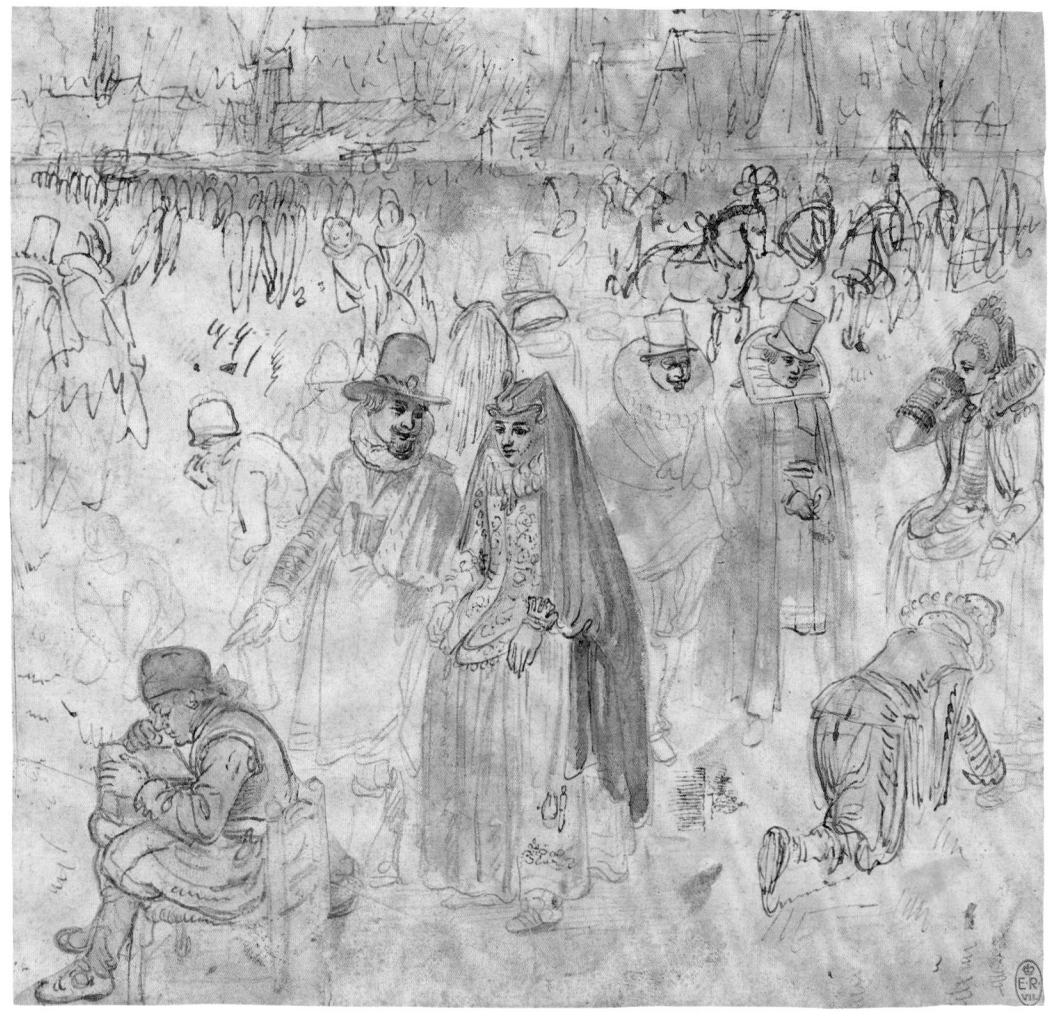

30

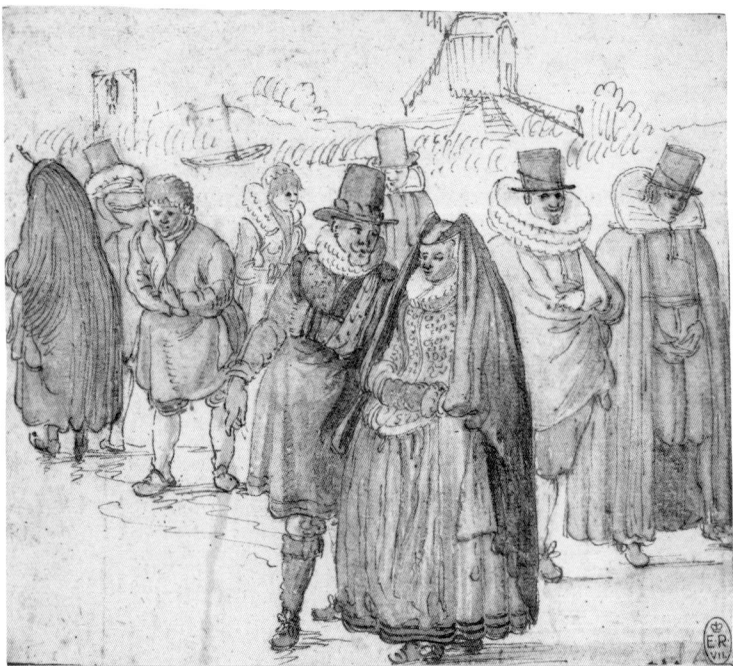

Hendrick Avercamp,
Elegantly Dressed Figures
Walking on the Ice
Pen and brown ink and
watercolor, $4\frac{1}{2} \times 5\frac{1}{4}$ in.
(115×133 mm)
(Royal Collection: Windsor
Castle, Royal Library:
W & C 254)

The figures of the couple and the two gentlemen behind them are repeated in another drawing at Windsor.[2] All four also appear in a signed *Scene on Ice*, on copper, formerly with L. Koetser.[3] The couple recur in the center of a picture formerly in the collection of J. de Frayter, Amsterdam.[4] The two men reappear in a drawing in Berlin and in a painted *Skating Scene*.[5] There is no reason to suppose, as has been suggested, that this couple represent Lambert Avercamp and his wife, with the artist's sister, Femmetje, on the extreme right.

31 *A Standing Girl with Her Hands under Her Apron*

$10\frac{3}{16} \times 5\frac{3}{16}$ in. (260 × 132 mm)

Black and red chalk

Coll: George III

Bibl: Welcker, no. T176; w & c 280
(RL 6506)

The drawing is an unusually large-scale figure study for the artist. The girl – or a very similar figure – recurs on the left-hand side of pictures of a *Scene on the Ice*, in the Edward Carter collection, Los Angeles,[6] and in the National Gallery of Art, Washington.[7]

[2] w & c 254.

[3] Previously Miss N. I. Nichols. Sale, Sothebys, London, 6 March 1957 (78).

[4] Welcker, no. S27. The couple may be the same models who appear in a drawing in the Rijksprentenkabinett, Amsterdam (Schatborn, p. 44, repr.).

[5] The drawing is Berlin 2230. The painting, in a private collection, is Welcker, no. S14.

[6] Welcker, no. S23, Fig. XXV; Walsh and Schneider, no. 1, repr.

[7] Inv. no. 2315; Ailsa Mellon Bruce Fund 1967.3.1. (PA).

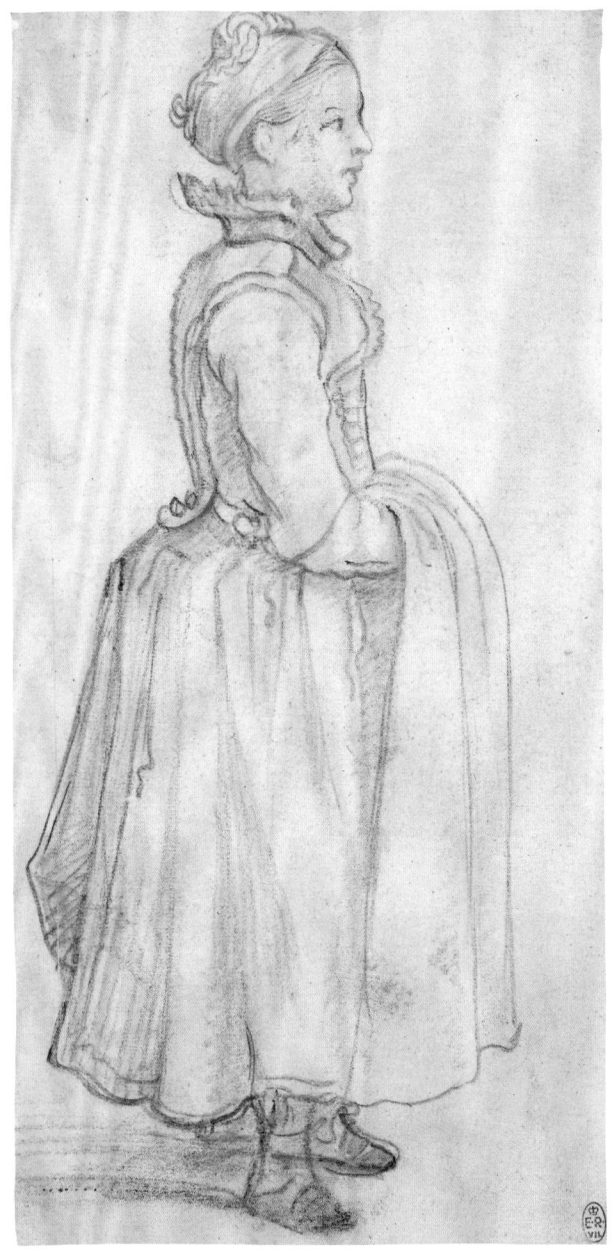

31

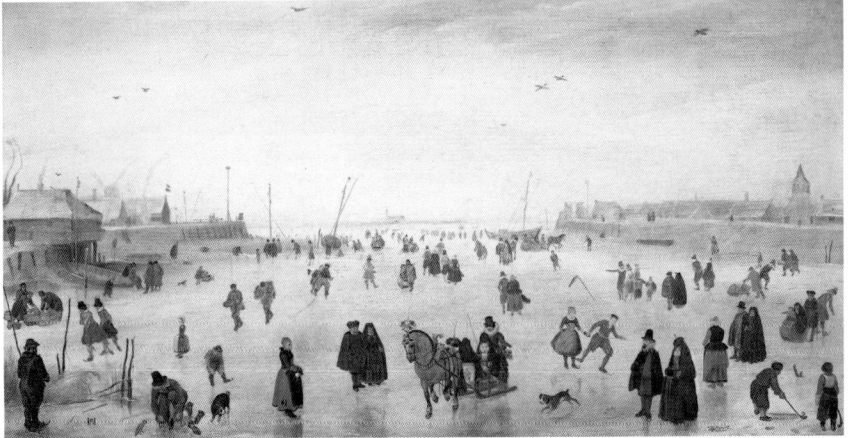

Hendrick Avercamp, *A Scene on Ice*
Oil on panel, $15\frac{7}{16} \times 30\frac{5}{16}$ in. (39.3 × 77.1 cm)
(Washington, National Gallery of Art, Ailsa
Mellon Bruce Fund: 1967.3.1 (PA); 2315)

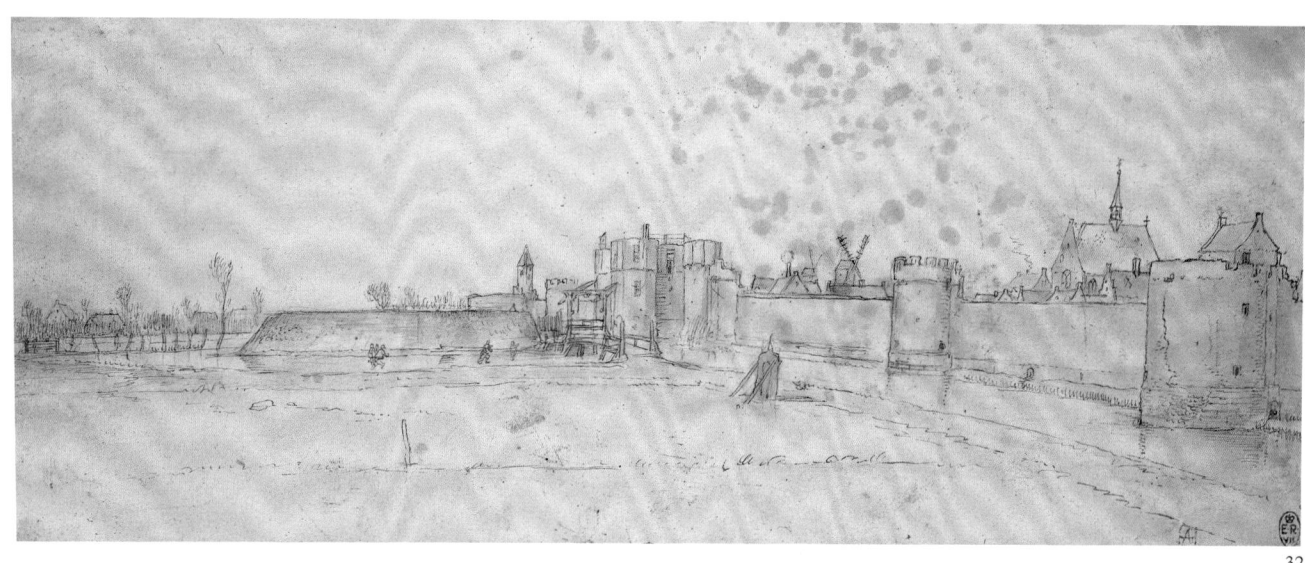

32 *A View of Kampen from outside the Walls*

$4\frac{13}{16} \times 12\frac{3}{16}$ in. (122 × 310 mm)

Pen and brown ink with watercolor over graphite

Signed lower right: *HA* (in monogram)

Verso: further views (scarcely legible) of Kampen from outside the walls

Coll: George III

Bibl: Welcker, no. T177; W & C 281 (RL 6507)

The town is seen from outside the moat and fortifications, looking towards the Broederpoort; on the right is the Mennonite parish church, formerly a conventual church. The drawing and the additional views on the *verso*, which was only revealed in 1993, are among the rare topographical studies made by Avercamp of Kampen, which more often appears as the background to the artist's various figure scenes.

Kampen, a member of the Hanseatic league in the fifteenth century, is situated on the River Ijssel in the province of Overijssel, near the Isselmeer. Avercamp lived in Kampen for much of his life.

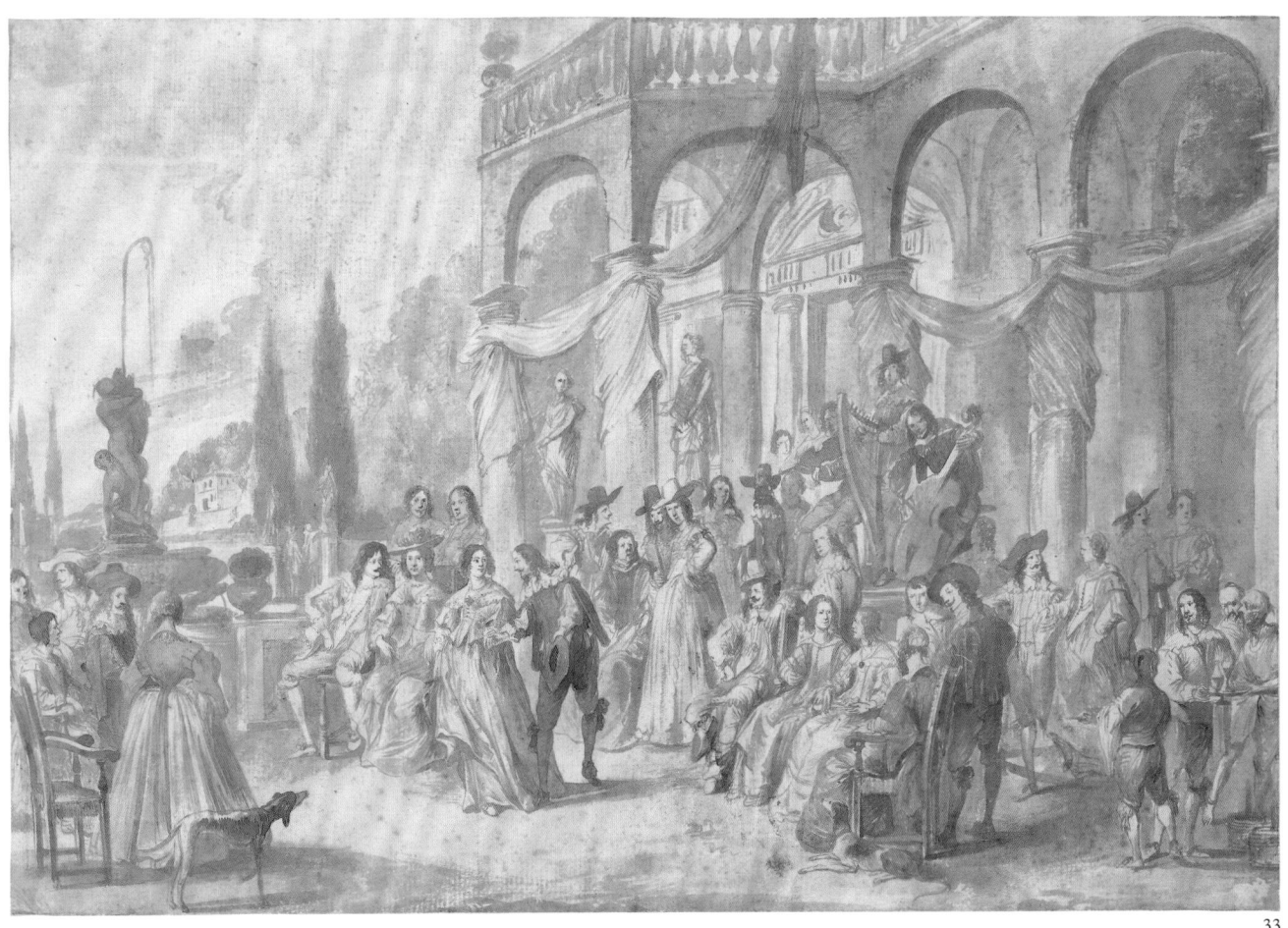

Cornelis de Wael

1592–1662

De Wael was trained by his father in Antwerp. In 1610 he went to Italy, settling three years later in Genoa where, apart from visits to Rome, he spent most of the remainder of his life. Van Dyck, a friend from his youth, lived with him during the former's visits to Genoa. De Wael produced paintings, drawings, and etchings of harbor scenes and genre and military subjects. He was a prolific and fluent draughtsman, if somewhat unvaried in style.

33 *A Garden Party*

$10\frac{3}{16} \times 15$ in. (260 × 382 mm)

Brush drawing in brown over traces of graphite

Coll: George III

Bibl: W & C 506 (RL 6456)

The event takes place before a loggia on the right, where a trio are playing to the assembled company. A garden with a large sculpted fountain and cypresses can be seen on the left. The present drawing differs from the majority of De Wael's drawings, which are executed in pen with loosely drawn shading. The use of the point of the brush and wash in No. 33 produces a more finished effect. It is not possible to determine whether the drawing was intended as an end in itself or was made as a preparatory study for a painting.

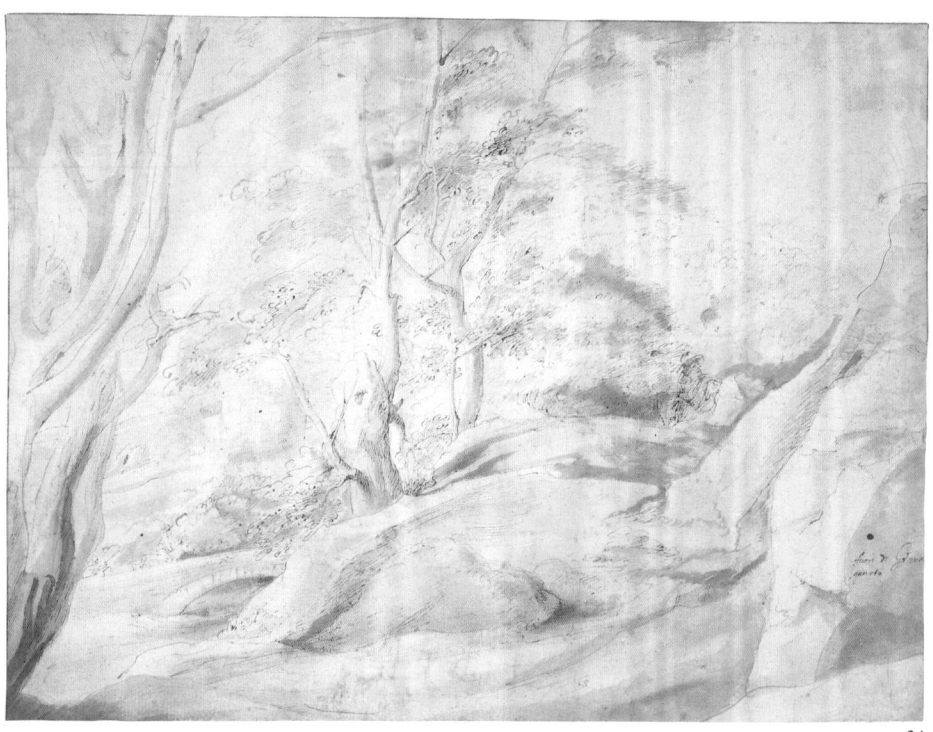

34

Antony van Dyck

1599–1641

Born in Antwerp, Van Dyck was a
pupil of Hendrick van Balen and was
made a master of the Guild of St.
Luke in 1628. He assisted Rubens,
who in 1620 described him as one of
his "disciples." In 1620/21 he paid a
brief visit to England, where he was in
the service of James I. By the end of
1621 Van Dyck was in Italy, where he
remained until 1627. He traveled
widely, going as far south as Sicily,
but he was mainly active as a painter
in Genoa. By 1628 he had re-
established his studio in Antwerp,
where he remained until 1632, when
he moved to England and became the
principal painter to Charles I. Van
Dyck was back in the southern
Netherlands during 1634 and early
1635, but apart from brief visits to
Antwerp and Paris at the very end of
his life, he remained resident in
London.

34 *Landscape near Genoa*

$10\frac{3}{4} \times 14\frac{9}{16}$ in. (273 × 370 mm)

Pen and grayish-brown ink and grayish-
brown wash, with some blue watercolor
in the sky. Some retouching (by another
hand?) in brown wash

Inscribed lower right by the artist: *fuori
di Genua | quarto* (outside Genoa, Quarto)

Coll: purchased from the Gore Ouseley
collection, Tenbury Wells (1919)

Bibl: Vey, no. 282; w & c 353 (RL 12972)

The inscription on the drawing, which
has clearly been cut, probably
identifies the locality as Quarto dei
Mille, situated outside Genoa on the
road to Nervi. Van Dyck was resident
in Genoa on several occasions during
his Italian journey between 1621 and
1627 and presumably made this study
on an outing from the city.

Apart from a rapid study of a *House
among Trees* on the *verso* of a drawing
connected with a Genoese
commission[1] and two sketches in his
Italian Sketchbook, which may
represent the mole and lighthouse at
Genoa,[2] this drawing remains Van
Dyck's only known Italian landscape.

There appear to be no further
landscape studies until the mid–1630s
when he was working in England.

35 *Nicolaas Rockox*

$11\frac{7}{8} \times 8\frac{1}{2}$ in. (302 × 217 mm)

Black chalk

Inscribed (by Ten Kate?) lower left: *A:
van Dijk*; and on *verso*: *Nicolaus Rockox*
and . . . *tot Antwerp*

Coll: (?) Alexander Voet (1689
inventory); Lambert ten Kate Hermansz.
(sale 1732); George III

Bibl: Vey, no. 193; w & c 354 (RL 6421)

Nicolaas Rockox (1560–1640) was a
distinguished collector, patron, and
scholar in Antwerp, who also served
as alderman and burgomaster of the
city on a number of occasions. A close
friend of Rubens, he was portrayed by
the artist on several occasions.

The sitter, who wears an old-

[1] *St. Matthew and the Angel*, in the Museum
Boymans-van Beuningen, Rotterdam
(Vey, no. 111, Pl. 149).

[2] In the British Museum (Adriani, f.1, Fig. 1,
and f.95 *verso*, not by Van Dyck).

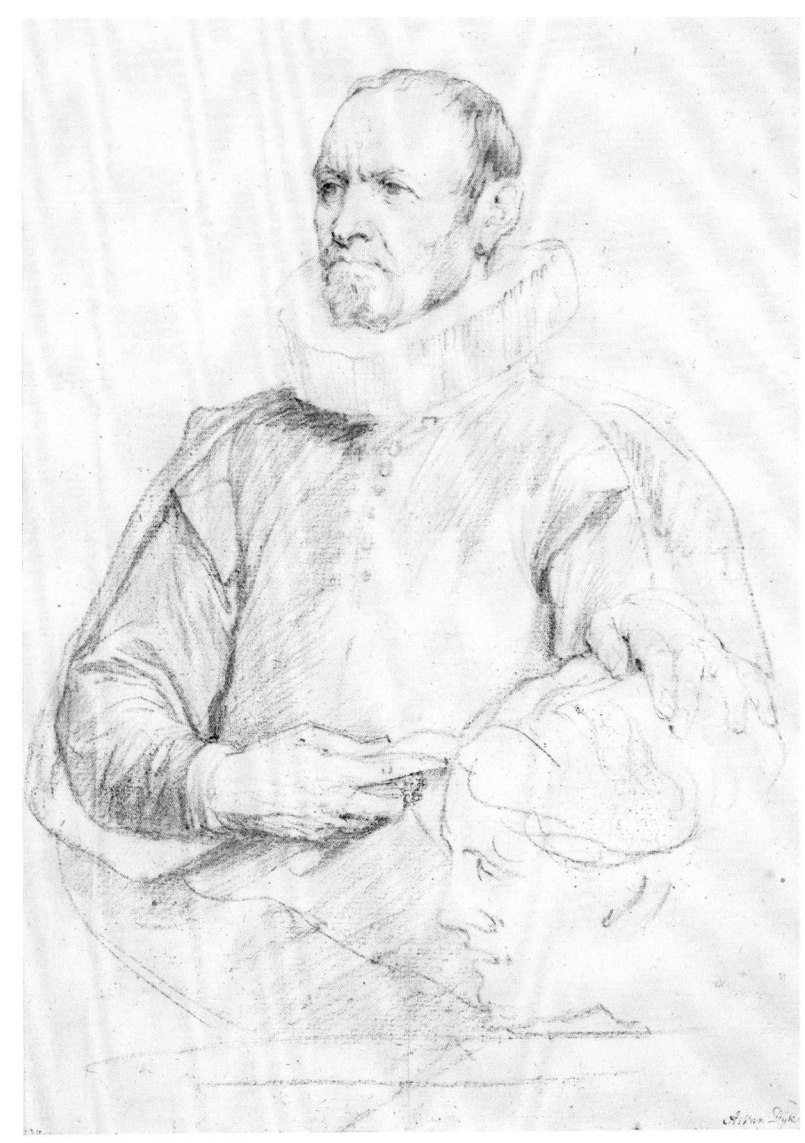

35

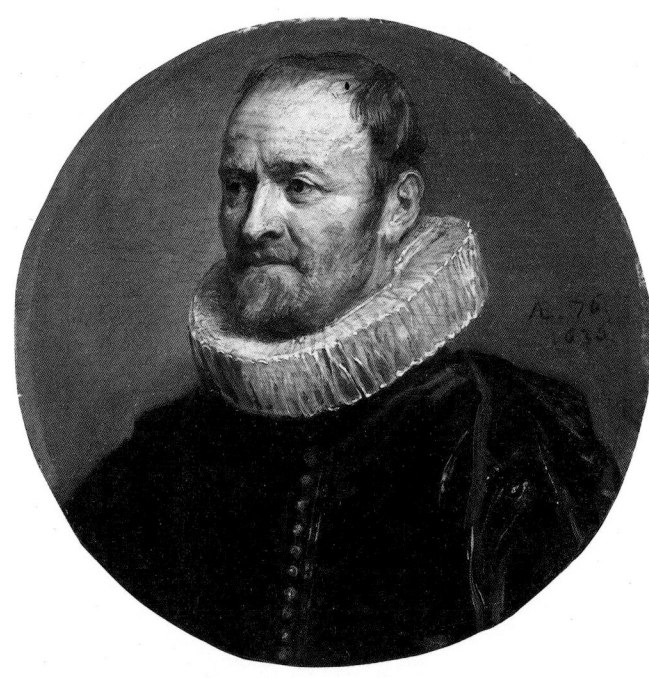

Antony van Dyck,
Nicolaas Rockox
Oil on panel,
diameter 6 in.
(15.2 cm)
(Washington,
Private Collection)

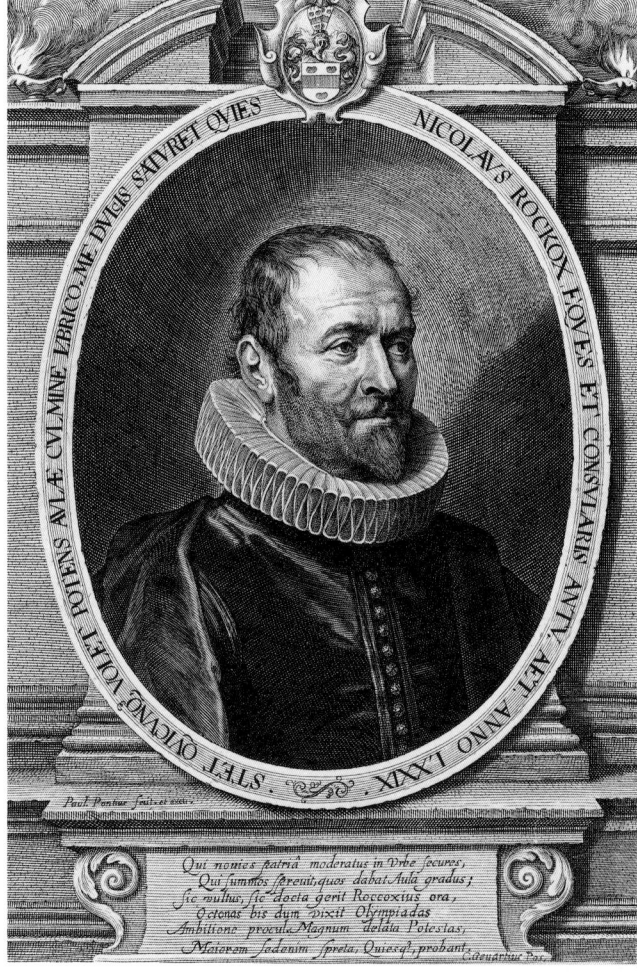

Paulus Pontius after
Antony van Dyck,
Nicolaas Rockox
Engraving,
10¼ × 7 in.
(260 × 176 mm)
(cut within
platemark;
London, British
Museum,
Department of
Prints and
Drawings)

fashioned millstone collar, rests his left hand on the head of a bust. The latter probably represents Athena, who can be seen with four classical male busts in the picture by Frans Francken the Younger of the *Dining Room in the House of Nicolaas Rockox*, in the Alte Pinakothek, Munich.[3] Van Dyck portrayed Rockox on several occasions; a portrait in the Hermitage, St. Petersburg, probably painted in 1621, shows him with another classical bust (of Plato ?).[4]

The present drawing, in which the sitter is considerably older than in the St. Petersburg portrait, was probably made between Van Dyck's return to Antwerp in 1627 and his departure for England in 1632, or – less likely in view of the sitter's age – during the artist's brief return to Antwerp in 1634/35. It may well be that it was made with the series of portraits for Van Dyck's etched and engraved *Iconography* in mind. Rockox would have been a natural subject for inclusion among the group of collectors.

The head in the drawing clearly served for the likeness in the recently discovered small roundel in grisaille of the head and shoulders of Rockox, dated 1636, in a private collection.[5] The roundel was, in turn, the basis of the preparatory grisaille (possibly by Paulus Pontius) and the engraving (certainly by Pontius) in 1639,[6] which was included in the second expanded edition of the *Iconography* published in 1645/46, after Van Dyck's death in 1641. The head of Rockox is drawn on a slightly larger scale in No. 35 than in Pontius's engraving; the head in the roundel is yet smaller.

[3] Munich, p.36, no. 858, Fig. 32.

[4] Larsen, no. 55, Pl. 129.

[5] Washington, no. 100, repr.

[6] Mauquoy-Hendrickx (1956), no. 115, repr. The artist responsible for the portrait was named as Rubens in the sixth state of Pontius's print; this was corrected to Van Dyck (*Ant. van Dyck pinxit*) in the eighth state.

Herman van Swanevelt

*c.*1600–1655

Swanevelt was a landscape painter, draughtsman, and etcher. Probably from Woerden, he seems to have visited Paris in 1623 before moving to Rome, where he resided from 1629 until 1641. There he lived with various French painters – he appears to have been in close contact with Claude Lorrain – and played an important role in the development of Italianate landscape. In later life he spent much of his time in Paris, where his work was greatly admired. He also paid several visits to his native Woerden.

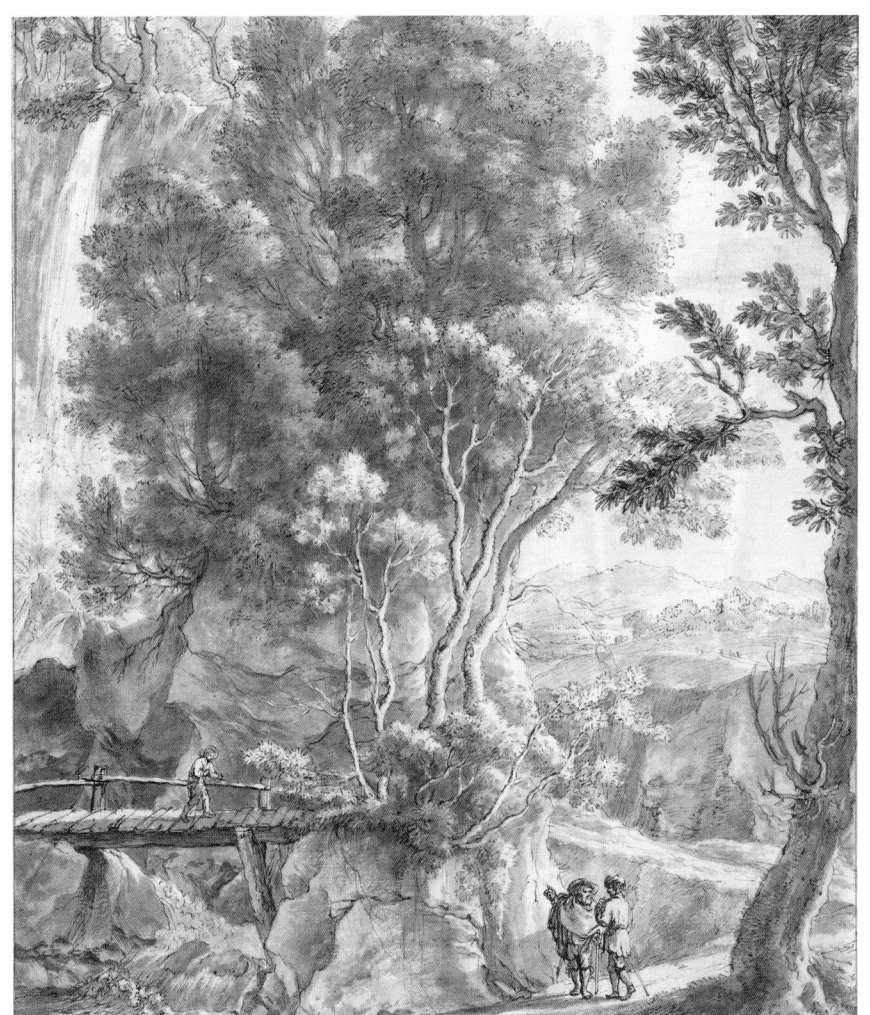

36

36 *A Winding Mountain Road with Travellers and a Bridge*

11⅝ × 9⁷⁄₁₆ in. (296 × 240 mm)

Pen and brown ink with gray wash over graphite

Coll: George III

Bibl: w & c 458 (RL 6291)

The drawing was executed *en suite* with three other drawings at Windsor Castle.[1] They were probably made when the artist was in Paris in the early 1650s, and they are similar in style and subject to the series of etchings of *Four Upright Landscapes*.[2] After his return to the north, Swanevelt continued to produce decorative landscapes with scenery reminiscent of what he had seen in Italy. But whereas his earlier drawings had an individual feeling for light and atmosphere very similar to what Claude was doing at the same time, his later works adopt a more general formula for the play of light over the landscape, which tends to lack variety. Nevertheless, they served to create attractive decorations in a classical style: for instance, those painted (with other artists) in the Cabinet de l'Amour in the Hôtel Lambert, Paris, in the mid-1640s.

[1] w & c 457 and 459–60.

[2] Hollstein, XXIX, pp. 91–93, nos. 99–102.

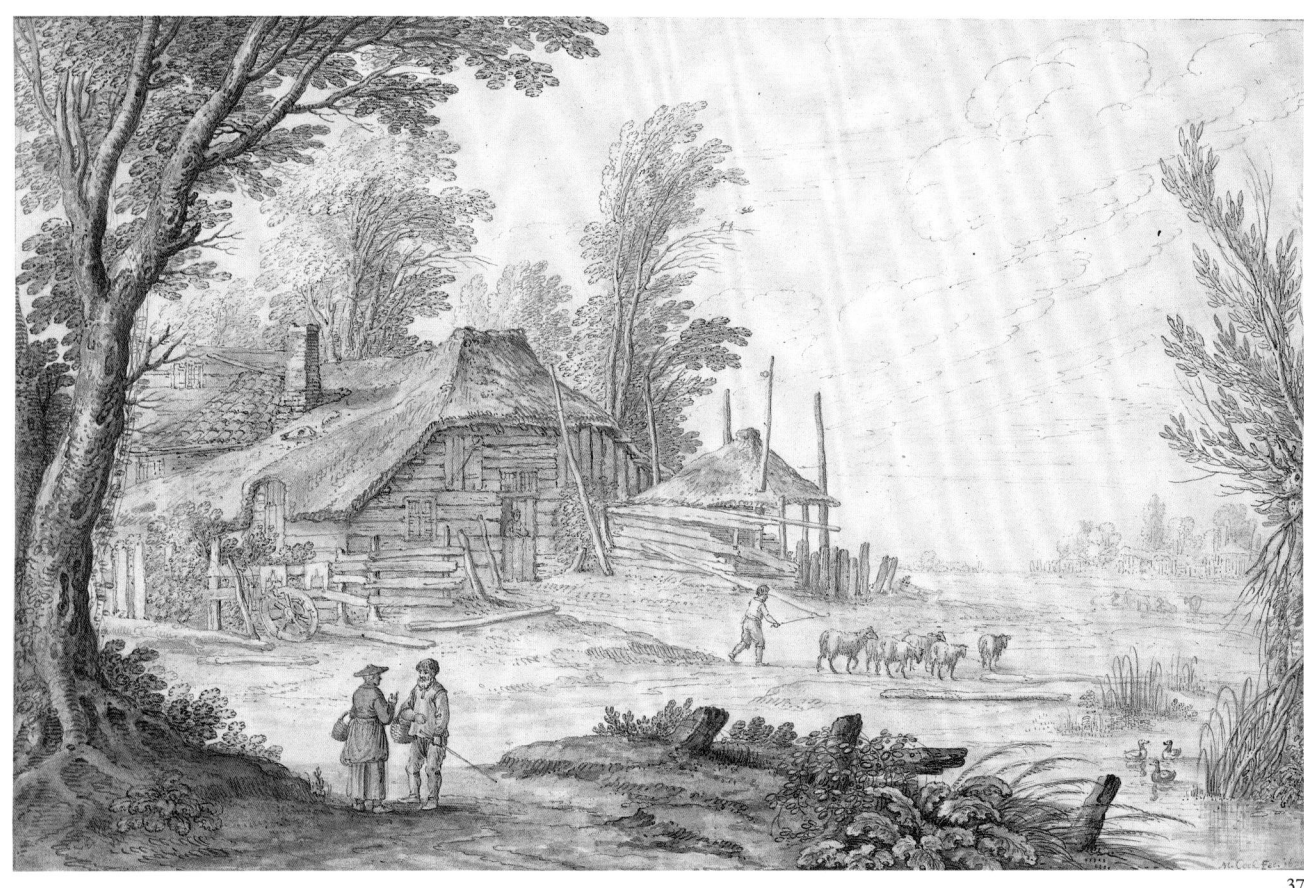

37

Marten de Cock

Active 1620–1646

Apart from a group of signed and dated landscape drawings from between 1620 and 1646, little is known of Marten de Cock. One drawing is signed and dated 1630 in London,[1] but otherwise the artist's presence in England is unrecorded. He may have worked in Amsterdam between 1620 and 1630, but according to Cornelis Ploos van Amstel he was born in Antwerp in 1578, which would explain the similarity of his style with the landscapes of Paul Brill. If there was direct contact between the two artists, this would have occurred in Rome before the latter's death in 1626. Such a meeting would also introduce the possibility that De Cock's Roman views were based on the artist's direct experience.

37 Farm Buildings with Figures and Sheep

$8\frac{9}{16} \times 13\frac{1}{4}$ in. (216 × 337 mm)

Pen and brown ink with watercolor over traces of black chalk

Signed and dated lower right: *M. Cock fec. 1629*

Coll: George III

Bibl: W & C 338 (RL 6267)

The present drawing is entirely characteristic of the artist's gentle rural scenes, executed in a combination of precise penwork and supporting wash, reminiscent of the style of Paul Brill. This type of populated landscape – centered around farm buildings – recalls both Abraham Bloemart's drawings, many of which were engraved, and what was being produced in Haarlem at the same period, notably the etchings of Esaias and Jan van de Velde.

---

[1] *A Walled Town*, in the Städelsches Kunstinstitut, Frankfurt (5539; repr. *Stift und Feder* (1926), no. 30).

68

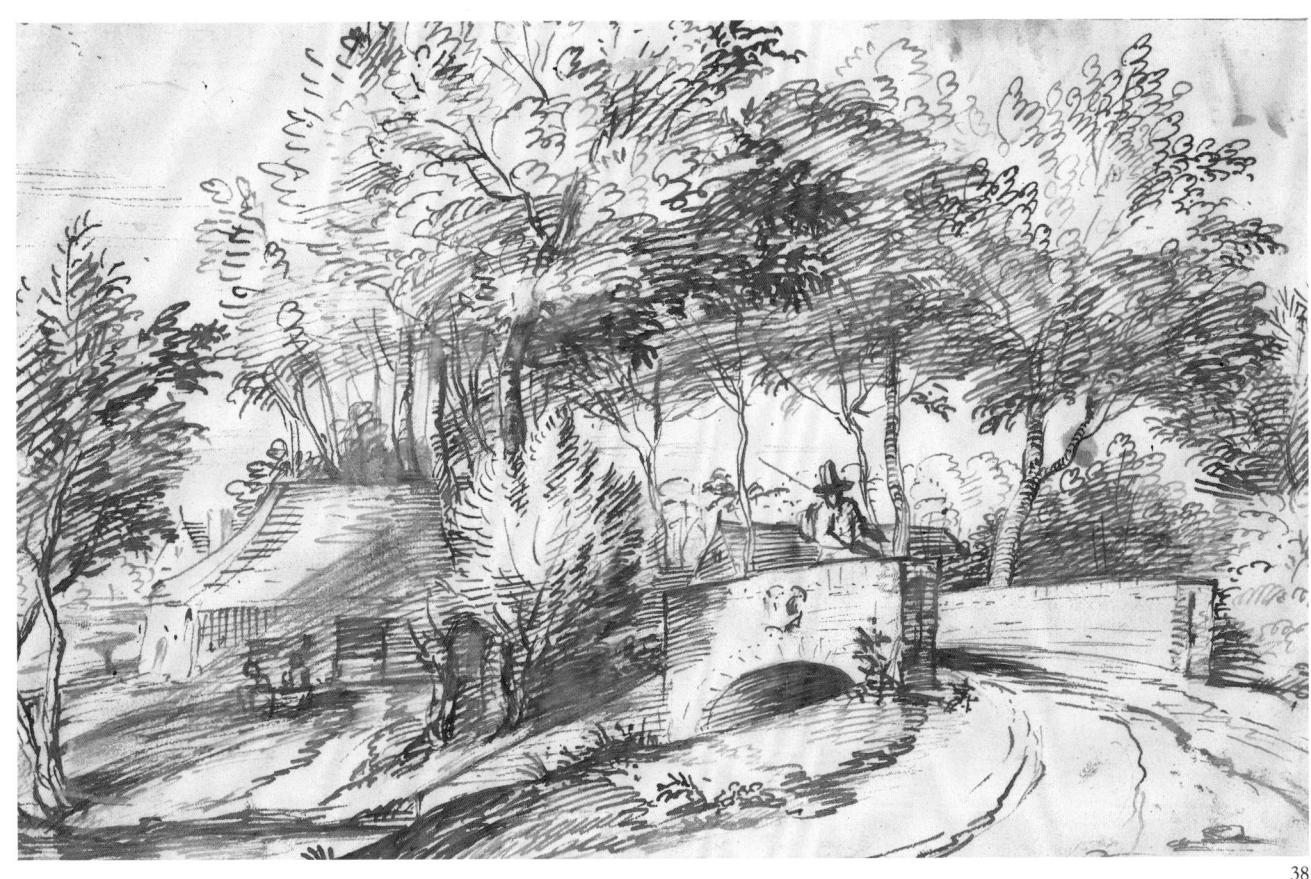

Jan Lievens

1607–1674

Born in Leiden, Lievens was a pupil there of Joris van Schooten, before studying under Pieter Lastman in Amsterdam. In the second half of the 1620s, he was back in Leiden, where he was a companion of Rembrandt. Lievens appears to have lived in England from 1631 to 1634, but was definitely in Antwerp from 1635 to 1644. Thereafter, apart from sojourns in The Hague and Leiden, he spent the remainder of his life in Amsterdam.

38 A Bridge Crossing a Stream with a Huntsman

9 × 14$\frac{5}{16}$ in. (229 × 364 mm)

Pen and brown ink

Coll: presumably George III

Bibl: Schneider, no. z220; w & c 382 (RL 6640)

In addition to his paintings and etchings, Lievens produced a large number of landscape and portrait drawings, which were largely in a very different style from that of Rembrandt. He created a wide repertory of landscape forms, sometimes based on actual views, on other occasions clearly imaginary, and scarcely repeated himself in his extensive group of landscape studies. The drawing is characterized by summary draughtsmanship and an emphasis on simplified patterns of light and on structural form, observed from a low viewpoint. These qualities are, unusually, reminiscent of Rembrandt's late drawing style, which in its turn is indebted to Titian. The drawing is probably a late work, possibly executed in the late 1660s.

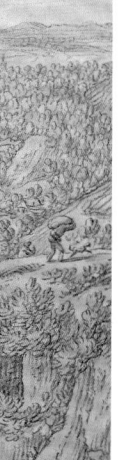

Herman Saftleven

1609–1685

Born in Rotterdam, Saftleven was a
member of a family of artists. He had
settled permanently in Utrecht by
1633, by which time he had come to
specialize as a landscape painter,
draughtsman, and occasional etcher.
He made several journeys along the
Rhine and Moselle, and in 1677 he was
resident at Elberfeld in the Rhineland.
As a result, mountainous river valleys
became the predominant theme of his
work.

39 Mountainous River Landscape with Boats and Figures

$7\frac{11}{16} \times 12\frac{3}{4}$ in. (195 × 325 mm)

Black chalk with watercolor

Signed and dated lower left:
HS (in monogram)/ *1677*

Coll: formerly framed at Buckingham
Palace; transferred to Windsor 1950

Bibl: W & C 447 (RL 12898)

The drawing belongs to a group of
landscapes executed in 1677,[1] which
are more or less freely based on the
Rhine. All are carefully drawn in black
chalk and completed in watercolor,
and they represent the culmination of
Saftleven's study of landscape.

[1] See Schulz (1982), nos. 870, 908, 911,
968–70, 1037–1038, 1159–60.

Style of **Adriaen van Ostade**

1610–1685

Adriaen van Ostade, who was a pupil of Frans Hals at the same time as Adriaen Brouwer, was a prolific genre painter and draughtsman, as well as an etcher. He spent virtually his whole life in Haarlem and was much imitated by a number of his contemporaries.

40 *Two Street Musicians at an Arched Doorway*

$7\frac{3}{4} \times 7\frac{3}{8}$ in. (197 × 188 mm)

Pen and brown ink with gray wash over black chalk

Coll: George III

Bibl: Schnackenburg, no. F 266; w & c 415 (RL 6523)

Followed by two children and a woman holding a baby, a man with a violin and a boy with a toy (a *rommelpot* or "rumbling pot") play to a young woman leaning over a half-door.

Although previously accepted as by Adriaen van Ostade, the drawing is now recognized as a variant of a genuine drawing by the artist in the Kupferstichkabinett, Berlin.[1] It may well be by his pupil Cornelis Dusart, who in his early drawings closely imitated his master to a degree that has led to confusion between the two artists (see No. 57). Although a draughtsman of spirit, Dusart's work lacks the variety and quality of that of Van Ostade.

[1] Schnackenburg, Pl. 53.

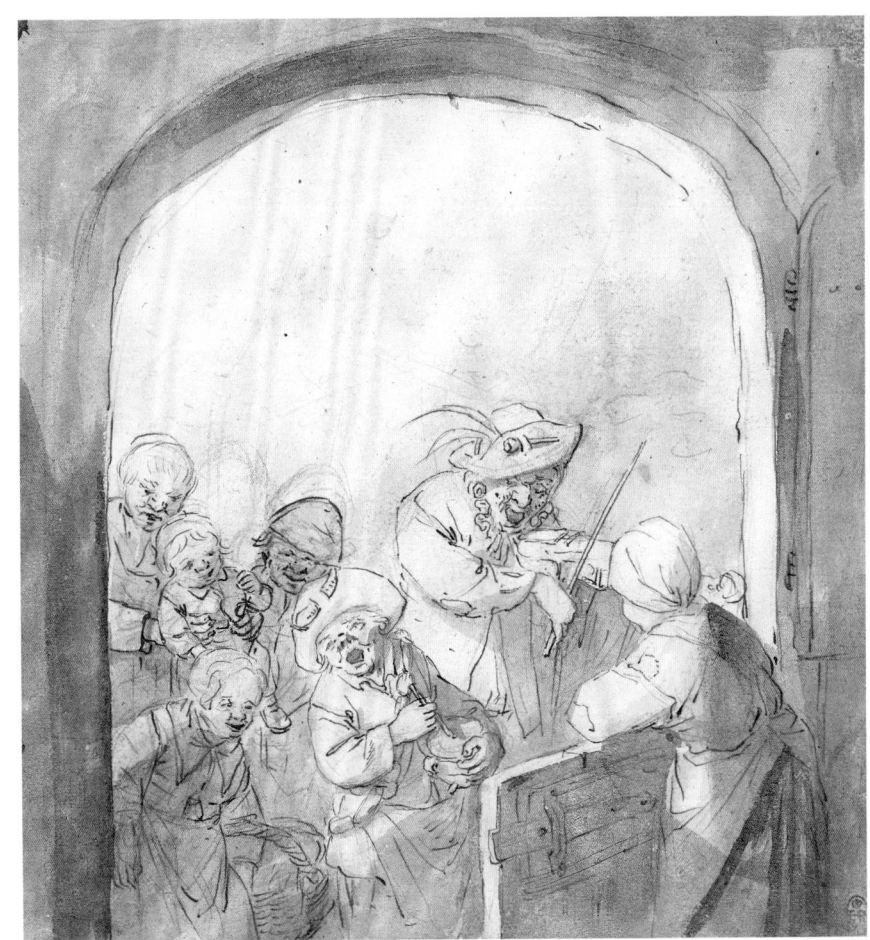

40

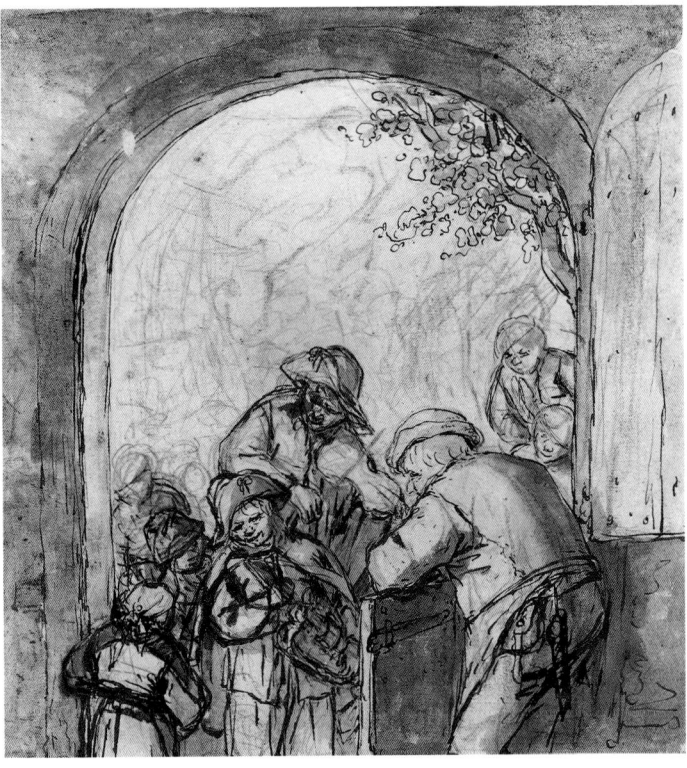

Adriaen van Ostade,
Musicians at the Door of a House
Pen and brown ink with brown and gray wash, over black chalk, $8\frac{13}{16} \times 8\frac{1}{4}$ in.
(224 × 210 mm) (Berlin, Staatliche Museen, Kupferstichkabinett: 4050)

Jan Asselyn

1615–1652

After probably training in Amsterdam under the battle-painter Jan Martsens the Younger, Asselyn appears to have gone to Rome around 1635, where he became primarily an Italianate landscape artist. He was a member of the society of Netherlandish artists in Rome, the *Bentveughels* (birds of a feather), among whom he was known as *Crabbetje* (little crab) on account of his deformed left hand. In 1644 he was in Lyon before going on to Paris, where he worked, *inter alia*, on the decorations in the Hôtel Lambert up to 1646. By the following year he was back in Amsterdam, where he stayed for the remainder of his short life.

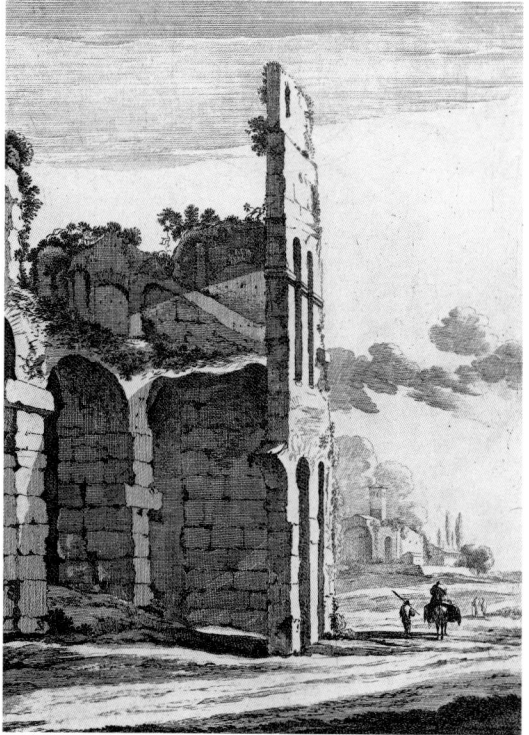

Gabriel Perelle after
Jan Asselyn, *Veue du Colisée*
Etching, $9\frac{3}{4} \times 7\frac{3}{16}$ in.
(248 × 182 mm)
(London, British Museum,
Department of Prints and
Drawings)

41 *The Ruins of the Colosseum, Rome, Seen from the South-East*

$9\frac{7}{8} \times 7\frac{1}{4}$ in. (252 × 184 mm)

Pen and brush with black ink and gray wash over traces of black chalk, indented for transfer

Verso: rubbed with black chalk for offsetting

Coll: possibly Amsterdam collection (sale 22 Nov. 1757, lot 10 or 11); George III

Bibl: Steland-Stief (1980), pp. 216, 219; Steland, no. 157; w & c 236 (RL 6568)

In the right foreground is part of the southern side of the Colosseum. In the left background can be seen the ruined Temple of Venus and Rome, with the tower of S. Francesca Romana behind, at the east end of the Forum.

The drawing is the preparatory study, in reverse, for the etching by Gabriel Perelle, inscribed *Veue du Colisée*, which forms part of a series of eighteen prints (by Perelle after Asselyn) of views of Roman antiquities in and around Rome.[1] When the drawing was lifted from its old backing sheet (in 1992) the *verso* was found to be coated with black chalk, to facilitate the transfer of outlines to the etching plate. The series is divided into three sets of six each. One set – including the present subject – is upright; the other two, horizontal. The carefully executed preparatory drawings, indented for transfer, of which eleven are now known,[2] were presumably made on commission in Paris, where Asselyn worked from about 1644 to 1646 on his return from Italy to Amsterdam. Another more freely executed drawing of the same view but seen from a marginally different viewpoint, in the Musées Royaux des Beaux-Arts, Brussels,[3] may have served Asselyn as the basis for the present drawing. The Colosseum, seen from different angles, is the subject of two other plates, one upright and one horizontal, in Perelle's series, for which similar preparatory drawings are in the Teylers Museum, Haarlem, and the Musées Royaux des Beaux-Arts, Brussels.[4] (See also No. 48.)

[1] Hollstein, I, p. 44, nos. 15–32. The *Veue du Colisée* with which No. 41 is associated is inscribed with the figure *3*.

[2] See Steland, p. 19.

[3] Steland, no. 39, Fig. 5.

[4] Steland-Stief (1980), Pls. 3 and 9 respectively.

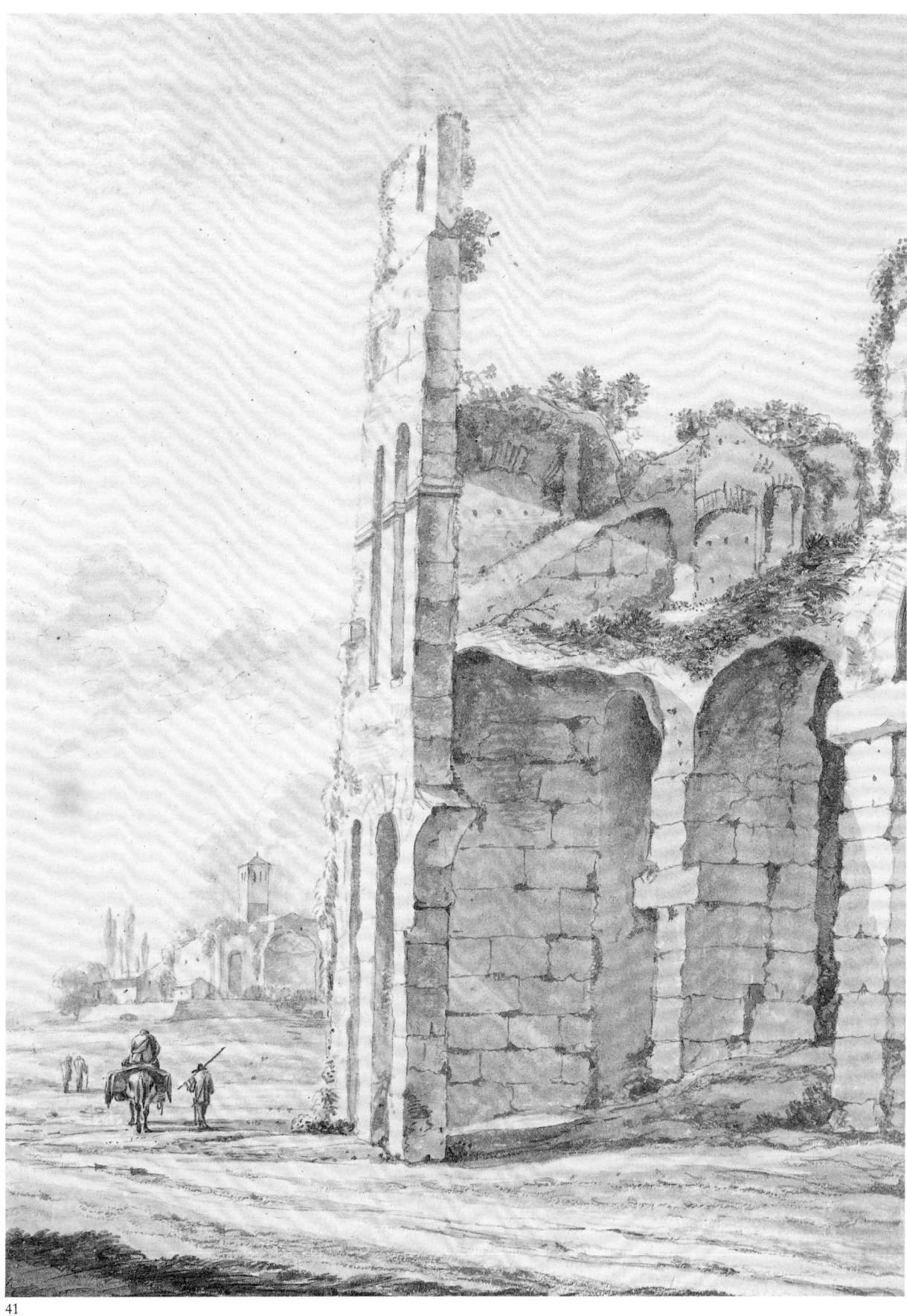

41

Ferdinand Bol

1616–1680

Born in Dordrecht, where he possibly trained under Jacob Cuyp, Bol moved in or shortly after 1635 to Amsterdam, where at first he appears to have had some association with Rembrandt. He remained in Amsterdam, becoming one of the leading portrait and history painters; he played a major role in the decoration of the New Town Hall and was much patronized by municipal bodies. Bol was also active as a draughtsman and etcher.

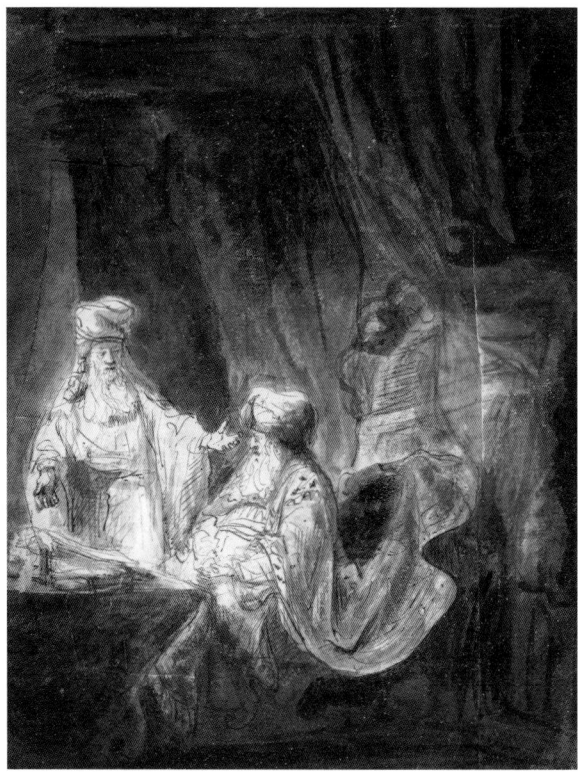

Ferdinand Bol,
Nathan Admonishing David
Pen and brown ink with brown wash, red and black chalk, with black bodycolor, heightened with white, $11\frac{5}{8} \times 9\frac{1}{8}$ in. (295 × 232 mm) (Royal Collection: Windsor Castle, Royal Library: W & C 319)

42 *Nathan Admonishing David*

$11\frac{5}{8} \times 7\frac{7}{8}$ in. (296 × 200 mm)

Pen and brown ink with gray and touches of brown wash over black chalk

Coll: George III

Bibl: Benesch (1973), II, under no. C31; Sumowski, I, no. 131; W & C 316 (RL 6514)

Taken from II Samuel 12: 7–14, the subject illustrates Nathan's remonstrations with King David over the latter's adulterous love for Bathsheba and the planned death of her husband, Uriah the Hittite, in battle.

This drawing, with another of the same subject at Windsor Castle,[1] can be attributed to Ferdinand Bol, who worked with Rembrandt from about 1636 until 1641. His exact role in Rembrandt's studio is unclear, since he had already undergone a traditional apprenticeship in his native Dordrecht. On account of their Rembrandtesque style, the drawings are probably to be dated in the later 1630s. (The drawings of the two artists during this period have sometimes been confused, and only recently has a convincing attempt been made to distinguish between them.)

No painting by Bol of the subject is known. The story of David was to become popular with Rembrandt in the 1650s, when he made three of his most powerful and moving drawings devoted to this particular incident in the king's life.[2]

[1] W & C 319. A drawing with a single figure corresponding with that of Nathan in the latter drawing is in the Staatliche Graphische Sammlung, Munich (Sumowski, I, no. 163).

[2] Benesch (1973), nos. 918, 947, and 948.

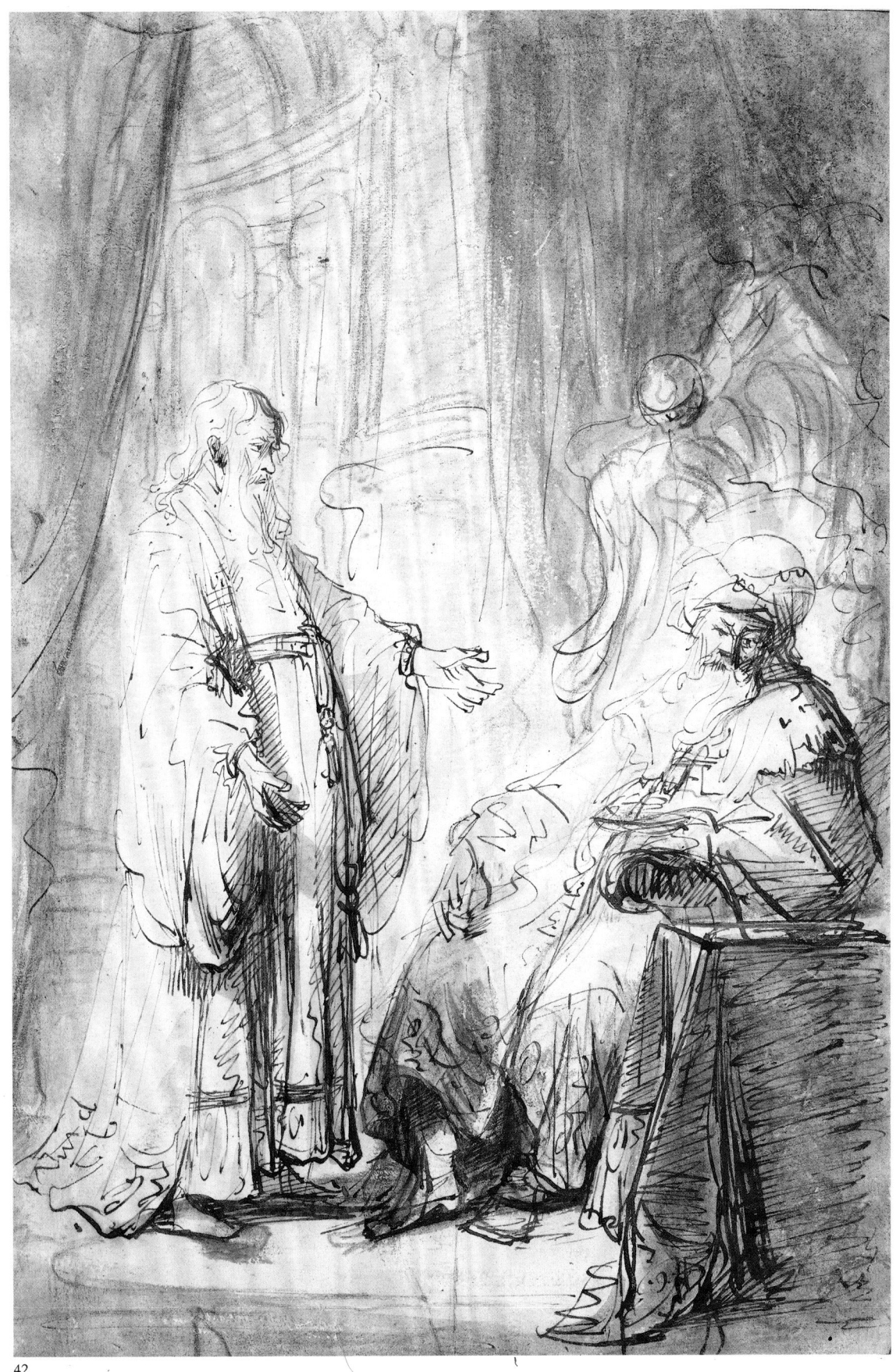

42

Nicolaes Berchem

1620–1683

Born in Haarlem, Berchem was a pupil of his father, the still-life painter Pieter Claesz. According to Houbraken, he studied with several other artists, including Jan van Goyen. His knowledge of the landscape of southern Europe makes a journey to Italy likely, and although there is no documentary evidence, it is very possible that he was there in the early 1650s. Thereafter Berchem is recorded at various times as living in Amsterdam and Haarlem. He was one of the most productive and financially successful artists of the period, and his work was particularly admired – and engraved – in the later seventeenth and eighteenth centuries.

43 Allegory on the Discovery of America

5¾ × 10¾ in. (146 × 274 mm)

Pen and brown ink with brown and gray wash over black chalk; indented for transfer

Signed upper right: *Berchem f.*

Verso: The Same Subject

Pen and brown ink with brown wash over black chalk

Watermark: the arms of Amsterdam

Coll: George III

Bibl: Schaar, p. 242; W & C 301 (RL 6441)

Surrounded by figures engaged in various occupations, a native ruler, dressed only in a feathered headdress and skirt, and shaded by an umbrella, is pointing to gold ingots piled on the ground at his feet. Immediately behind him is a large rectangular block, on the face of which is represented a scene with numerous figures in adoration before a ruler or image seated in a circular temple, with a large star above. There are two serpents on top of the block.

The drawing is the preparatory study for the cartouche at the bottom of an engraved map of America included in the *Atlas contractus orbis terrarum praecipuas ac novissimas complectens tabulas* (concise world atlas containing excellent and most recent maps), engraved by Jan de Visscher and published in Amsterdam by Nicolaes Visscher the Elder, probably sometime between 1657 and 1677. (The watermark on the drawing suggests a date in the mid-1660s.) After completing the drawing on the *recto* (which must always have been intended for engraving) the artist traced the main outlines through to the *verso*, thus reversing the images and making them appear as they would be seen in the print. The composition is considerably simplified in both the *verso* drawing and the print. In the printed map, the front of the tablet, which is blank in this drawing, is inscribed: *Novissima et Accuratissima Totius Americae Descriptio* (newest and most accurate description of the whole of America).

Although better known as an Italianate landscapist, Berchem made other designs for Visscher's *Atlas*, one of several important topographical publications produced in Holland at the time, and he may well have played an extensive role in the preparation of the volume. There is another version of this subject with a similar native figure in the Metropolitan Museum of Art, New York, which was probably intended as a frontispiece or illustration to an atlas or book.[1]

[1] Honour, no. 95, repr.

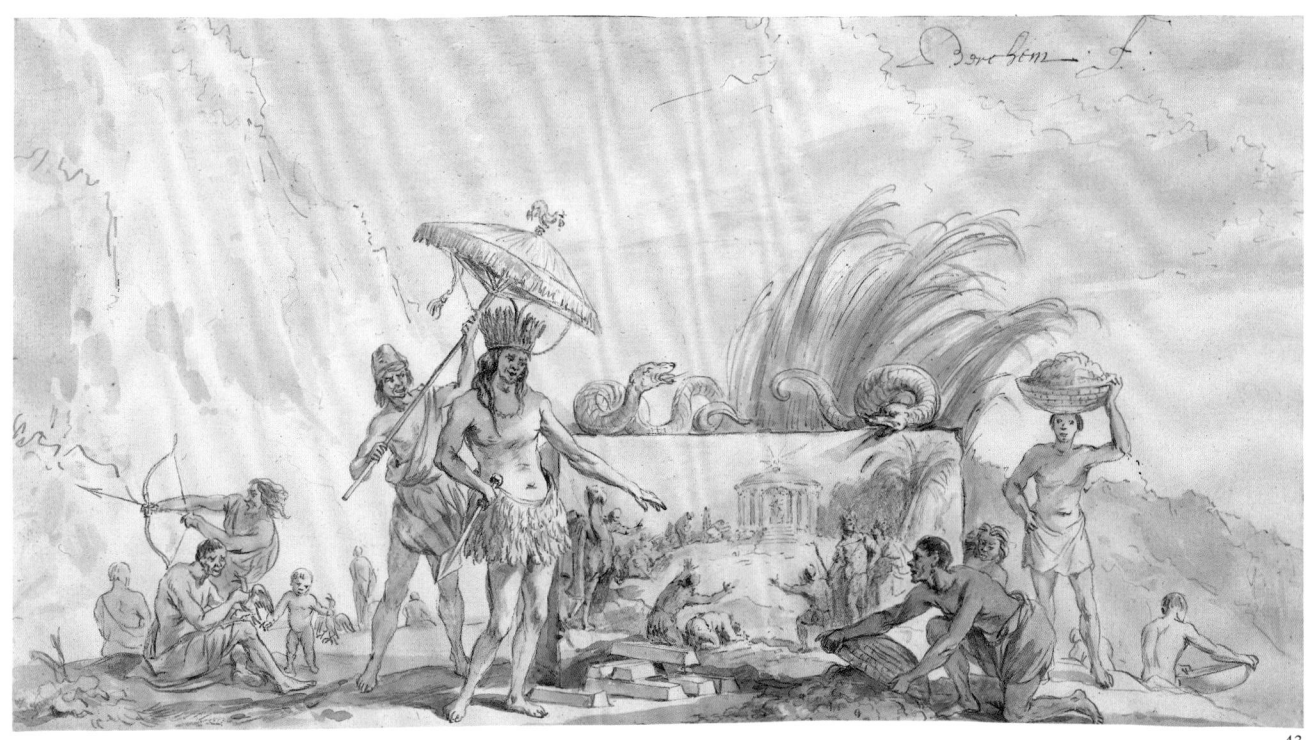

43

(*Right*) Nicolaes Berchem, *verso* of No. 43.
Allegory on the Discovery of America
Pen and brown ink with brown wash over black
chalk

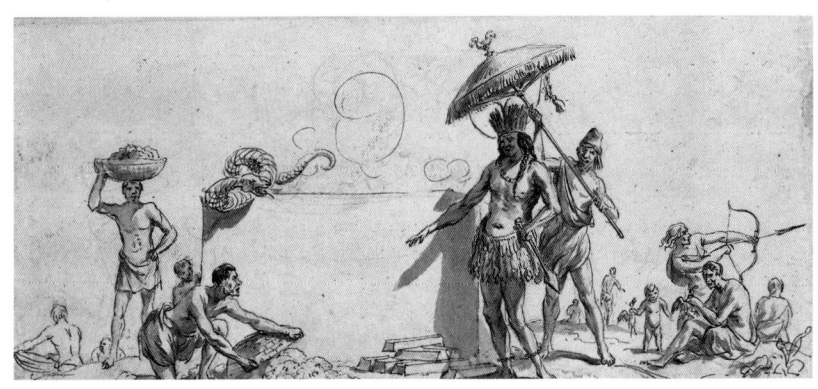

(*Right*) Jan de Visscher after Nicolaes Berchem,
Cartouche from the Map of America
(from N. Visscher, *Atlas contractus orbis terrarum*)
Engraving. (London, British Library, Map Room)

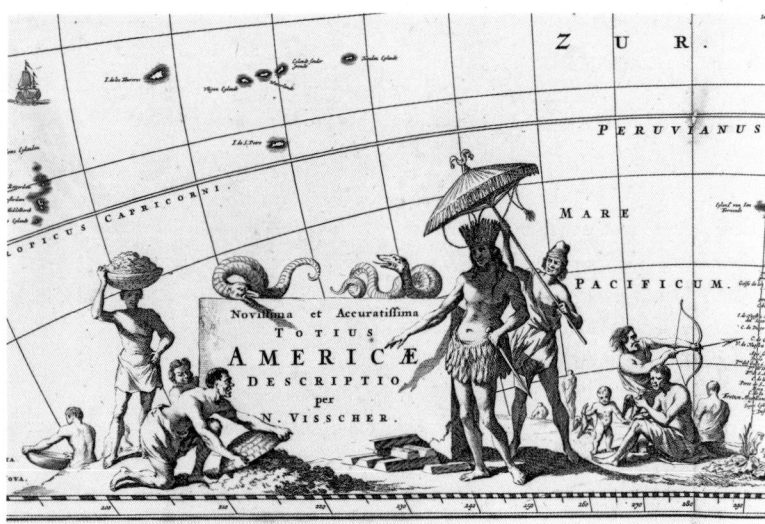

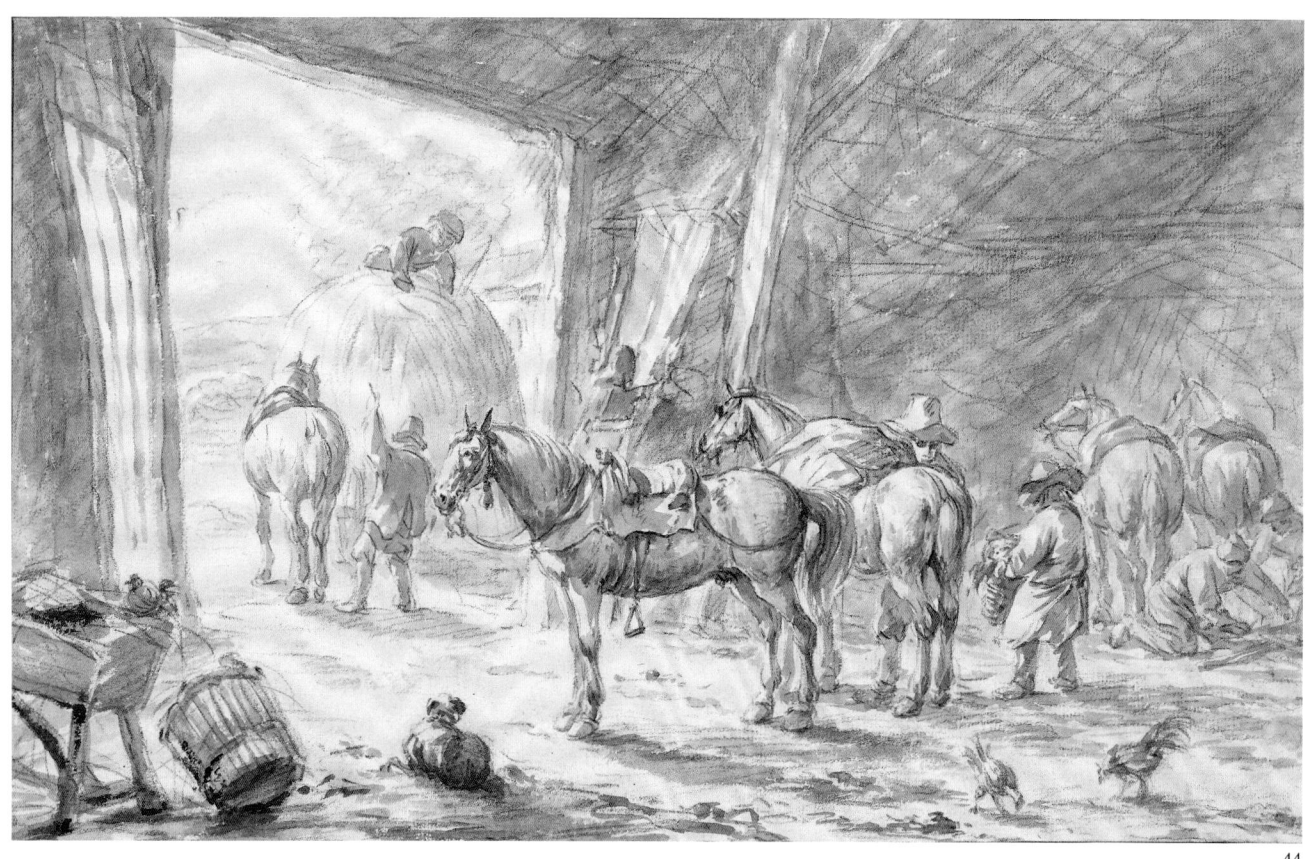

44

Barend Gael

1630/40 – after 1681

Little is known of this pupil of Philips Wouwermans, who was born in Haarlem and died in Amsterdam.

44 The Interior of a Barn with Men and Horses

$7\frac{1}{8} \times 11\frac{11}{16}$ in. (182×297 mm)

Black chalk with gray wash

Coll: George III

Bibl: w & c 364 (RL 6627)

With its free brushwork and shadows executed in broad, bold strokes, the drawing is typical of Gael's work. He produced a number of drawings on this theme, for example, *Peasants and Horses in a Stable*, in the Yale University Art Gallery, New Haven.[1]

[1] Haverkamp-Begemann and Logan, no. 374, Pl. 242.

Willem Romeyn

c.1622 – after 1695

Romeyn was born in Haarlem and was a pupil of Nicolaes Berchem. In 1650 and 1651 he visited Italy. After his return to Haarlem in 1652, he continued to produce Italianate scenes up to the time of his death.

45 A Cowherd with Cattle Resting before Roman Ruins

$10\frac{1}{8} \times 7\frac{9}{16}$ in. (258×192 mm)

Brush drawing in gray over black chalk with gray wash

Signed and dated top left: *WROMEYN 1694* (*WR* in monogram)

Coll: George III

Bibl: w & c 431 (RL 6632)

As in Romeyn's other very late works, this drawing shows the influence of the work of Karel du Jardin. The tower, which resembles the Torre delle Milizie in Rome, recurs in the background of other drawings by Romeyn. However, the setting appears to be imaginary and is characteristic of the southern landscapes evoked by the artist.

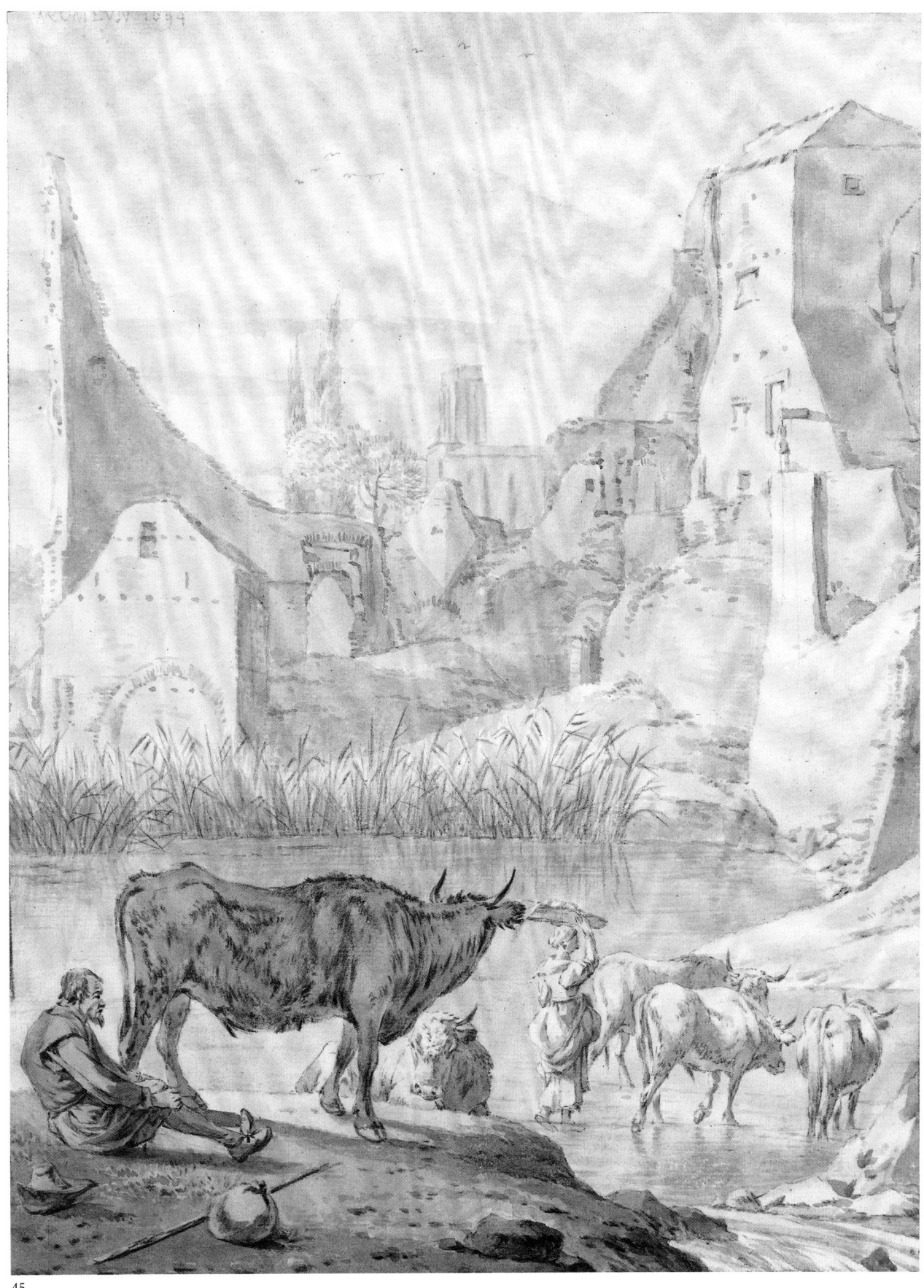

45

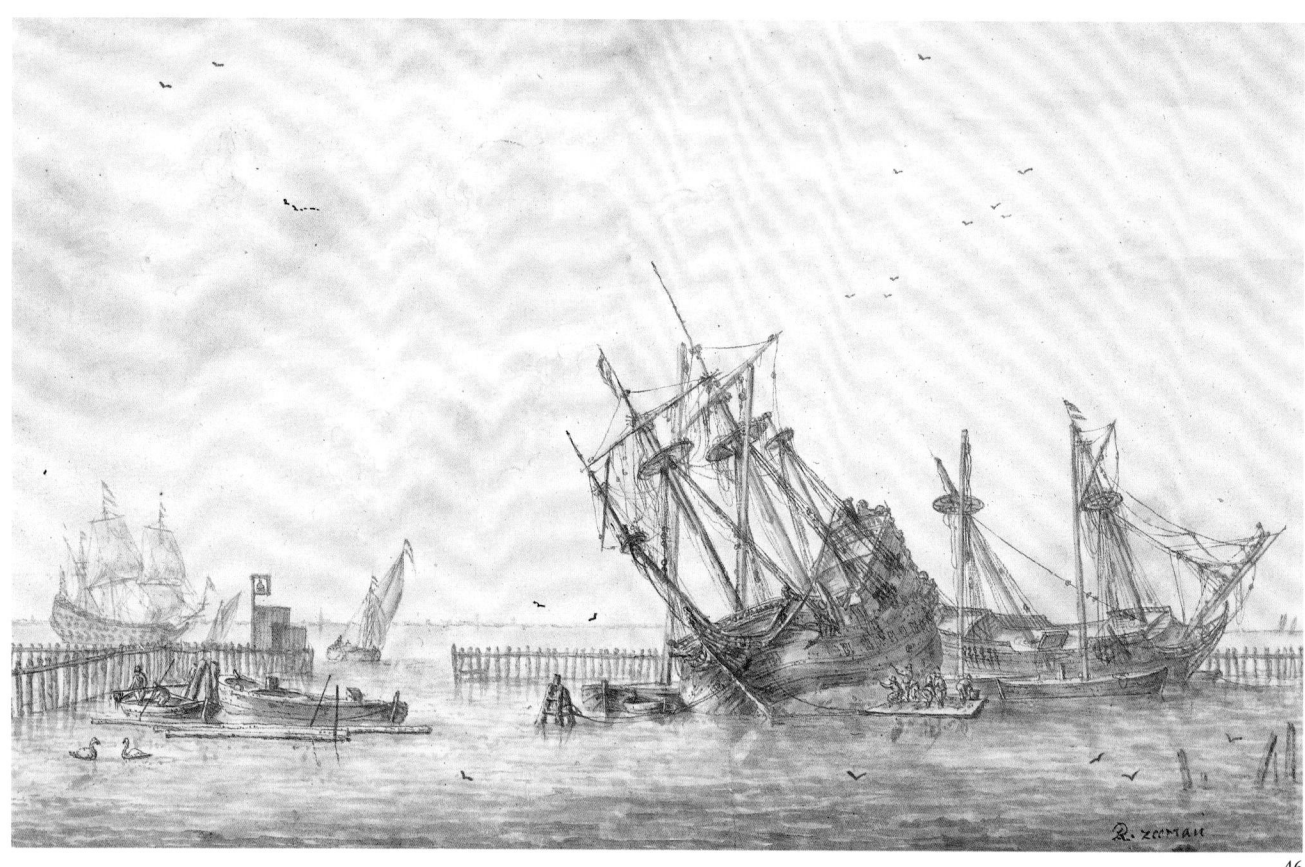

46

Reynier Nooms, called Zeeman

*c.*1623–1664

Little is known of Nooms's life, although in addition to being a painter, draughtsman, and etcher, he may also have been a sailor, which would explain his expertise as a marine artist, as well as his knowledge of African and Mediterranean coastal scenery. His familiar name, "Zeeman," can be translated as "seaman." He was active in Paris from 1650 to 1652, producing etched views of the city as well as shipping subjects. Thereafter, he appears to have lived in Amsterdam.

46 *Two Vessels Being Careened for Repairs beside Two* Onderleggers *within a Palisade*

$7\frac{3}{8} \times 11\frac{13}{16}$ in. (187 × 301 mm)

Pen and brown ink and brush drawing in black and gray

Signed lower right: *R. zeeman*

Watermark: foolscap

Coll: George III

Bibl: W & C 516 (RL 6277)

To right of center a large careened vessel is being repaired from a raft alongside. On the left are a mastless *onderlegger* and a small boat with two men; possibly the masts floating behind their boat are to be fixed to the *onderlegger*. Beyond, a *kaag* approaches the entrance to the palisade with a larger vessel behind and land in the distance. The subject of vessels being careened was popular with the artist, who treated it in painting, drawing,

and etching. Similar views appear in Zeeman's etched series *Sailing Vessels* of 1652, the *Thirteen Naval Scenes*, and *Various Embarkations*.

Zeeman's drawings are for the most part finished compositions, executed, as here, in a mixture of pen and brushwork.

Lambert Doomer

1624–1700

Doomer was born in Amsterdam and is described as a pupil of Rembrandt at some time after 1640. Although he produced some paintings, Doomer is principally known as a prolific landscape draughtsman. Much of his work was based on the sketchbooks he filled on his frequent journeys, sometimes in the company of other artists (e.g. with Willem Schellinks in the Loire valley in 1646), throughout the Netherlands and various European countries, including France, Germany, and Switzerland. Apart from living in Amsterdam, he was resident in Alkmaar between 1669 and 1693/95.

47 *The Angel Opening Christ's Tomb* (after Rembrandt)

$18\frac{3}{16} \times 12\frac{3}{4}$ in. (463 × 325 mm)

Pen and brown ink with brown, gray, and pink wash

Signed lower left: *Rembrandt pinx/ LDoomer f* (LD in monogram)

Coll: George III

Bibl: Schulz (1974), no. 41; Sumowski, II, no. 376; *Rembrandt Corpus*, under no. A127; W & C 349 (RL 6518)

Taken from Matthew 28: 1–4, the subject shows the angel lifting the stone covering the tomb, on which one soldier was reclining, while others flee; in the lower right, the two Marys look on.

Both on account of its size and the fact that it is a copy of a painting by another artist, the drawing is unusual in Doomer's *oeuvre*, and it may possibly have been executed on commission. It is based on Rembrandt's painting of the *Resurrection*,[1] which was one of the Passion series executed for the Stadholder, Frederick Henry.

[1] In the Bayerische Staatsgemäldesammlungen, Alte Pinakothek, Munich (397). See *Rembrandt Corpus*, III, under no. A127.

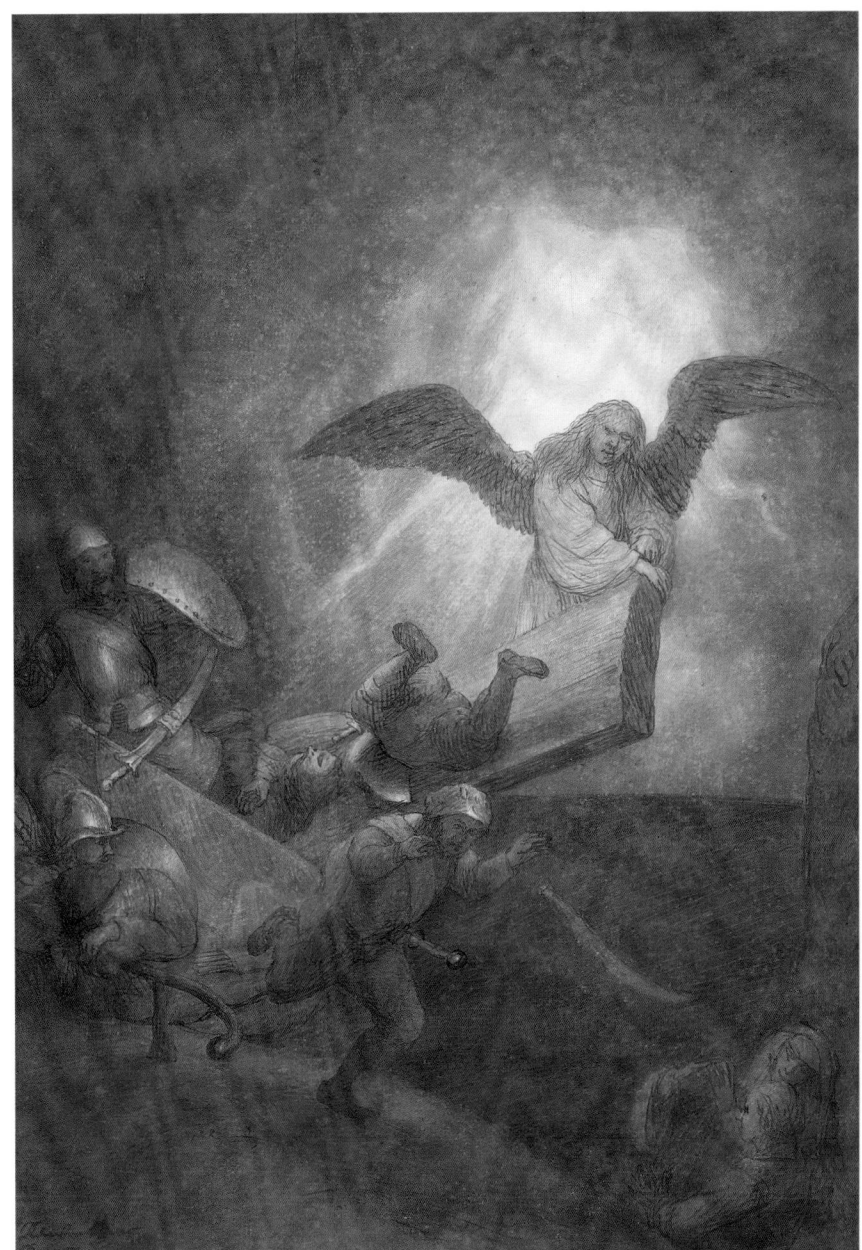

Rembrandt van Rijn,
Resurrection
Oil on canvas,
$36\frac{3}{16} \times 26\frac{3}{8}$ in.
(91.9×67 cm)
(Munich, Bayerische
Staatsgemäldesamm-
lungen, Alte
Pinakothek: 397)

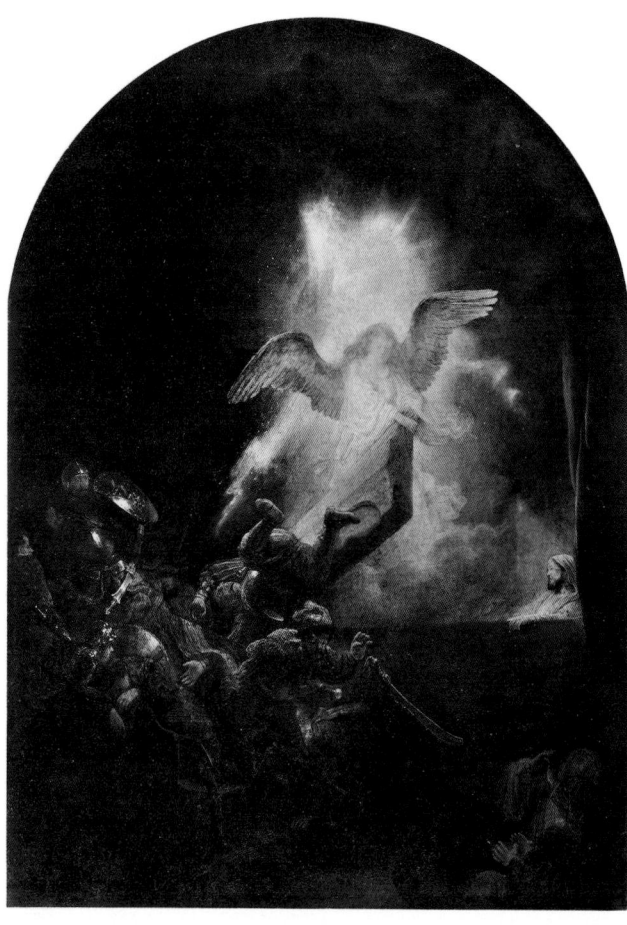

Willem Schellinks
*c.*1627–1678

A pupil of Karel du Jardin, Schellinks was primarily a prolific landscape draughtsman, although he also produced some paintings and etchings. A native of Amsterdam, he was, like Lambert Doomer, an extensive traveler throughout Western Europe, where he made a large number of topographical drawings. He also kept a diary and published a volume of poems in 1654.

48 Interior of Roman Ruins (the Colosseum, Rome?) with a Man and Three Packhorses

$11\frac{15}{16} \times 9\frac{1}{4}$ in. (304×235 mm)

Pen and brown ink with brown and gray wash over graphite

Signed(?) lower left: *W. Schellinghs*

Coll: George III

Bibl: Steland-Stief (1986), pp. 99–100; W & C 449 (RL 6301)

The drawing may depict the interior of the Colosseum, which was the subject of several studies by Schellinks. Although he was in Italy for some time between 1661 and 1665, when with Jacques Thierry he undertook a European tour, it has been argued[1] that this study – and other Roman drawings by Schellinks – were executed earlier, during the 1650s, and were based on views made by Jan Asselyn rather than studied *in situ*. (For a view of the Colosseum by Asselyn see No. 41.)

Although only completed in 1639, the painting was already "more than half done" as early as 1636. Moreover, the composition was considerably modified in the course of execution by the inclusion of the figure of Christ arising (not in Matthew's account of the event) and more soldiers. This copy, however, records the earlier stage. The apparently mature style of Doomer's drawing makes it most unlikely that it is a very youthful work done in Rembrandt's studio, where

Doomer worked as a pupil some time after 1640. (Doomer's father was a well-known framemaker, and he and his wife were portrayed by Rembrandt in 1640.) The drawing was almost certainly executed much later in the century and, therefore, is based on another work recording Rembrandt's first design, possibly the signed copy by Ferdinand Bol,[2] with which it agrees apart from several minor details.

[2] Also in the Bayerische Staatsgemäldesammlungen, Munich (4874; *Rembrandt Corpus*, p. 285, Fig. 5). For further discussion of Doomer's source, see W & C 349.

[1] Steland-Stief, *loc. cit.*

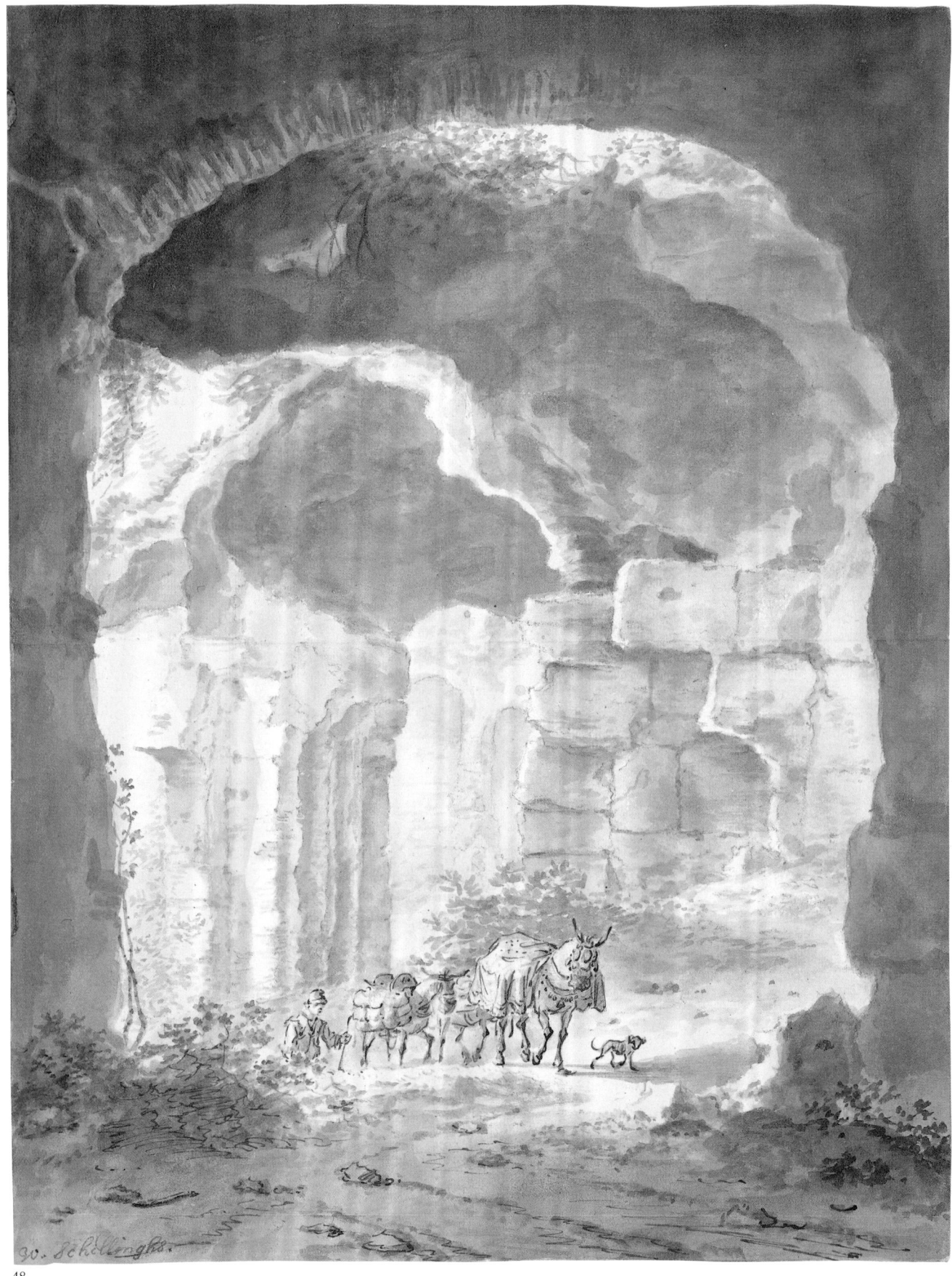

30. Schellinghe.

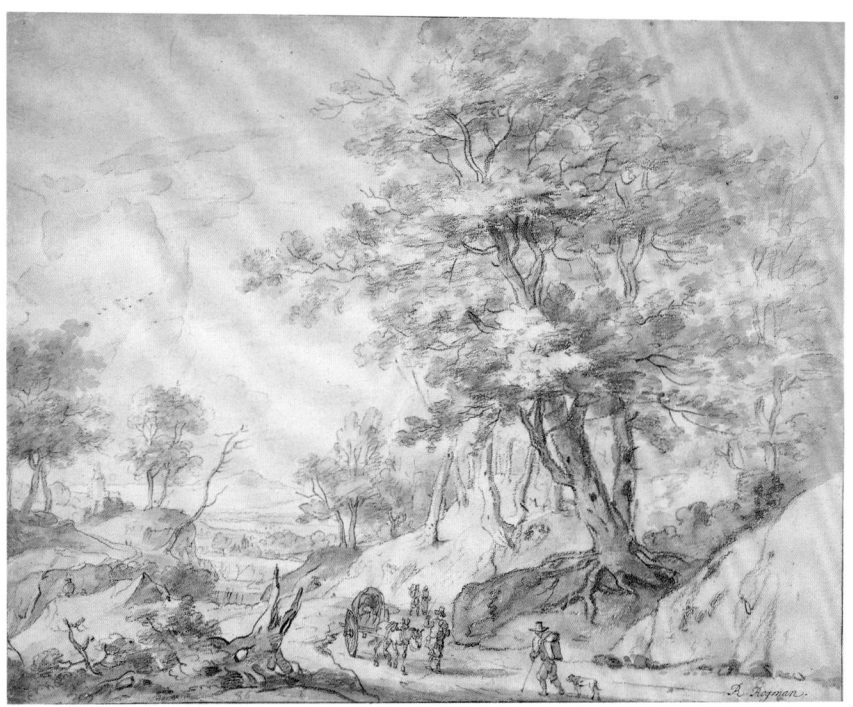

49

Roelant Roghman

1627–1692

A native of Amsterdam, Roghman was a landscape painter, draughtsman, and etcher. He is particularly noted for his series of 241 topographical drawings of castles and country houses in the Netherlands. According to Houbraken, he was a close friend of Rembrandt, the influence of whose work can be seen in some of his imaginary landscapes.

49 Hilly Landscape with a Road and Travellers

14$\frac{3}{16}$ × 17$\frac{15}{16}$ in. (361 × 453 mm)

Black chalk and gray wash

Inscribed lower right: R. *Roghman*

Bibl: Sumowski, X, no. 2272^x; w & c 429 (RL 12840)

This study can be placed among a group of large-scale landscape drawings made by Roghman, possibly in the mid-1650s. Unlike his more carefully executed topographical studies, the present drawing – clearly of an imaginary landscape – is drawn with greater freedom and stronger, more broken areas of tone. In such works he produced some of the finest landscape compositions of the period.

Jacob van Ruisdael

c.1628/29–1682

Born in Haarlem, Jacob was possibly a pupil of both his father, Isaack Jacobsz. van Ruisdael, and his uncle, Salomon van Ruysdael. About 1650 he visited Bentheim on the German border, probably in the company of Nicolaes Berchem. In 1657 he settled in Amsterdam, where he remained, apart from some possible journeys in Holland. He was arguably the greatest Dutch landscape painter of the century and had numerous followers and imitators; Meyndert Hobbema was his best known pupil. Jacob van Ruisdael was a prolific painter and draughtsman; he also made a series of etchings at the beginning of his career.

50 A Windmill and Cottages beside a Footbridge over a River

7$\frac{5}{8}$ × 11$\frac{1}{2}$ in. (194 × 292 mm)

Black chalk with gray wash

Signed lower right: *JvR* (in monogram)

Coll: George III

Bibl: Giltay, pp. 159, 201; Slive, no. 75; w & c 444 (RL 6607)

The same stone footbridge, seen from the opposite side of the river, occurs in a drawing (in the same technique and in the same scale) in the Historisch Museum (Fodor Collection), Amsterdam.[1] The latter is inscribed (in another hand) on the back *bij Alkmaar*, although a copy of that drawing by Gerrit Lamberts (1776–1850), in the Museum Boymans-van Beuningen, Rotterdam, is inscribed *de hoge voetbrug by Amersfoort*. It has not so far proved possible to locate a similar bridge in the vicinity of either Alkmaar or Amersfoort.

Both the Windsor and the Amsterdam drawings were probably executed during the second half of the

[1] Inv. A 10305, Slive, no. 74, repr.

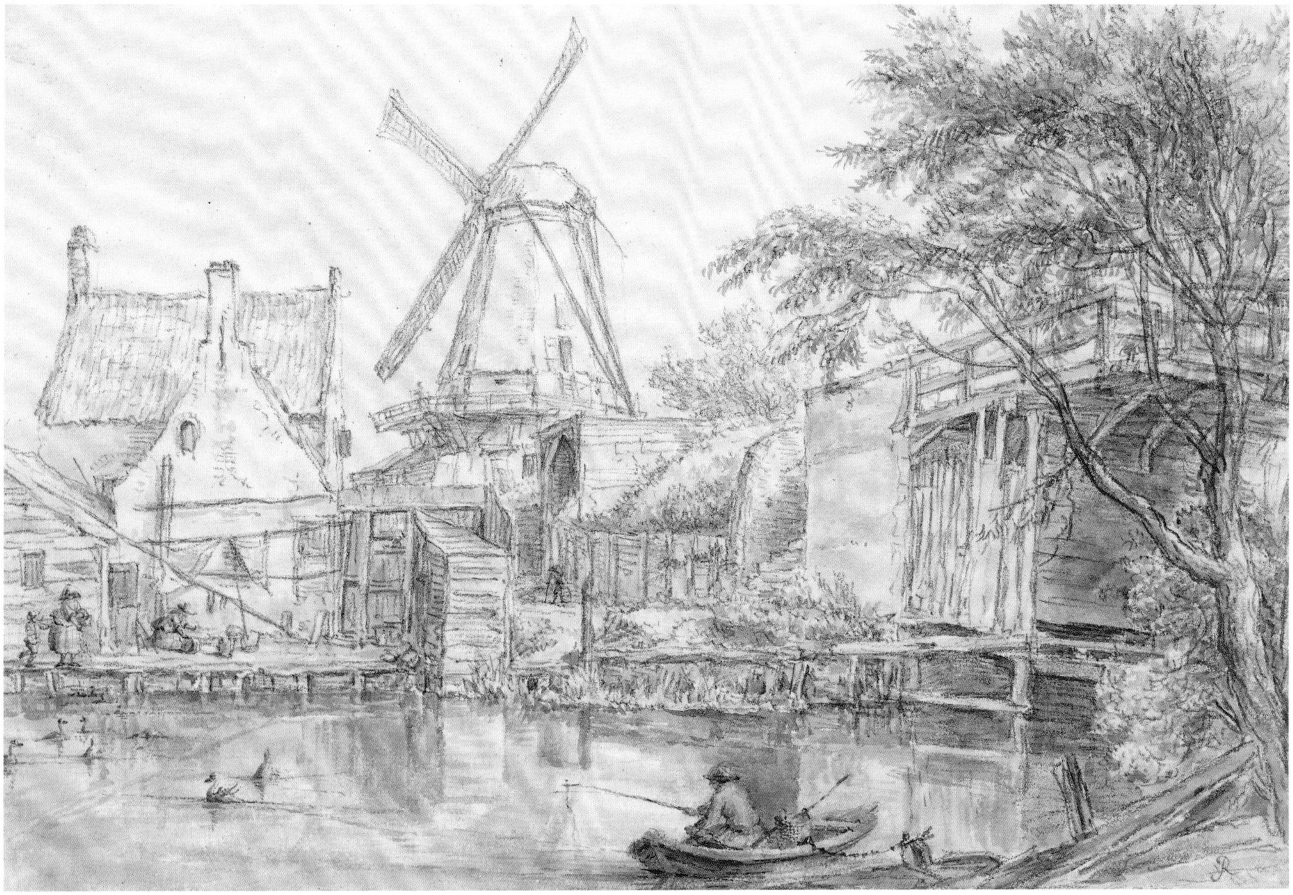

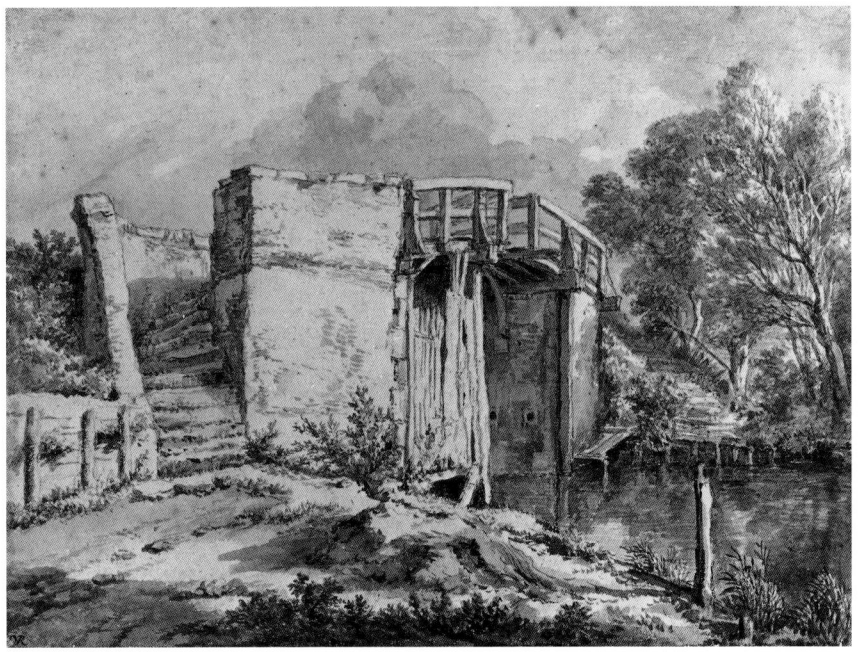

1650s, presumably after the artist's
move to Amsterdam. Whereas the
bridge is the powerful central motif in
the Amsterdam drawing, here it is
absorbed into its setting, seen beneath
a beautiful play of light and shadow.
This drawing ranks as one of the
artist's more complete studies,
enlivened by figures and ducks.

Jacob van Ruisdael, *A Footbridge over a River*
Black chalk with gray wash, $7\frac{13}{16} \times 10\frac{13}{16}$ in.
(199 × 274 mm) (Amsterdam, Amsterdams
Historisch Museum: A10305)

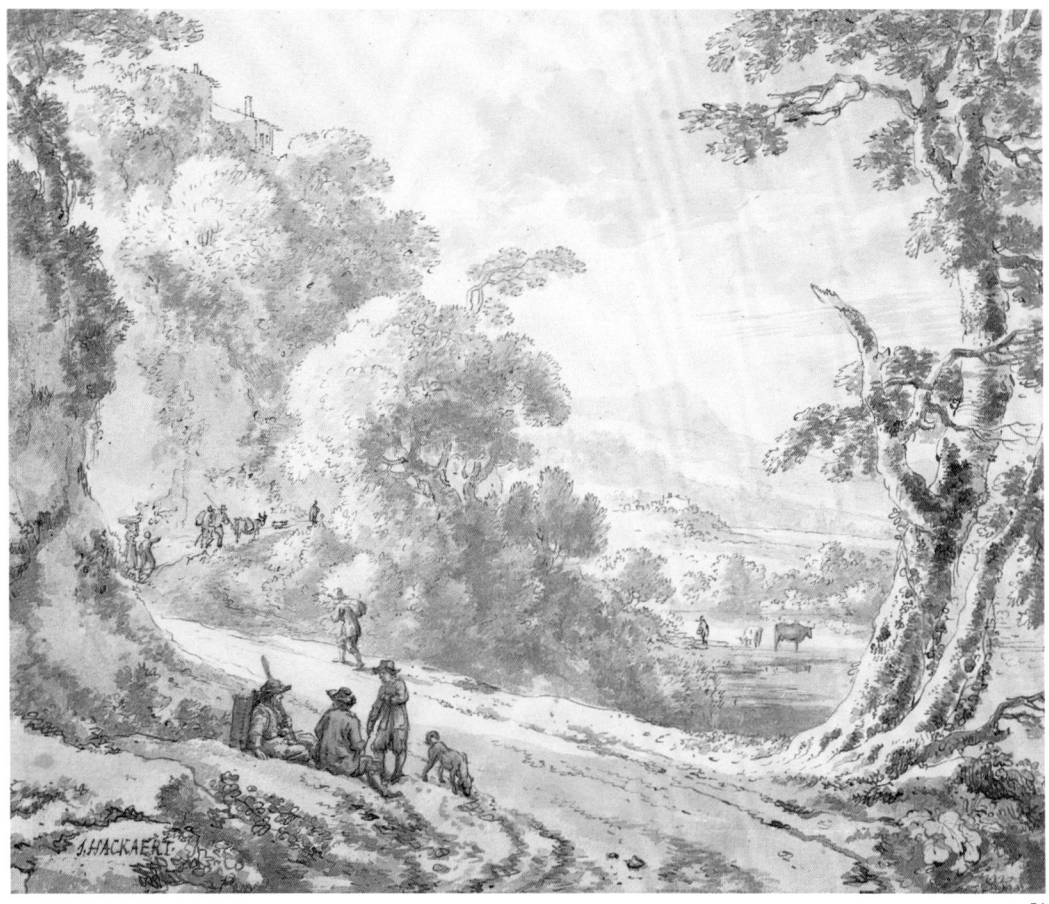

51

Jan Hackaert

*c.*1629 – after 1685

Hackaert was an Amsterdam painter,
draughtsman, and etcher, principally
of Italianate landscapes. He may have
been a pupil of Jan Both and was
certainly influenced by him. Little is
known of Hackaert's life, apart from a
journey to Switzerland between 1653
and 1656. It is possible that he visited
Italy at this time, although there is no
direct evidence for such a voyage.

51 *A Road with Travellers and Animals*

$8\frac{1}{8} \times 9\frac{7}{8}$ in. (207 × 252 mm)

Pen and brown ink with brown and gray
wash over graphite

Signed lower left: *J. HACKAERT*

Coll: George III

Bibl: W & C 372 (RL 6303)

The present drawing shows imaginary
wooded hilly scenery generally
reminiscent of the southern European
landscape, which Hackaert either saw
himself or which was derived from the
works of such artists as Jan Both and
Jan Asselyn. In addition, his drawings
achieve through their feeling for the
rendering of trees and the rich
patterns of light – here conveyed in a
combination of gray and brown
washes – a calm and grandeur which is
one of the principal qualities of the
Dutch Italianate tradition.

Cornelis Visscher

1629–1658

Visscher was a draughtsman and etcher largely of portraits. He was probably a pupil of Pieter Soutman (see No. 26) in Haarlem. For the last three years of his life he lived in Amsterdam. His finely executed portrait drawings, most of which are on vellum (as here), with dates between 1652 and 1658, were clearly intended as finished works of art. Five drawings by Visscher were noted in George III's collection.

52 *Portrait of a Young Man in a Wide-brimmed Hat*

$11\frac{3}{8} \times 8\frac{7}{8}$ in. (290 × 226 mm)

Black chalk and graphite on vellum

Signed and dated upper right: *A° 1655.| C. Visscher| fecit*

Coll: Jonathan Richardson the Elder (L. 2184); George III

Bibl: W & C 497 (RL 6425)

The sitter is seated on a chair beside a table with a book on the left, and before a column on the right. There is a version of this drawing, also on vellum but paler in tone, in the Museum of Fine Arts, Boston.[1] It is cut at the sides and below, and is probably a copy. No etching or engraving relating to this drawing is known, and no identification has been proposed.

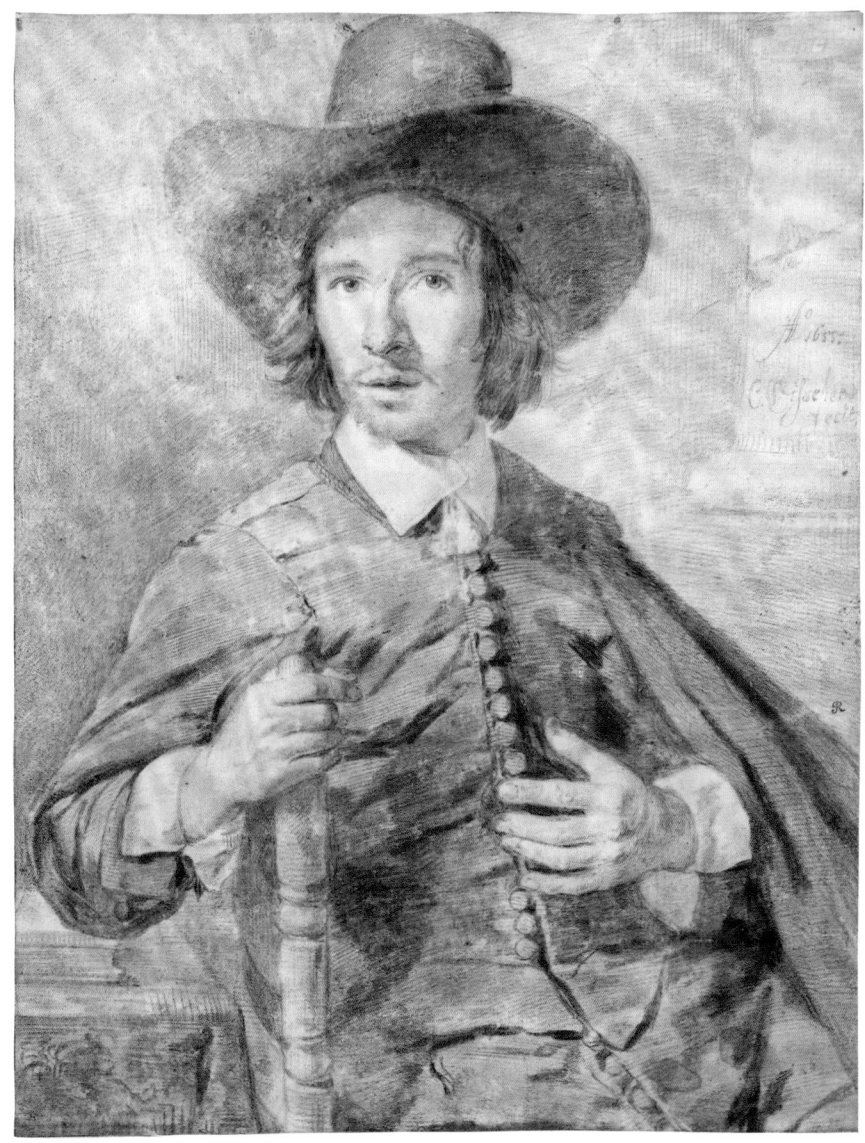

52

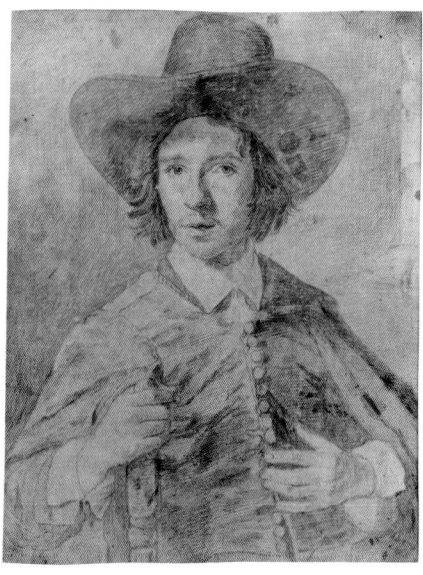

After Cornelis Visscher, *Portrait of a Young Man in a Wide-brimmed Hat*
Black chalk and graphite on vellum,
$9\frac{7}{16} \times 7\frac{3}{8}$ in. (240 × 187 mm) (Boston, Museum of Fine Arts, Francis Bartlett Fund: 15.1266)

[1] Inv. no. 15.1266.

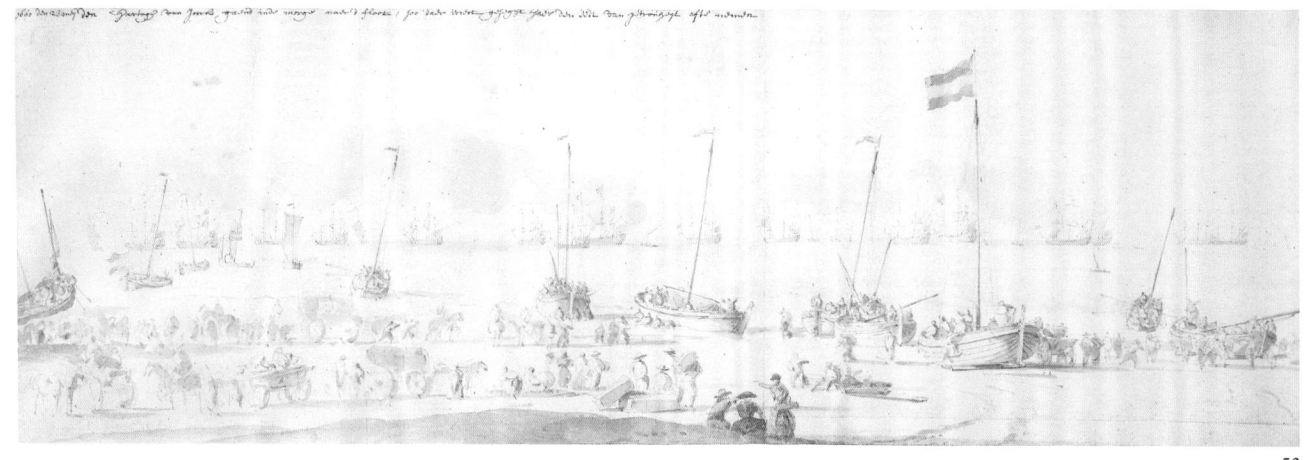

53

Willem van de Velde the Younger

1633–1707

Van de Velde was born in Leiden, but his family moved to Amsterdam in 1636, where he was a pupil of his father Willem van de Velde the Elder. (His younger brother was Adriaen van de Velde.) He may also have studied under Simon de Vlieger in Weesp. Following the French invasion of Holland in 1672, Willem and his father moved to England where, apart from some brief visits back to Holland, they spent the remainder of their lives. They were extensively employed by both Charles II and James II in recording specific vessels and naval events; until 1691 they had their studio in the Queen's House at Greenwich.

53 The Visit of the Duke of York to the Fleet at Scheveningen before the Departure of King Charles II for England in 1660

$7\frac{1}{4} \times 21\frac{7}{8}$ in. (184 × 557 mm)
On two sheets of paper, with an addition at the bottom right.
Brush drawing in black with gray wash over graphite

Inscribed by the artist along the top:
1660 den 23 meij den Hartogh van Jorck gaend inde morge naer d floot, soo daer wiert geseght haer den eedt van getrouheijt afte nemen (The 23 May 1660 the Duke of York going to the fleet in the morning, it is said to administer the oath of allegiance).

Watermark: the arms of Amsterdam (on both sheets of paper)

Bibl: Robinson, II, p. 859; W & C 484 (RL 12848)

At the time of the Restoration of the British monarchy, the English fleet was despatched to Holland to collect Charles II. The fleet arrived off the Dutch coast at Scheveningen on 14 May, but poor weather delayed their departure until 23 May. The shore at Scheveningen is here shown crowded with people, carriages, carts, and horses. A number of Dutch pinks (small open fishing boats) are shown both on the beach and being rowed towards the English fleet, which lies at anchor in the distance. In the center of the fleet can be seen the *Naseby*, the ship which had been sent to collect Charles II and his family and which, as a result, was renamed the next day the *Royal Charles*. To the left is the rear-admiral of the fleet, Stayner, in the *Swiftsure*, and to the right, the vice-admiral of the fleet, Lawson, in the *London*.

The inscription gives the date in the old (English) style and was presumably only added by the artist after his arrival in England, possibly at the same time as his father, in 1672. According to the Earl of Sandwich's journal, although the Duke of York (later James II), the brother of the king, went on board the *Naseby* on 22 May (O.S.), the following day he returned on board with the king; there is no mention of a visit by the Duke alone on 23 May. (At this time there was a discrepancy of ten days between the dates used in England (O.S.) and on the Continent (N.S.). The date of the King's departure from Scheveningen was 2 June according to the Continental method of dating.)

Both Willem van de Velde the Elder and the Younger were present at Charles II's departure from Scheveningen. The drawings by the Elder of "His Maties embarkation in Holland and his landing at Dover by way of a Journall" have not survived. Willem van de Velde the Younger made at least one painting and a number of drawings of the event. See also No. 56.

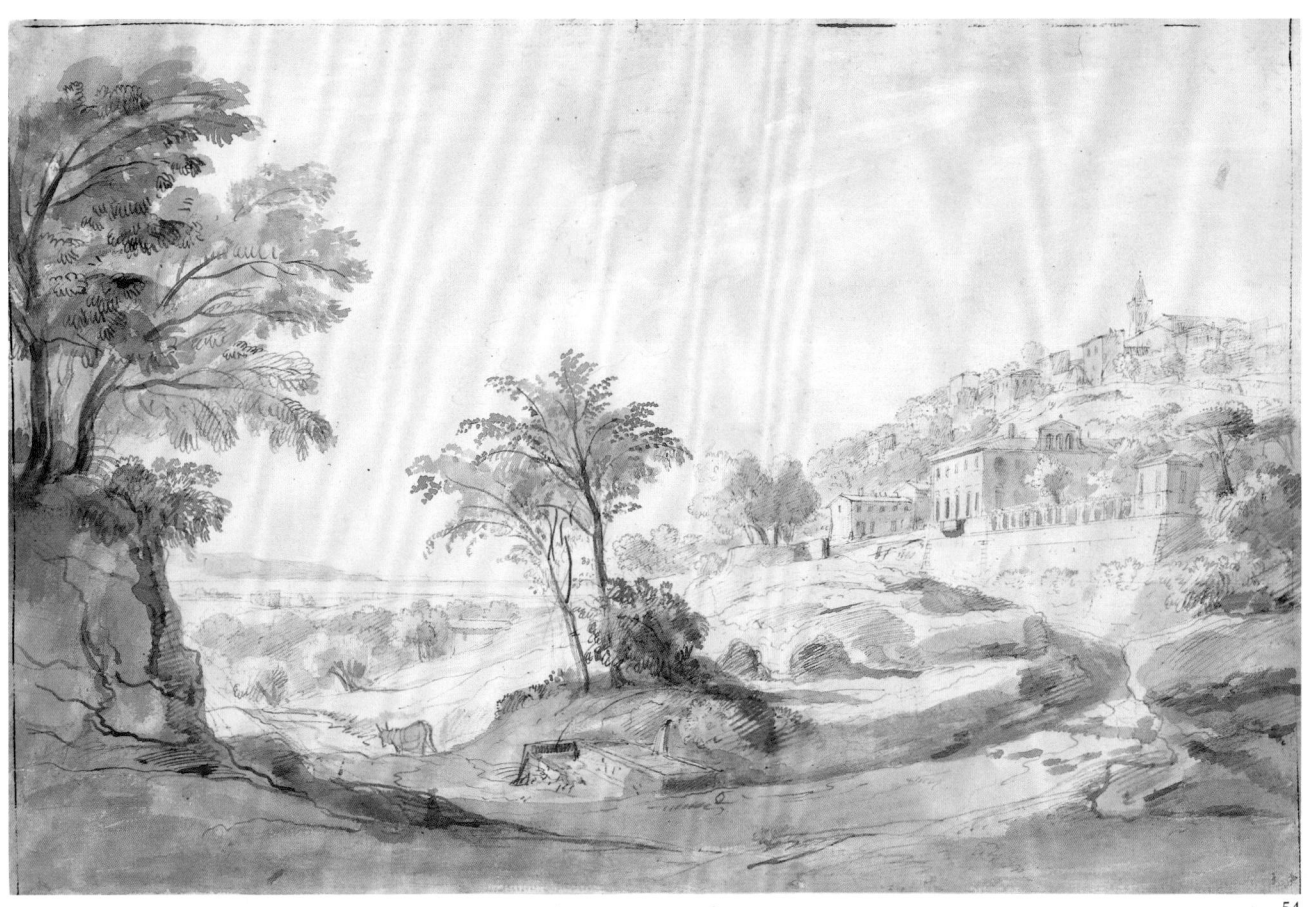

54

Gaspar van Wittel

1652/53–1736

A pupil of another Amersfoort artist, Mathias Withoos, Van Wittel left Holland for Italy around 1674, settling in Rome, where he studied under Cornelis Meyer and Abraham Genoels. In Italy he became generally known as Gaspare Vanvitelli. He visited other Italian cities, including Naples, Florence, and Venice, and became a very accomplished painter and draughtsman of townscapes. He produced a large number of studies for his paintings; those of Venice influenced such artists as Luca Carlevaris, Francesco Guardi, and Canaletto.

54 *Italian Landscape with a Villa and a Village on a Hillside*

10$\frac{11}{16}$ × 16$\frac{1}{4}$ in. (272 × 413 mm)

Pen and brown and gray ink with gray wash over graphite. Some ruled margins in black ink

Coll: George III

Bibl: w & c 694 (RL 5798)

In addition to his precisely rendered townscapes, Van Wittel made a large number of drawings of more generalized landscapes based on Italian scenery, as can be seen in this and the following drawing. Whether or not this drawing – showing the village with its church on the hillside and the substantial villa and gardens below on the right – is based on an actual view cannot be determined, but the artist has clearly completed the subject by artificially composing the foreground.

55 View of a Coastal Town

$7\frac{3}{8} \times 10\frac{1}{8}$ in. (187×258 mm)

Pen and brown ink with gray wash

Watermark: fleur-de-lys in double circle

Coll: George III

Bibl: W & C 701 (RL 6595)

The landscape, clearly Italianate in character, appears to be imaginary, possibly inspired by the scenery in the vicinity of Naples. Like the previous drawing, it is executed in Van Wittel's preferred medium – at least for his more general landscapes – of brown ink combined with gray wash.

Pieter Bout

1658–1719

Pieter Bout was born in Brussels, where he spent most of his life, apart from several years' activity in Paris and an apparent journey to Italy. He was a landscape and figure painter and etcher, who sometimes contributed the staffage to landscapes by other artists.

56 The Embarkation of King Charles II at Scheveningen in 1660

$10\frac{15}{16} \times 18\frac{7}{8}$ in. (278×480 mm)

Pen and brush with black ink and gray wash

Signed lower left: *P. bout*

Coll: George III

Bibl: W & C 323 (RL 6283)

For a description of the event see No. 53. The spire of the church at Scheveningen (from which Charles II embarked for England) can be seen on the right. An eyewitness account describes how "many hundreds of carriages could be counted, still more carts, spectators and horses. Pedestrians blackened the road from The Hague to Scheveningen, and, as for the beach, as far as the eye could see. Never have more people been seen together in Holland."[1] Samuel Pepys, who was present (as secretary, on board the *Naseby*), described how the King took leave of his hosts, the States General, on the beach, before embarking on a pink that had been drawn up for the purpose on the shore. The pink, decorated with three crowns representing his three kingdoms, is visible in the left middle distance in No. 56. There then followed "an infinite shooting off of the guns, and that in a disorder on purpose, which was better then if it had been otherwise"; the guns, with smoke, can be seen lined up on the beach beyond the pink.

Several artists, including Jan de Bisschop and the elder and younger Willem van de Veldes (see No. 53), were at Scheveningen.[2] The subject became very popular with Dutch artists. There are numerous paintings, drawings, and prints of *The Embarkation*, many of which are derivative. Since Pieter Bout was only two years old in 1660, it was formerly believed that No. 56 showed William III's embarkation for England at Hellevoetsluys. However, it is demonstrably a later recreation of the earlier event. The high degree of finish suggests that it was done preparatory to a painting or a print.

[1] *Hollandtse Mercurius* (Haarlem, 1660), XI, p. 95.

[2] For further discussion of the subject and its treatment, see White, no. 98.

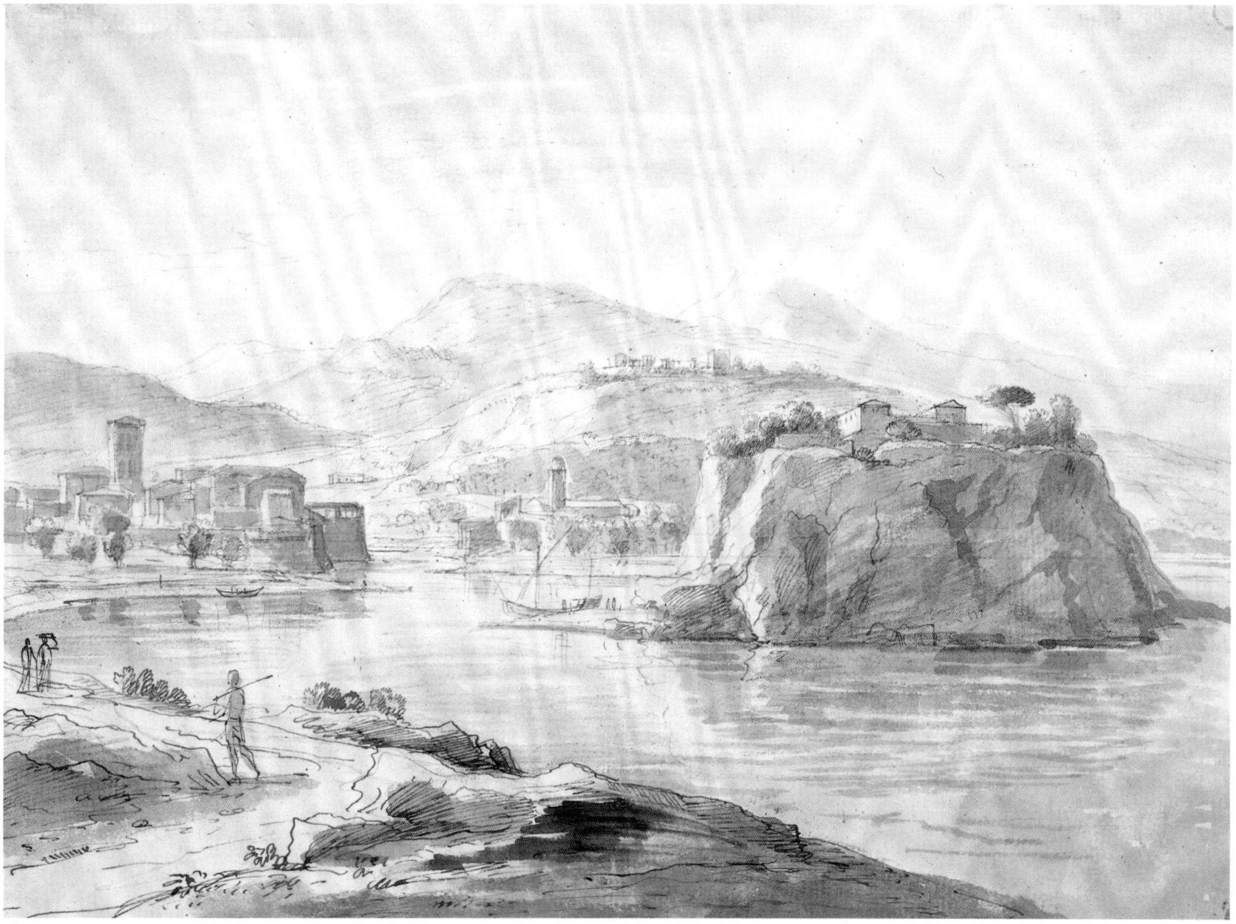

55

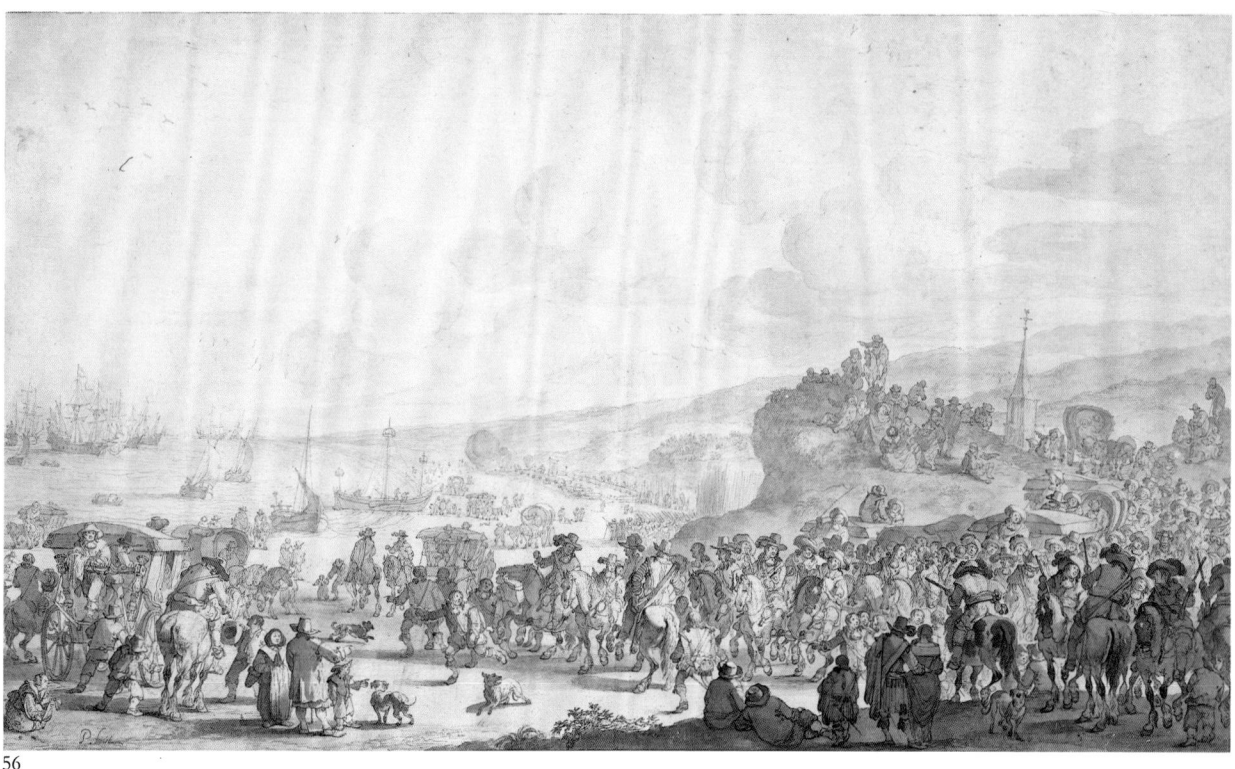

56

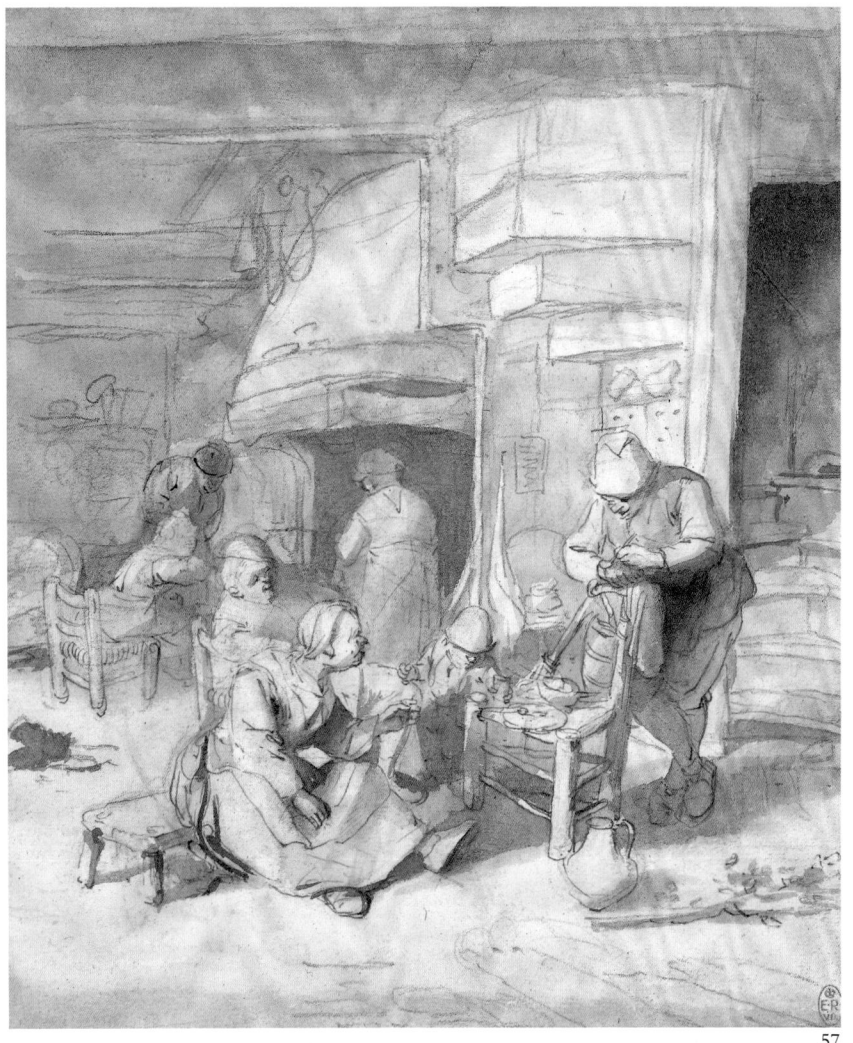

57

Cornelis Dusart

1660–1704

Born in Haarlem, where he spent his life, Dusart was a pupil of both Jan Steen and Adriaen van Ostade. As well as a painter and etcher of genre subjects, he was also a prolific draughtsman. His drawings vary from rapid sketches from life to highly finished colored studies, sometimes executed on vellum, which must have been regarded as finished works of art.

57 The Interior of a Cottage

$8\frac{7}{16} \times 7\frac{1}{8}$ in. (215 × 182 mm)
Pen and brown ink with gray wash over graphite

Verso: Several Figures around a Table

Pen and brown ink over black chalk. Inscribed: *Dusart*

Watermark: foolscap with seven points

Coll: George III

Bibl: Schnackenburg, no. F265; W & C 350 (RL 6522)

This study belongs to a group of drawings, which, although in the style of Adriaen van Ostade (see No. 40), lack the quality and variety of his draughtsmanship. They are now generally thought to be by his pupil Cornelis Dusart, done either early in his career or somewhat later when he was still working under the influence of his master.

The drawing on the *verso* of No. 57 is an unfinished sketch, which may have been abandoned when the artist turned over the sheet.

Cornelis Dusart, *verso* of No. 57.
Several Figures around a Table
Pen and brown ink over black chalk

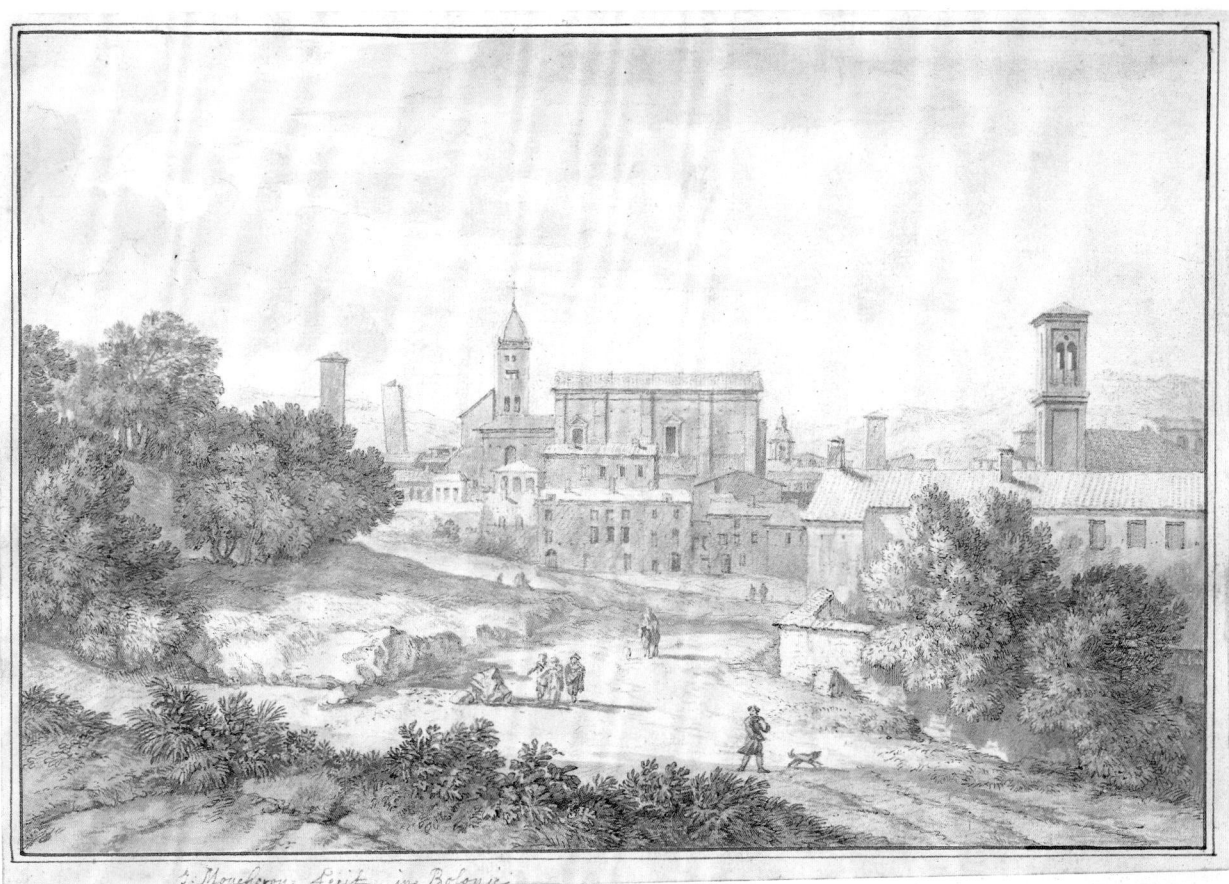

Isaac de Moucheron

1667–1744

Isaac was the son and pupil of the Amsterdam landscape painter Frederick de Moucheron. Following the example of his father, he completed his artistic education in Italy from 1694 to 1697. In Rome his early ability was recognized by his appointment as an instructor in painting by the *Bent*, the local society of Dutch and Flemish artists. After his return to Amsterdam, Isaac de Moucheron also developed a successful career as a painter of decorative murals in private houses and as a designer of gardens and façades.

¹ Sotheby's, 25 March 1982, lot 68; inscribed: *buijten Bologna I Moucheron fecit.*

58 *View of the Basilica of S. Petronio, Bologna*

$6\frac{5}{16} \times 9\frac{1}{16}$ in. (160 × 235 mm)

Pen and gray ink with gray wash over traces of graphite

Inscribed in the margin below:
I: Moucheron fecit in Bolonie

Coll: George III

Bibl: W & C 630 (RL 6305)

The view shows the Basilica of S. Petronio seen from the west with the two leaning towers in the Piazza di Porta Ravegnana further back to the left.

The artist's inscription indicates that he made the drawing in Bologna, presumably on his way to Rome in 1694 or on his way back to the Netherlands three years later. There is at least one other similarly inscribed landscape made outside Bologna, which was sold in London in 1982.¹

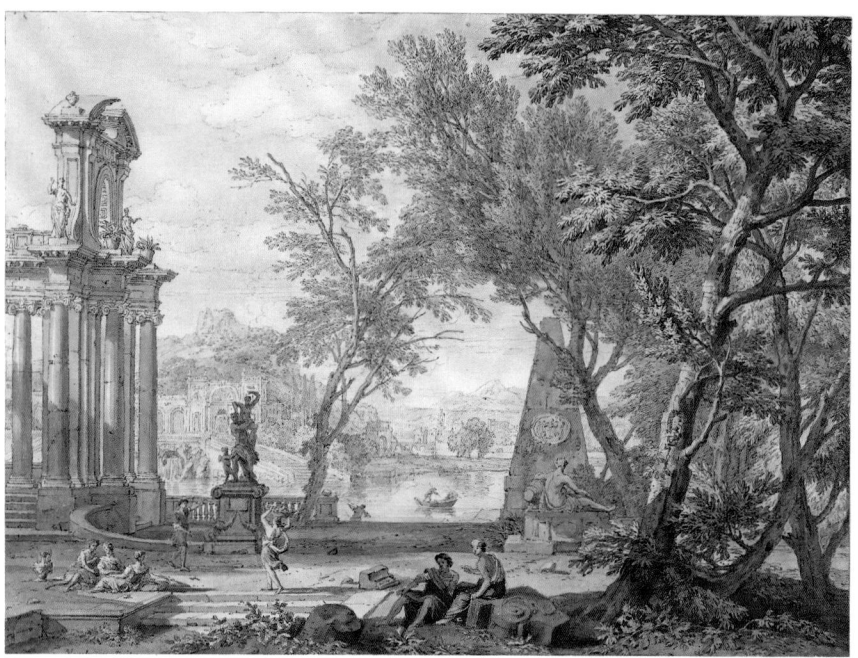

59

59 Classical Architecture in an Imaginary Landscape

8 9/16 × 11 13/16 in. (218 × 300 mm)

Pen and brown and gray ink with watercolor

Signed in bottom left corner (partly cut): *Moucheron Fecit.*

Coll: George III

Bibl: W & C 637 (RL 6312)

The imaginary landscape filled with fanciful classical architecture and figures in classical costume is typical of Moucheron's ideal landscapes, which form a substantial part of his *oeuvre* from the 1730s onwards. They clearly owe much to the examples of the Flemish artist Frans van Bloemen (Orizzonte), who had arrived in Rome in 1688, six years before Moucheron, and ultimately to the work of Claude Lorrain. Moucheron's classical landscapes were much imitated by his Dutch contemporaries.

Cornelis Troost

1697–1750

Troost was born and lived in Amsterdam. A pupil of the portrait painter Arnold Boonen, he is the most famous Dutch artist of the eighteenth century. With his gently satirical and humorous depictions of everyday life and theatrical subjects, which form a substantial part of his *oeuvre*, he can be seen as a Dutch equivalent of William Hogarth, although he lacks the acerbic wit of the latter. He worked extensively in watercolor and bodycolor as well as in oil, and his work was greatly admired and collected by his contemporaries.

60 'De Verloren Schildwacht' (The Lost Sentry), 10th Scene

13 5/16 × 9 11/16 in. (336 × 247 mm)

Watercolor and bodycolor over traces of graphite

Signed and dated in the sentry box: *C. Troost/ 1745*

Coll: [Cornelis Ploos van Amstel (sale 1800); G. van Nijmegen (sale 1809);] purchased by the Prince Regent (later George IV), 1815

Bibl: Niemeijer, no. 444T; W & C 664 (RL 12858)

On the left, a fashionably dressed young man, the student Leander, declares his love to Isabel, who leans over the balcony above the front door. Ostensibly Leander is making a speech to the sentry (sent to guard Isabel by her brother Lodewijk), who stands by the doorway with a blackened face, dressed in a harlequin costume over which he wears a lady's dress and lace cap.

The drawing is an illustration of the tenth scene in J. Pluymer's *De Verloren Schildwacht* (possibly adapted from F. L. de Sevigny's *Philippin sentinelle*), editions of which were published in 1686 and 1730. The subject of the drawing was identified in the catalogue of the collection of the artist's son-in-law, Ploos van Amstel, and although the sentry in fancy dress is not described, the situation accords with that in the play.

There appears to have been a second version of the subject, which was last recorded in the D. Vrijdag sale in 1825. It is possible that the first two references in the provenance given here (Ploos van Amstel and Van Nijmegen) relate to the Vrijdag drawing rather than the Windsor version.

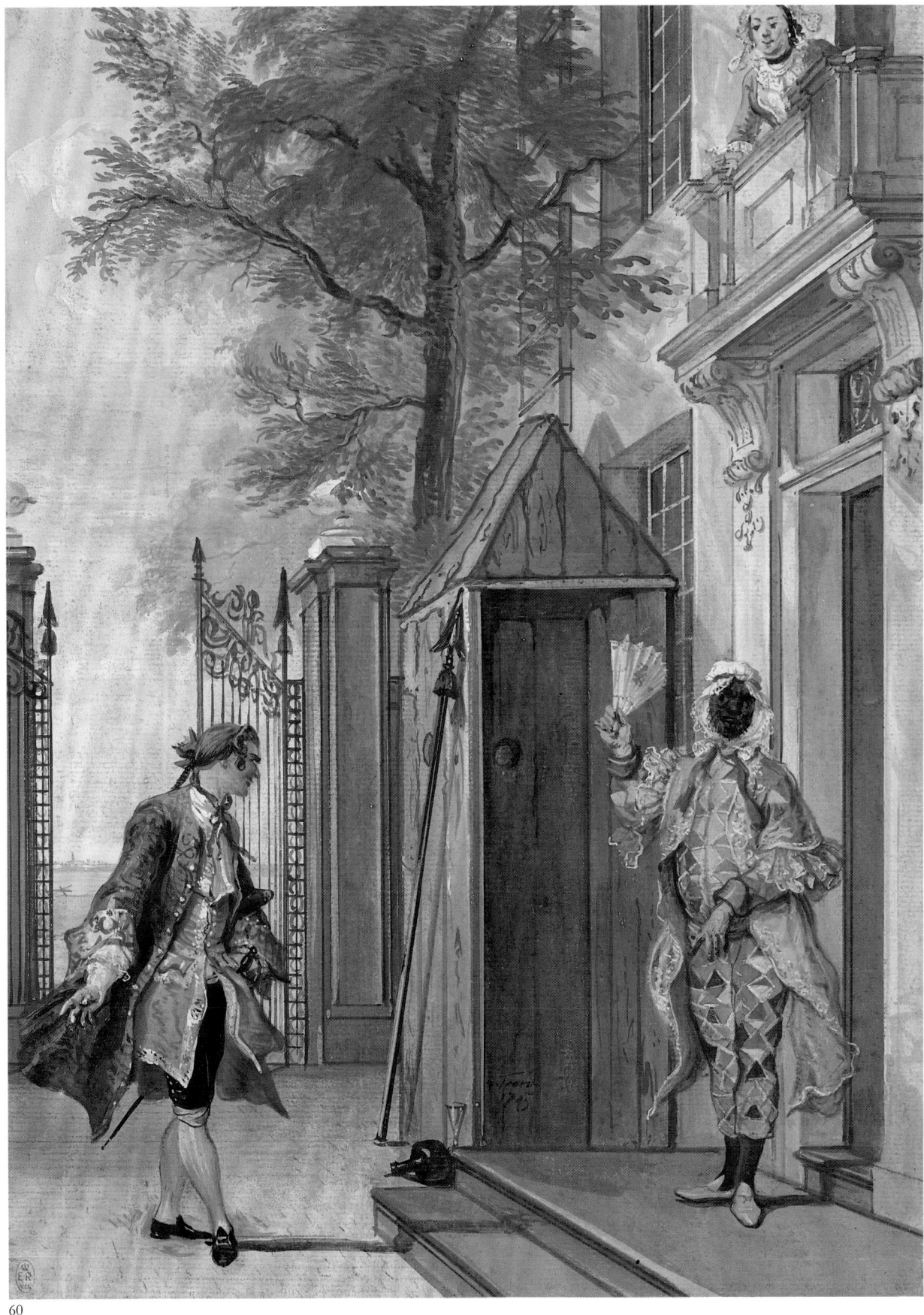

60

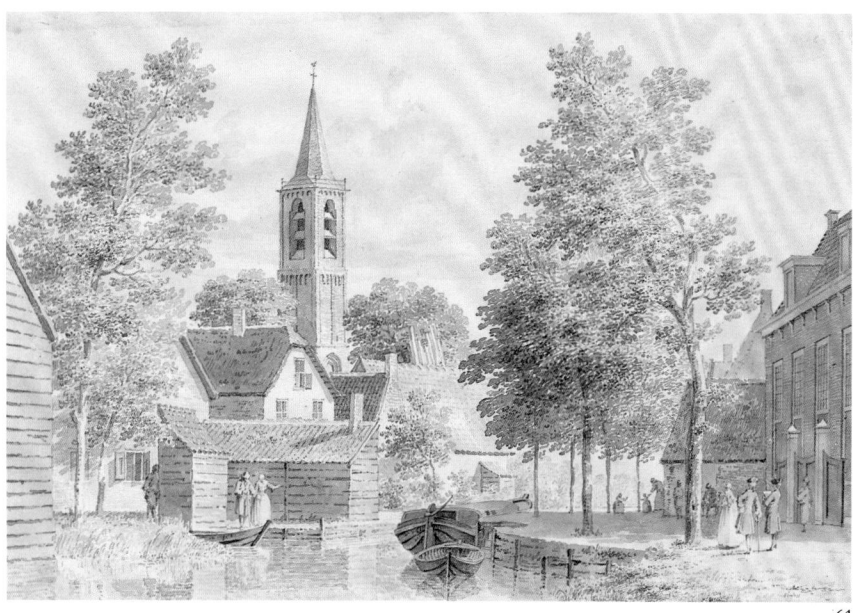

61

Attributed to **Paulus van Liender**

1731–1797

In Amsterdam, Van Liender became a pupil of Cornelis Pronck, whose influence can be seen in the feathery foliage and graceful, elongated figures. His drawings were much sought after by contemporary collectors. He was also a painter and etcher who later became co-director of the Haarlem Academy.

61 *The Village of Linschoten, between Utrecht and Gouda*

5¼ × 7¹³⁄₁₆ in. (133 × 199 mm)

Brush drawing in gray

Faintly inscribed top right: *Linschoten*

Coll: George III

Bibl: W & C 622 (RL 6243)

The village of Linschoten is situated between Utrecht and Gouda on the river Ijssel.

Formerly given to Abraham Rademaker, the drawing was attributed to Van Liender by Dr. L. J. van der Klooster. The delicacy of touch suggests that it is an early work by Van Liender.

Jan Anthonie Langendijk

1780–1818

Jan Anthonie Langendijk was a pupil of his father Dirck, whose style he closely imitated and whose sketches he worked up and amplified. He was frequently on the move between Amsterdam, Rotterdam, The Hague, and Brussels. He worked principally in watercolor, producing a large number of scenes of everyday and military life. There is a very substantial group of military subjects by both the elder and the younger Langendijk in the Royal Collection.[1]

62 *A Town Fair with 'The Capture of Cairo'*

12¼ × 16⅜ in. (311 × 417 mm)

Pen and brown ink and watercolor over traces of graphite

Signed and dated in bottom left corner: *J; A: Langendijk. Dzⁿ invᵗ et delinᵗ 1803.* Inscribed on the building second from the right: *DE | VEROVERING | VAN CAIRO* (The Capture of Cairo), and *GRO[OTE] SCH[IM]MEN* (large ghosts or shadows) (partially obscured), and over an entrance at left: *BIER | EN |*

JENEVE | TE | KOOP (beer and gin for sale)

Verso: inscribed £7–17–6

Coll: purchased by the Prince of Wales (later George IV), 1807

Bibl: W & C 608 (RL 15239)

The fair takes place in a crowded town square. On a stage erected in front of a building on the right, actors can be seen performing in front of painted backdrops, the uppermost of which is inscribed with what is presumably the title of the entertainment. There is a pendant to this drawing at Windsor, also signed and dated 1803,[2] which shows a town fair with a puppet show. Despite the similarities between the two, the locations are, however, different. In addition to these two studies, Langendijk produced several other drawings of fairs in 1803.

---

[1] These are discussed in A.E. Haswell Miller and N.P. Dawnay, *Military Drawings and*

Paintings in the Collectin of H.M. The Queen, 2 vols. (London, 1970).

[2] W & C 607. The price still inscribed on the verso of No. 62 is precisely that paid by the Prince of Wales to Colnaghi's in 1807: fifteen guineas for the two drawings.

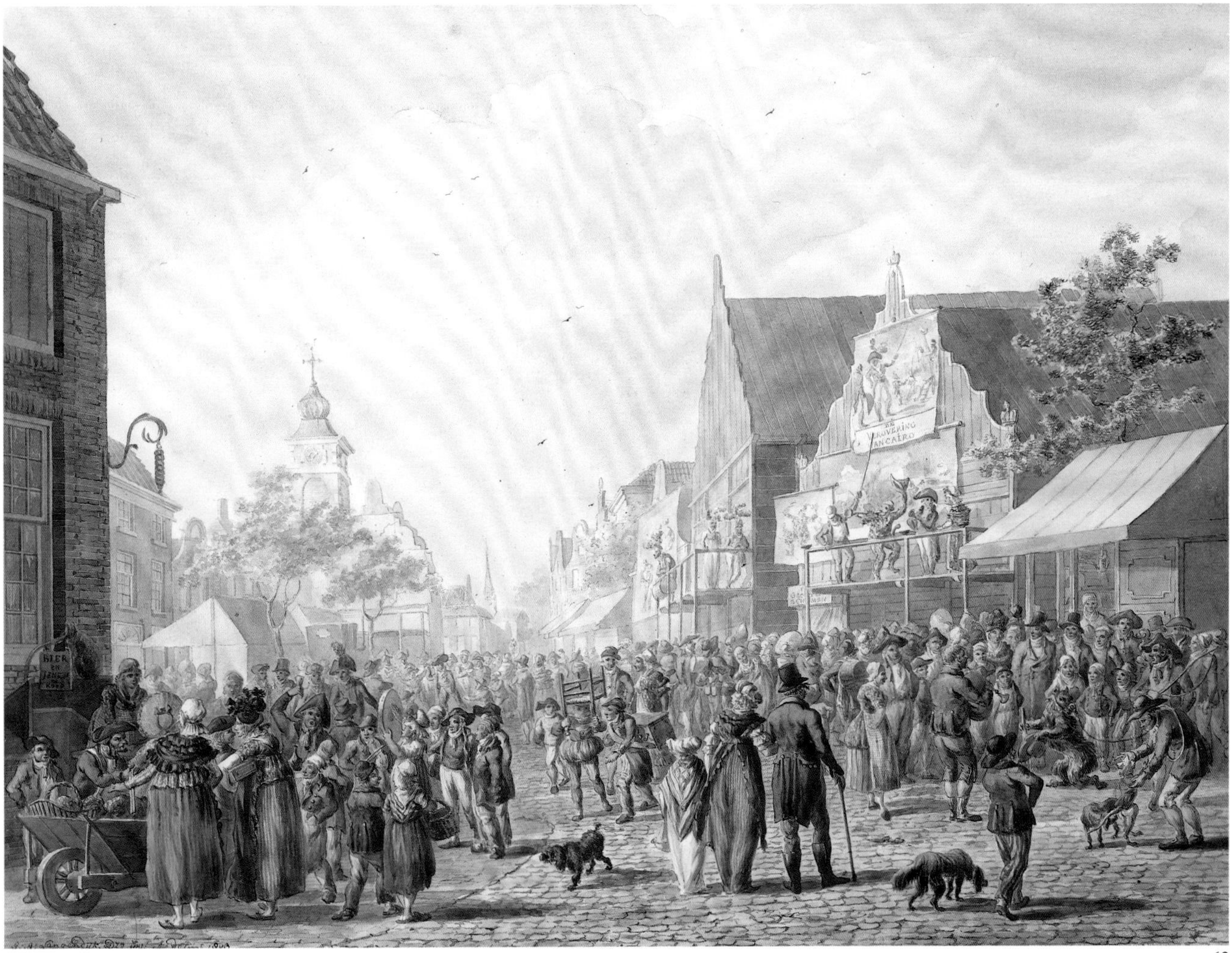

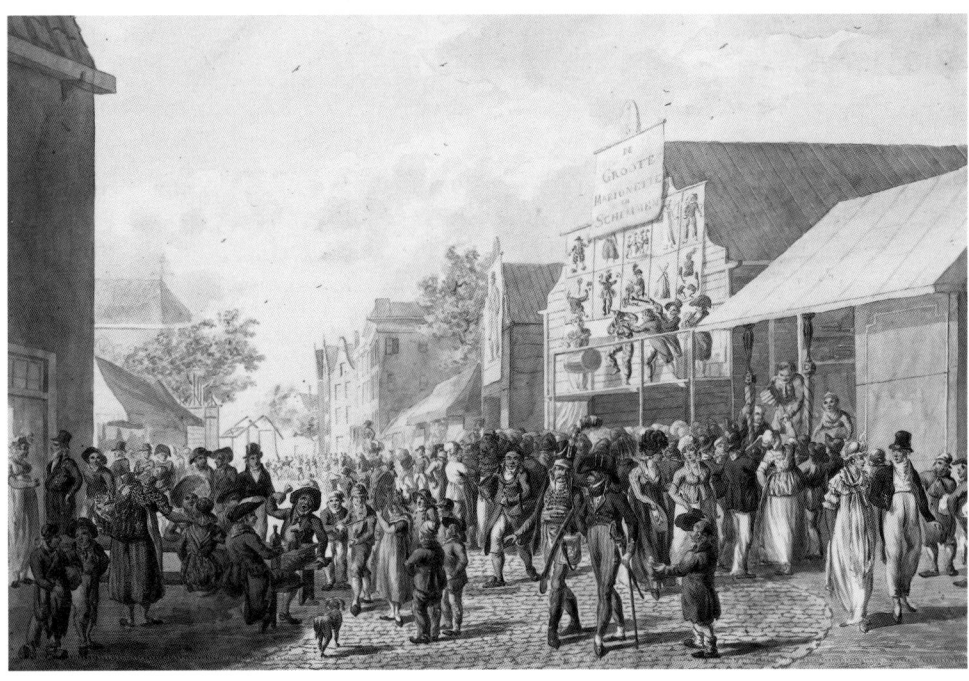

62

Jan Anthonie Langendijk,
A Town Fair with a Puppet Show
Watercolor over graphite,
10¾ × 16¼ in. (273 × 413 mm)
Signed and dated 1803
(Royal Collection:
Windsor Castle, Royal Library:
w & c 607)

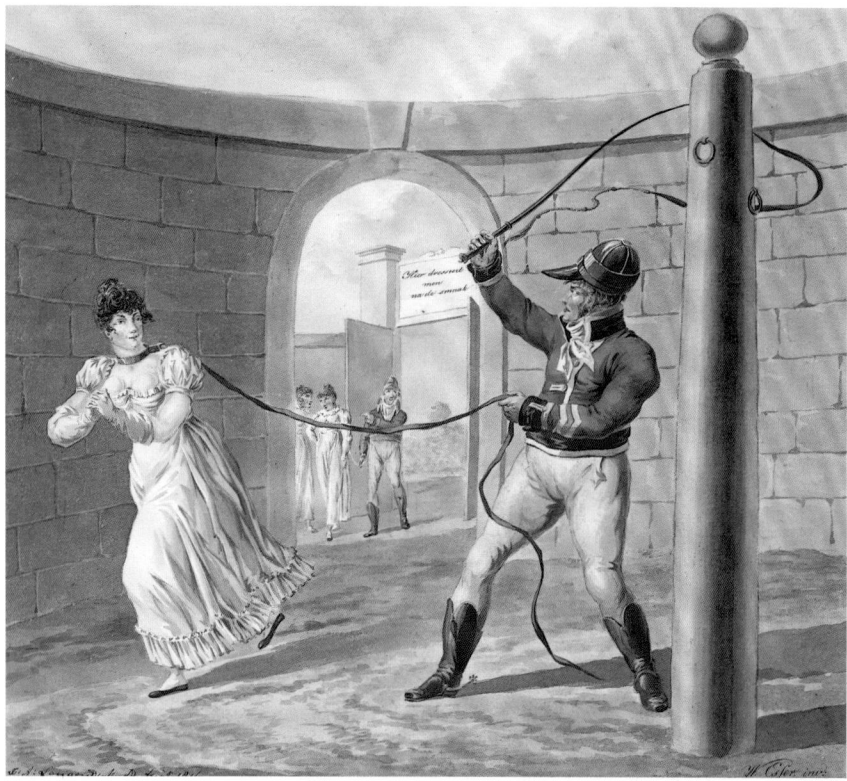

63

63 'The Female Manège' – A Trooper with a Woman on a Lunging Rein (after Wijnand Esser)

$19 \times 11\frac{1}{4}$ in. (254×287 mm)

Watercolor over traces of graphite

Signed and dated in bottom left corner: *J: A: Langendyk Dz fecit 1814.* Inscribed in a different hand bottom right corner: *W. Esser inv:* and over the door in the distance: *Hier dresseert/ men/ na den smaak* (Here one drills as one likes)

Coll: purchased by the Prince Regent (later George IV), 1815

Bibl: w & c 617 (RL 15249)

In a circular *manège*, a savage-looking trooper is cracking his whip as he glares at a woman with a lunging rein around her neck. Through the arched entrance can be seen a man with two women, one of whom wears a neck rein, who presumably have just arrived for a "drilling" session.

A pendant at Windsor,[3] also signed and dated 1814, shows a complementary subject of a married couple with the wife wearing the trousers. Likewise inscribed as being based on a design by Esser, it establishes Langendijk's practice of copying the latter. (See also No. 64.)

[3] w & c 616.

Wijnand Esser

1779–1860

or **Jan Anthonie Langendijk** after **Esser**

1780–1818

64 *Queen Hortense of Holland Haunted by Napoleon*

$13 \times 9\frac{9}{16}$ in. (332×244 mm)

Pen and black ink and watercolor over traces of graphite, with a broad line and wash border

Inscribed below: *DE DAGMERRI BERYD HORTENSIA / Geweese Koningin van Holland* (The Daymare

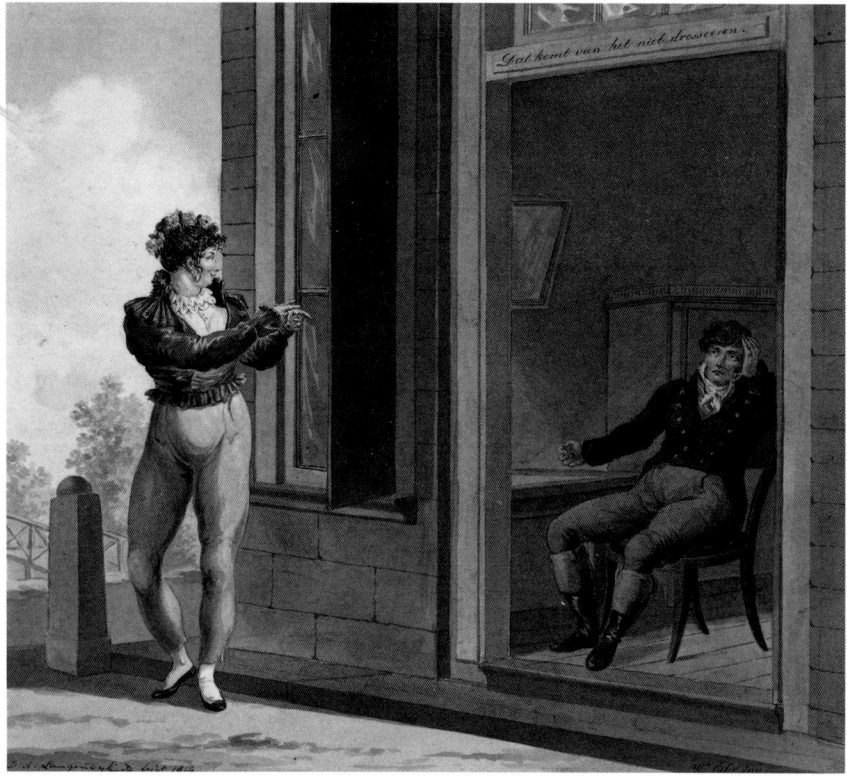

Jan Anthonie Langendijk, *A Married Couple with the Wife Wearing the Trousers* Watercolor over traces of graphite, $10 \times 11\frac{5}{16}$ in. (255×287 mm) Signed and dated 1814 (Royal Collection: Windsor Castle, Royal Library; w & c 616)

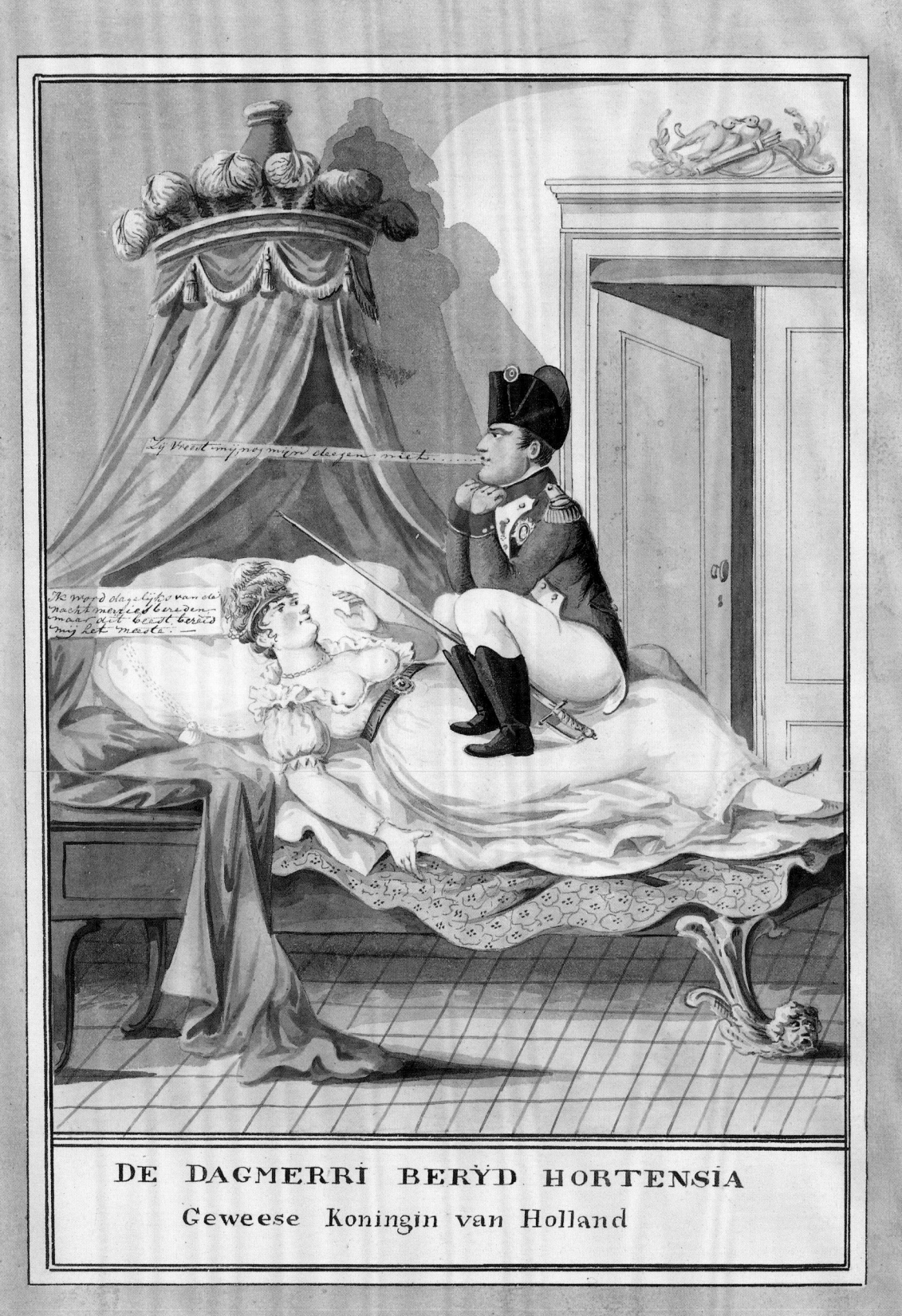

DE DAGMERRI BERŸD HORTENSIA

Geweese Koningin van Holland

64

Wijnand Esser, or Jan Anthonie Langendijk after Esser, *Napoleon Seated at His Desk at Elba* Pen and black ink and watercolor over traces of graphite, with a broad line and wash border, $14\frac{5}{16} \times 10\frac{1}{2}$ in. (372×266 mm) (Amsterdam, Rijksmuseum, Rijksprentenkabinet)

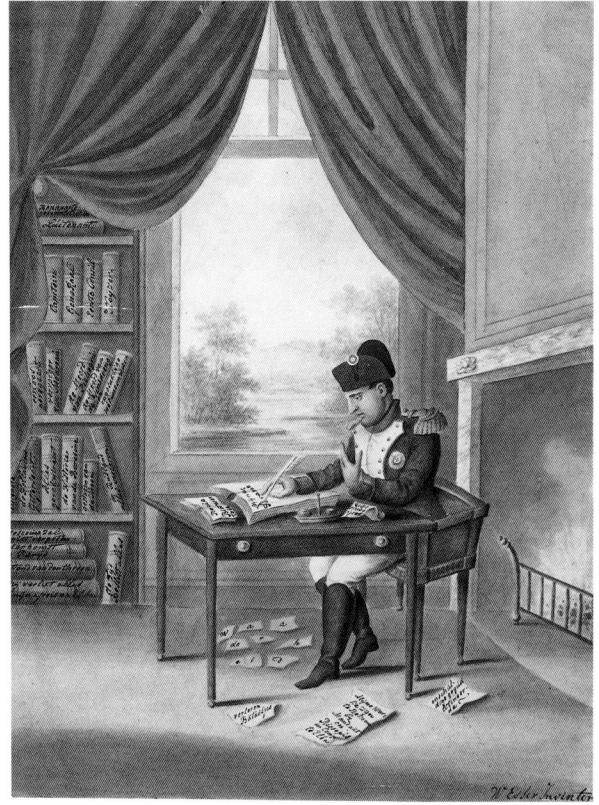

riding Hortensia, former Queen of Holland). Inscribed in a cartoon bubble from Napoleon's mouth: *Zij vreest mij, nog mijn deegen niet...* (She fears neither me nor my sword), and in another bubble to the left of the Queen's head: *Ik word dagelijks van de | nachtmerries bereden | maar dit beest bereid | mij het meeste.–* (Every day I am nightmare ridden, but this beast is the heaviest rider.)

Coll: purchased by the Prince Regent (later George IV), 1815

Bibl: W & C 583 (RL 12896)

Queen Hortense (1783–1837) was the daughter of Napoleon's wife, the Empress Josephine, by her first marriage to Alexander Beauharnais. In 1802 Napoleon arranged for the marriage of Hortense to his brother Louis Bonaparte, who from 1806 to 1810 ruled the Netherlands as King. It is clear from the inscription at the bottom of the present drawing that it was executed after 1810. Although in the early years of Hortense's unhappy marriage there had been rumors of a liaison between her and Napoleon, and even that Hortense's first son had been fathered by the Emperor, there is no record of any contact between the pair after Louis's abdication.

The present drawing may be a pendant to another satirical piece about Napoleon. A drawing in the Rijksmuseum, Amsterdam,[1] dated 1813 and inscribed *W. Esser Invintor*, represents Napoleon, identically dressed, seated at his desk in his study on the island of Elba. Given the inscription on the latter drawing, and the fact that there are two humorous drawings at Windsor inscribed as by Langendijk after Esser (see No. 63), it is uncertain whether the present drawing is by Esser or a copy after him by Langendijk. Both artists worked in a similar style, but very few works are known by Esser, who remains a shadowy figure.

[1] Inv. no. 48:302.

Bibliography and List of Abbreviations

Adriani
G. Adriani, *Anton van Dyck. Italienisches Skizzenbuch* (Vienna, 1940).

Antwerp
Hessenhuis, Antwerp, *Antwerp: Story of a Metropolis* (exhib. cat., ed. J. van der Stock, 1993).

Béguin
S. Béguin, 'An Unpublished Drawing by Jan Soens at Windsor Castle,' *Master Drawings*, XXVIII (1990), pp. 275-79.

Benesch (1928)
O. Benesch, *Die Zeichnungen der niederländischen Schülen des 15. und 16. Jahrhunderts, Albertina* – Kat. II (Vienna, 1928).

Benesch (1951)
O. Benesch, 'A Drawing by Arnout Mytens,' *Burlington Magazine*, XCIII (1951), pp. 351-52.

Benesch (1973)
O. Benesch, *The Drawings of Rembrandt*, 6 vols. (2nd. ed., London, 1973).

Benisovich
M. Benisovich, 'The drawings of Stradanus (Jan van der Straeten) in the Cooper Union Museum for the Arts of Decoration, New York,' *Art Bulletin*, XXXVIII (1956), pp. 249-51.

Blunt
A. Blunt, *Supplements to the Catalogues of Italian and French Drawings ... at Windsor Castle* (London and New York, 1971).

Bowron
E. Bowron, *European Paintings before 1900 in the Fogg Art Museum* (Cambridge, Mass., 1990).

Bruges
Musée Gruuthuse, Bruges, *Bruges et la Tapisserie* (exhib. cat. by G. Delmarcel and E. Duverger, 1987).

Burchard and d'Hulst
L. Burchard and R.-A. d'Hulst, *Rubens Drawings*, 2 vols. (Brussels, 1963).

Byam Shaw
J. Byam Shaw, *Drawings by Old Masters at Christ Church, Oxford*, 2 vols. (Oxford, 1976).

Ertz
K. Ertz, *Jan Brueghel der ältere: Die Gemälde* (Cologne, 1979).

Garff and de la Fuente Pedersen
J. Garff and E. de la Fuente Pedersen, *Rubens Cantoor. The Drawings of Willem Panneels*, 2 vols. (Copenhagen, 1988).

Gerhardt
C. Gerhardt, 'Die Zeichnung 4761 von Windsor, ein neuer Gutenberg-Beleg,' *Gutenberg-Jahrbuch* (1972), pp. 44-49.

Ghent
Musée des Beaux-Arts, Ghent, *Roelandt Savery 1576-1639* (1954).

Giltay
J. Giltay, 'De tekeningen van Jacob van Ruisdael,' *Oud Holland,* XCIV (1980), pp. 141-208.

Haverkamp-Begemann and Logan
E. Haverkamp-Begemann and A.-M. Logan, *European Drawings and Watercolors in the Yale University Art Gallery*, 2 vols. (New Haven and London, 1970).

Held (1959), (1986)
J. Held, *Rubens Selected Drawings*, 2 vols. (London, 1959; 2nd revised ed., Oxford, 1986).

Held (1980)
J. Held, *The Oil Sketches of Peter Paul Rubens. A Critical Catalogue*, 2 vols. (Princeton, 1980).

Hind
A. M. Hind, *Engraving in England in the Sixteenth and Seventeenth Centuries,* I (Cambridge, 1952).

Hollstein
F. W. H. Hollstein, *Dutch and Flemish Etchings, Engravings and Woodcuts,* I ... (Amsterdam, 1949-92).

Honour
H. Honour, *The European Vision of America* (Cleveland, 1975).

Jaffé
M. Jaffé, *Rubens: catalogo completo* (Milan, 1989).

Judson
J. R. Judson, *Dirck Barendsz.* (Amsterdam, 1970).

Kunst voor de beeldenstorm
Rijksmuseum, Amsterdam, *Kunst voor de beeldenstorm: Noordnederlandse kunst 1525-1580* (exhib. cat., 1986).

L.
F. Lugt, *Les marques de collections de dessins et d'estampes* (Amsterdam, 1921); *Supplément* (The Hague, 1956).

Larsen
E. Larsen, *The Paintings of Anthony van Dyck*, 2 vols. (Freren, 1988).

Liedtke
W. Liedtke, *Flemish Paintings in the Metropolitan Museum of Art*, 2 vols. (New York, 1984).

Logan (1977)
A.-M. Logan, 'Rubens exhibitions 1977,' *Master Drawings*, XV (1977), pp. 403-417.

Logan (1987)
A.-M. Logan, review of Held (1986), *Master Drawings*, XXV (1987), pp. 63-82.

Mauquoy-Hendrickx (1956)
M. Mauquoy-Hendrickx, *L'Iconographie d'Antoine Van Dyck*, 2 vols. (Brussels, 1956).

Mauquoy-Hendrickx (1978)
M. Mauquoy-Hendrickx, *Les estampes de Wierix ...*, I (Brussels, 1978).

Munich
Alte Pinakothek, Munich, *Katalog I* (Munich, 1961).

Niemeijer
J. W. Niemeijer, *Cornelis Troost* (Assen, 1973).

Norman
P. Norman, 'On an Allegorical Painting in Miniature by Joris (George) Hoefnagel, and some other works by this artist,' *Archaeologia*, LVII (1901), pp. 321-25.

Nuti
L. Nuti, 'The mapped views by Georg Hoefnagel ... ,' *Word & Image,* IV (1988), pp. 545-70.

Popham (1926)
A. E. Popham, 'Hugo van der Goes?' *The Vasari Society*, 2nd series, Part VII (1926).

Popham (1928)
A. E. Popham, 'Notes on Flemish Domestic Glass Painting,' *Apollo*, VII (1928), p. 178.

Rembrandt Corpus
J. Bruyn *et al.*, *A Corpus of Rembrandt Paintings*, III (Dordrecht, Boston, and London, 1989).

Reznicek (1961)
E. Reznicek, *Die Zeichnungen von Hendrick Goltzius*, 2 vols. (Utrecht, 1961).

Reznicek (1964)
E. K. J. Reznicek, *Gabinetto Disegni e Stampe degli Uffizi, XVIII: Mostra di Disegni Fiamminghi e Olandesi* (Florence, 1964).

RL
The numerical inventory of drawings and watercolors in the Royal Library, Windsor Castle.

Roberts (1986)
The Queen's Gallery, London, *Master Drawings in the Royal Collection* (exhib. cat. by J. Roberts, 1986).

Roberts (1989)
J. Roberts, 'The Limnings, Drawings and Prints in Charles I's Collection' in *The Late King's Goods* (ed. A. MacGregor; London and Oxford, 1989), pp. 115–29.

Robinson
M. Robinson, *The Paintings of the Willem van de Veldes*, 2 vols. (London, 1990).

Schaar
E. Schaar, 'Zeichnungen Berchems zu Landkarten,' *Oud Holland*, LXXI (1956), pp. 239–43.

Schatborn
P. Schatborn, *Dutch Figure Drawings from the Seventeenth Century* (The Hague, 1981).

Schilling
E. Schilling, 'Zwei Landschaftszeichnungen des Georg Hoefnagel,' *Kunstgeschichtliche Studien für Hans Kauffmann* (Berlin, 1956).

Schnackenburg
B. Schnackenburg, *Adriaen van Ostade, Isack van Ostade. Zeichnungen und Aquarelle*, 2 vols. (Hamburg, 1981).

Schneider
H. Schneider, *Jan Lievens* (Haarlem, 1932).

Schulz (1974)
W. Schulz, *Lambert Doomer sämtliche Zeichnungen* (Berlin, 1974).

Schulz (1982)
W. Schulz, *Herman Saftleven 1609–1685. Leben und Werke. Mit einem kritischen Katalog der Gemälde und Zeichnungen*, (Berlin and New York, 1982).

Seilern
[A. Seilern,] *Flemish Paintings & Drawings at 56 Princes Gate SW7: Addenda* (London, 1969).

Slive
Mauritshuis, The Hague and Fogg Art Museum, Cambridge, Mass, *Jacob van Ruisdael* (exhib. cat. by S. Slive, 1981-82).

Spicer
J. A. Spicer, *The Drawings of Roelandt Savery*, 2 vols., (Ann Arbor, 1979).

Stainton
British Museum, London, *British Landscape Watercolours 1600–1860* (exhib. cat. by L. Stainton, 1985).

Stampfle
F. Stampfle, *Netherlandish Drawings of the Fifteenth and Sixteenth Centuries and Flemish Drawings of the Seventeenth and Eighteenth Centuries in the Pierpont Morgan Library* (New York, 1991).

Steland
A. Steland, *Die Zeichnungen des Jan Asselijn* (Fridingen, 1989).

Steland-Stief (1980)
A. Steland-Stief, 'Zum zeichnerischen Werk des Jan Asselyn,' *Oud Holland*, XCIV (1980), pp. 213–58

Steland-Stief (1986)
A. Steland-Stief, 'Zu Willem Schellinks' Entwicklung als Zeichner,' *Niederdeutsche Beiträge zur Kunstgeschichte*, XXV (1986), pp. 79–108.

Strong
R. Strong, *Portraits of Queen Elizabeth I* (London, 1963).

Sumowski
W. Sumowski, *Drawings of the Rembrandt School*, 9 vols. (New York, 1979–85).

Thiem (1958), (1959)
G. Thiem, 'Studien zu Jan van der Straet, genannt Stradanus,' *Mitteilungen des Kunsthistorischen Institutes in Florenz*, VIII (1958), pp. 88–111, IX (1959), pp. 155-65.

Van Mander
C. van Mander, *Het Schilder-Boeck* (Haarlem, 1604).

Van Sasse van Ysselt
D. van Sasse van Ysselt, 'Johannes Stradanus: de decoraties voor intochten en uitvaarten aan het hof van de Medici te Florence,' *Oud Holland*, CIV (1990), pp. 149–79.

Venturi
A. Venturi, *Storia dell' Arte Italiana*, 25 vols (Milan, 1901–1940).

Vey
H. Vey, *Die Zeichnungen Anton van Dycks*, 2 vols. (Brussels, 1962).

Vivian
F. Vivian, *The Consul Smith Collection* (Munich, 1989).

Vlieghe
H. Vlieghe, *Corpus Rubenianum Ludwig Burchard. Portraits*, Part XIX, vol. II (London, 1987).

W & C
C. White and C. Crawley, *The Dutch and Flemish Drawings of the Fifteenth to the Early Nineteenth Centuries in the Collection of Her Majesty The Queen at Windsor Castle* (Cambridge, 1994).

Walsh and Schneider
Los Angeles County Museum of Art (and elsewhere), *A Mirror of Nature: Dutch Paintings from the Collection of Mr. and Mrs. Edward William Carter* (exhib. cat. by J. Walsh and C. Schneider, 1982).

Washington
National Gallery of Art, Washington, *Anthony van Dyck* (exhib. cat., 1991).

Wayment
H. Wayment, *King's College Chapel Cambridge. The Side-Chapel Glass*, (Cambridge, 1990).

Wegner and Pée
W. Wegner and H. Pée, 'Die Zeichnungen des David Vinckboons,' *Münchner Jahrbuch der bildenden Kunst*, XXXI (1980), p. 35–128.

Welcker
C. J. Welcker, *Hendrick Avercamp ... en Barent Avercamp ...* (Zwolle, 1933; 2nd ed., 1979).

White
C. White, *Dutch Pictures in the Collection of Her Majesty The Queen* (Cambridge, 1982).

Concordances

Index of Artists

References are to catalogue numbers.